REFORMING
MEDICINE

REFORMING MEDICINE:

lessons of the last quarter century

edited by
VICTOR W. SIDEL and RUTH SIDEL

PANTHEON BOOKS
NEW YORK

RA
395
A3
R 38
1984

Library of Congress Cataloging in Publication Data
Main entry under title:
Reforming medicine.
   1. Medical care—United States. I. Sidel, Victor W.
II. Sidel, Ruth.
RA395.A3R38   1984   362.1'042   83-42814
ISBN 0-394-50213-2
ISBN 0-394-72159-4 (pbk.)

Manufactured in the United States of America

First Edition

Designed by Naomi Osnos

contents

introduction

Victor and Ruth Sidel

I t is difficult to believe as we write this introduction, in early
1983, that beginning in the late 1950s—a quarter century ago
—there existed a widespread feeling that medicine in the United
States could be effectively reformed, bit by bit, piece by piece, to
meet human needs.

The need for change was obvious to the reformers. Infant mortality in the United States was higher for the poor than for the well-
off, and was twice as high for black babies as for white babies. The
rate of doctor visits was higher among whites and the well-off than
among racial minorities and the poor, even though members of the
latter two groups had considerably higher rates of illness and disability. The growth of technology, and of the costs of care, was
rapid and uncontrolled. Most of the elderly, who were an increasing
fraction of the population, and others living on fixed or low incomes
could not afford the growing costs, and even well-off families could
be financially destroyed by catastrophic illness. In many rural areas
and in the poor parts of large cities, access to adequate care was
difficult if not impossible. The medical profession was a bastion
largely populated and dominated by white males, who had begun
to earn incomes far higher than those of other health workers and
of others—even many other highly paid professionals—in the soci-

ety. Finally, there was a feeling that much of the caring was disappearing from health care, that what should be a humane service for everyone in need was as racist, sexist, ageist, distant, and unfeeling as other U.S. institutions and perhaps in some ways even more so.

A few observers, a quarter century ago, maintained that piecemeal reform could not solve fundamental problems in the health care system: the dependence on a largely entrepreneurial, fee-for-service, profit-making structure; the dominance by a profession that appeared to care more for income and perquisites than for the needs of communities and at times even of patients; and the absence of significant planning and control, and usually even of significant input, by the members of the community and by the patients the medical care system was to serve. These observers believed that nothing short of fundamental restructuring of the medical care system—along the lines of a national health service, as in Great Britain, or at least of universal, comprehensive, national health insurance, as in most of the industrialized countries of the world—could produce the needed change. Furthermore, they wondered whether the requisite changes could be made in the medical care system without fundamental change in the rest of the society.

But most medical reformers, while often recognizing the structural problems, were emboldened by piecemeal reforms that appeared to work in other elements of the society. At the beginning of the 1960s, the election of John F. Kennedy seemed to provide an opening for reform. The protest against nuclear fallout apparently led to a ban on atmospheric nuclear testing. As the decade lurched forward, the civil rights movement gave both heart and political techniques to other efforts to move toward greater equity and justice: the welfare rights movement, the women's movement, and ultimately the anti–Vietnam War movement. The dramatic results included civil rights and voting rights legislation, an end to much of the overt discrimination in public places in the South, fair housing laws, expansion of the welfare rolls and limited welfare reform, efforts at community control of urban schools, and legal aid for the poor. It was clear that political action, particularly when spearheaded by community groups demanding their rights, could produce change.

It was as part of these general reform efforts and feelings of optimism that serious attempts to reform the U.S. medical care system were begun. Health care was affected both directly and indirectly by the reform efforts in the society at large. First, it was influenced by the widespread feeling that change was possible. The civil rights movement, in particular, made it evident that a mass constituency for change existed and that this constituency, largely black and poor, was willing to take significant risks to participate in bringing about that change. On a more direct level, reform efforts in health care were influenced, as several authors in this volume point out, by the participation of health professionals in the civil rights movement and later in the Medical Committee for Human Rights, which began as a support group for civil rights efforts. Their participation taught health professionals much-needed political action and community organizing techniques, and especially the art of working together with others, above all with nonprofessionals, outside the customary hierarchy of medical settings. These newly acquired skills were to become crucial to health workers' efforts at reform within the health care system.

Just as liberals and reformers thought that blacks could have a fairer share of the American dream if legislation and regulation ensuring their civil rights were implemented, so those involved in health care felt that, by the use of similar techniques, the system could be reformed and be made significantly more equitable, accessible, and acceptable. If we provided health care for little or no cost to the elderly and the poor, the two groups most afflicted with health problems and least able to pay for care; if we shifted admissions to medical school just enough to allow more minority people and women into the profession, in order to give them a fairer opportunity and provide better care for disadvantaged populations; if we created health centers accessible financially, geographically, and culturally to the urban and rural poor, staffed with personnel who were able to relate to the poor and offered services relevant to their needs; if we permitted community people and patients to play a part in decisions that affected their health and their very lives—if we did all these things, then the United States, it was argued, would go a long way toward reforming its health care system. Thousands of health workers took part in these efforts and devoted years of their lives to making the dream come true.

The attempt to reform American health care occurred at various levels of the system: at the national level through the financing of health care for large segments of the population; at the local level through the creation of new institutions to provide care; and at the professional level through the recruitment of health professionals from groups that had been grossly underrepresented in the field and through the development of new kinds of health workers. Some reforms endeavored to cut across many levels—giving greater attention to occupational health and safety issues, involving the community in decision making in health care, or bringing about dramatic changes in the field of mental health.

This volume presents an analysis of several of these efforts. Each chapter, written by an expert in that particular field who either was or, in many instances, still is actively involved in the reform effort, traces the historical background of that aspect of health care, outlines the situation in the 1960s, describes the reform effort itself, and evaluates its results. As editors we have encouraged the authors to write within this format without, we hope, interfering unduly with their sense of how the material should be handled. Our hope was that this approach would yield an in-depth and coherent, yet highly personal, examination of reform efforts in the 1960s and 1970s in one profession based largely on the experiences of the authors themselves. Mao Zedong's dictum "All genuine knowledge originates in direct experience" is nowhere more applicable than in the risky, unpredictable, often uncharted efforts to make significant change in this highly individualistic society, which lacks established political parties dedicated to movement toward equity. It is only through analysis by those who participated, as individuals and in ad hoc groups, during those tumultuous and often exhilarating years that we can evaluate the successes, the failures, and, above all, the future directions.

Part I discusses the attempts at institutional reform. Jack Geiger, in his chapter on the rise and fall of community health centers, sums up the rediscovery of poverty in America: "It was . . . a land of hunger, slums, deprivation, illiteracy, unemployment, and racial oppression, suddenly made visible in one of the cyclic (though usually brief) swings of public attention and concern that have characterized Western capitalist societies regularly ever since the industrial revolution." With the perception of poverty came the equally clear perception that adequate medical care was a luxury that only the affluent could afford and that the health status of the poor—particularly the poor of the rural South and of the northern urban ghettos—was shockingly deficient and in a number of ways more comparable to the health status of people living in developing countries than to that of the population of industrialized societies.

As part of the Great Society's "War on Poverty," the neighborhood health center program was proposed to the Office of Economic

Opportunity in 1965, and in November 1966 the OEO Comprehensive Health Services Program was funded by the U.S. Congress. As Geiger notes, the neighborhood health center program, whose conception owes much to earlier models from England, China, Puerto Rico, and South Africa, attempted not merely to remove financial barriers to health care but also to create a new kind of health care institution and to assure the poor a role in both the planning and the administration of their own services. In the light of these goals, Geiger analyzes the central issues, problems, and strengths of this massive effort and attempts to evaluate its short- and long-term impact.

Quentin Young then describes the post–World War II shift to high-technology, hospital-based care and the subsequent problems that urban public hospitals faced. Through a close examination of Cook County Hospital, in Chicago, Young details the efforts to combat racism both in the hiring of health workers and in the treatment of patients, to defend patients' rights, to support the unionization of health workers, and to protest inadequate care of the poor. Finally, he evaluates the results of these efforts and offers guidelines for future attempts to reform the health care system.

E. Richard Brown, in the chapter on Medicare and Medicaid, continues the discussion of broad attempts at institutional reform. After examining the background of the "landmark reform legislation" that established Medicare and Medicaid, including the decades of discussion and debate about the establishment of a national health insurance program and the adamant and well-financed opposition by the AMA, he analyzes the factors that produced the momentum for Medicare and Medicaid and the compromises necessary to assure its passage by Congress. He proceeds to discuss the political reasons for the differences between Medicare and Medicaid, and the consequences of those differences, and then documents the spiraling cost of medical care, which was preordained by the shape of the Medicare/Medicaid legislation, and evaluates the impact of these reforms on health care for the elderly and poor.

In Part II we move from efforts to change health care institutions to efforts to provide services for special groups; the examples we have selected are workers and women. Molly Coye, Mark Smith, and Anthony Mazzocchi detail the multiple hazards that faced workers in the late 1960s: the dangers of the workplace; the inadequate compensation for work-related injury and particularly for work-related illness; the lack of basic research into occupational disease; and the lack of awareness among workers themselves about these issues. During the 1970s a coalition fought to modify industry's behavior and to alter the health care system to make it more responsive to the problems of occupational health and safety. The authors describe the establishment and development of the Occupational Safety and Health Administration and the National Institute for Occupational Safety and Health as well as the developments on the state and local level. After evaluating the results of a decade of reform, the authors raise crucial issues, such as the trade-off between productivity and health and the relative importance of job exposure versus individual life-style in producing illness.

The significant advances in woman's health care that have taken place since the late 1960s are described by Helen Rodriguez-Trias. Noting that women's perception of their health needs was clearly tied to the raising of women's consciousness generally, she asserts that as "patriarchy in the family was questioned, so was patriarchy in the doctor-patient relationship." Focusing on specific issues like sterilization abuse, experimentation on Third World women, abortion rights, and the role of women in the health professions, she details the development of the women's health movement, putting particular emphasis on the class conflicts that have emerged in it. Rodriguez-Trias points out that although the women's health movement is one reform effort that has cut across class, racial, and ethnic barriers, middle-class women concerned about health issues have nevertheless been in constant danger of being co-opted by the medical establishment and settling for token reforms that would leave a fundamentally sexist system intact.

Part III deals with reforms involving health workers—with efforts in the 1960s and 1970s to alter the recruitment and education of medical students, to encourage and train physicians to work in underserved areas of the United States, and to promote two new kinds of health workers, nurse practitioners and physician's assistants. After briefly reviewing the events that shaped medical education during the first half of this century and the numerous pressures to alter it, Rocio Huet-Cox details the attempts to modify the education of physicians during the 1960s and 1970s. Through the expansion of existing medical schools, the creation of new ones, and the reduction of the length of study in a limited number of schools, the number of physicians trained was significantly increased. Curriculum changes were made in order to produce physicians better prepared to deal with health problems related to environmental, behavioral, and occupational factors. Efforts were made to humanize the medical school curriculum and to enroll larger numbers of minority students and women. Huet-Cox then evaluates the extent of these changes in medical education and raises the question whether the 1980 graduate is truly better equipped than the 1960 graduate "to influence positively the factors that cause ill health, after being trained in this 'reformed' medical education system."

Hal Strelnick and Richard Younge discuss the panoply of programs, from those at the precollege level through those to retain minority students already in medical school, that supported affirmative action in medical education, particularly during the early 1970s. They stress the pivotal role the federal government plays both in financing affirmative action programs and in withdrawing support from them. Also, the implications of the *Bakke* case and the overall progress in the training of minority students are evaluated.

In his examination of the effort of the U.S. Public Health Service to provide health services for communities with inadequate health care Fitzhugh Mullan traces the development of the National Health Service Corps, created by Congress in 1970. In 1972 a National Health Service Corps scholarship program was authorized; this program offered full tuition and a monthly stipend in return for service in a federal program—most often the NHSC. Finally, Mullan evaluates the NHSC through the 1970s, weaving together the complex issues of medical need and shifting political ideology.

In the last chapter in Part III, Molly Backup and John Molinaro trace efforts during the 1960s to train physician's assistants and nurse practitioners. They outline the reasons organized medicine supported the development of midlevel health workers and go on to describe the specific programs. They conclude by evaluating the performance of these health workers and by questioning their future role in an era of oversupply of physicians and continued reliance on fee-for-service health care.

Part IV focuses on the highly complex issue of nonprofessional participation in health care. Addressed in passing in earlier chapters, it is the central topic of the chapter by John Hatch and Eugenia Eng. From a discussion of the increasing fragmentation, alienation, and violence in America's cities, the authors move to an analysis of the "strategy of community participation and control in the 1960s." Community action and participation, mandated by the Economic Opportunity Act of 1964, was an integral part of efforts to improve health care for the urban and rural poor. Hatch and Eng discuss the problems, conflicts, and positive results of community participation, paying particular attention to the difficulties of identifying local, indigenous leadership.

Larry Sirott and Howard Waitzkin explore another aspect of consumer control of health services—holism and self-help. They discuss some of the major problems that characterize modern technological medicine: fragmentation, alienation, professional dominance, and high cost. They proceed to explore the ways in which the self-help movement fosters increased individual autonomy and control of health services and to raise questions about the movement, particularly its victim-blaming aspects.

In the concluding chapter, we attempt to discuss the results and implications of these efforts—both for the medical profession and for reform efforts in the broader society. We hope that this collective book will help to lead the way, particularly during this dismal period when many of the reform efforts of the past fifty years are being undermined and in many cases actually dismantled, to a more just and equitable health care system—and indeed to a more just and equitable society—for all Americans.

This book is, of course, the product of its contributors; we are indebted to them not only for the clarity and cogency of their contributions but also for their collegiality and for making our job as editors so exciting and pleasurable. We are grateful as well to James Peck, our editor; to Dan Cullen and Otto Sonntag at Pantheon Books; and to Barbara Aiken, Eve Teitelbaum and Edythe Weber at the Department of Social Medicine at Montefiore Medical Center for helping to bring this book to fruition.

part I

HEALTH CARE INSTITUTIONS

1.

community
health centers:

HEALTH CARE AS AN INSTRUMENT
OF SOCIAL CHANGE

H . Jack Geiger

I n the United States in the early 1960s—while the stock market boomed, hundreds of millions of dollars were allocated to launch the race to put men (and flags) on the moon as a demonstration of national power, and affluent citizens bought fallout shelters—another America was rediscovered.[1] It was the United States as the poor experienced it: a land of hunger, slums, deprivation, illiteracy, unemployment, and racial oppression, suddenly made visible in one of the cyclic (though usually brief) swings of public attention and concern that have characterized Western capitalist societies regularly ever since the industrial revolution.

In the first half of the decade, as poverty and its correlates were made a part of the national political agenda, it became clear that the land of the poor was also a land of pain, suffering, needless disability, and early death. The evidence grew that health care was still essentially a privilege with a price tag and that for the poor it was unavailable, inaccessible, inappropriate in its organization and focus, and ineffective in its delivery. One medical observer, summarizing an extensive survey of health and poverty in the rural South and in northern urban ghettos, wrote:

We saw hundreds of people whose only hope of obtaining medical care was to become an emergency which could not be turned away. . . . Most of these people live constantly at the brink of medical disaster, hoping that the symptoms they have or the pain they feel will prove transient or can somehow be survived, for they know that no help is available to them. . . . We saw people with most of the dreadful disorders that weaken, disable, and torture, particularly the poor. High blood pressure, diabetes, urinary tract infections, anemia, tuberculosis, gall bladder and intestinal disorders, eye and skin diseases were frequent findings among the adults. . . . Most of the children had chronic skin infections. Chronically infected, draining ears with resulting partial deafness occurred in an amazing number of the smaller children. We saw rickets, a disorder thought to be nearly abolished in this country. Every form of vitamin deficiency known to us that could be identified by clinical examination was reported.[2]

When the national responses to such observations and to the simultaneous and closely linked pressures of the civil rights movement coalesced in 1964 as the "War on Poverty," health care was a part of the initial Great Society package—but not in terms of structural change in the health care system. The centerpieces of the liberal reform effort, Medicaid for the poor and Medicare for the elderly (poor and nonpoor alike), were limited to the *financing* of health care. They reimbursed physicians and hospitals—by and large on their own terms and without significant change in the location, organization, or control of their services—for their usual and customary efforts, delivered in their usual and customary ways. A third component, the maternal- and child-health program, offered inducements to existing medical care providers to extend and organize services to these high-need groups more coherently, and did establish minimum standards as criteria for funding.

But in early 1965 a fourth component—the neighborhood health center program—was proposed to the Office of Economic Opportunity.[3] Like the others, this program was designed to remove financial barriers to access to health care, but it emphasized additional and much wider goals. These included (1) *providing* care, not merely assuring its funding; (2) creating a new kind of institution in the health care delivery system—neighborhood or community health centers, serving defined communities and populations, and combining curative and preventive services; (3) shifting the locus of services from hospital to local community, and the emphasis from complex tertiary care to primary care; (4) establishing new patterns of professional organization, with emphasis on multidisciplinary teams that included paraprofessionals recruited from the target communities; (5) broadening the scope of "medical" services to include health-related environmental and social concerns; and (6) giving the poor an assured role in the design and control of their own health services.

Beyond these structural changes in the health care system, the initial neighborhood health center proposal articulated a still broader goal, extending beyond that system: social and political change to affect those powerful determinants of health status that lie in the economic and social order. Health care services, it was argued, should be deliberately used as a point of entry for such broader social change.[4]

These ideas fueled the development and growth of neighborhood health centers for almost a decade and established them—in the minds of their initiators, proponents, and participants, at least—as part of a social movement, with an ideology of liberal reform. In 1974—nine years into the development of a national health center network—analysts observed:

> The centers are not merely projects that implement a series of improvements in primary health care. They also express and carry a social movement defined by several impulses toward change that converged in the 1960s. It is impossible to understand the current generation of centers without viewing them as a social movement . . . they are in large part the product of several streams of reform. . . . It is important to analyze the health centers at least in part in terms of the extent to which they represent a playing out of larger political themes.[5]

A second decade of experience and growth is now almost completed. There are more than 800 health centers now, serving some 4.2 million people. They constitute a small but significant part of the national health care system. They have survived innumerable local political and professional assaults and, during the Nixon years, one prolonged attack by a hostile national administration, which questioned their costs and efficiency but not their commitment to the poor. In the process, the movement has faltered, changed, and grown again.

Now—in a very different national political climate, during the early years of the Reagan administration—they are undergoing the most determined assault of all. This time, however, the attack is aimed not so much at their effectiveness or efficiency as at the fundamental principles that gave rise to health care reform. Now there are overt challenges to the ideas that health care is a right, not an economic privilege; that the health of the poor is an appropriate governmental concern, requiring direct governmental intervention; that only the federal government can adequately protect the poor against regional, racial, and economic discrimination in health care; and that small-scale, locally accountable institutions, not gigantic health care corporations, should deliver primary care.

Any pertinent review of the health center movement, therefore, must now ask not only what the health care problems to be solved were, how they were addressed, and how it all worked, in health care terms. It must also consider what happened to the social movement and its ideology, what the effect was of political shifts in the larger society, and where—in political terms—we must go from here, if this health care effort is to continue.

POVERTY, ILLNESS, AND MEDICAL CARE: THE HEALTH GAP

The decade following the close of World War II was marked by massive governmental investment in biomedical research and in hospital construction and expansion. The dramatic yield in new knowledge—new drugs, vaccines, and technologies—was paralleled by steady improvement in national health indices (owing also to improvement in the national economy). Medical care was seen as a definite social good, promising miracles; at the same time, the hub of the system shifted decisively from doctor's office to hospital, and the costs of care increased substantially.

From 1948 to the early 1960s, a series of campaigns to establish a national health insurance system drew intermittent attention to the fact that improvements in health status and access to care were far from uniformly distributed. Each effort was fought off, however, by the determined opposition of the American Medical Association, the American Hospital Association, and private insurance companies. With the exception of the elderly—whose medical care began to be an insupportable burden to the middle class—the public was content to believe that the system worked, and that "charity medicine," public hospitals, and local welfare systems protected the poor.

What changed in the early 1960s were not the data but the amount of attention paid to them, attention stimulated by the struggle over Medicare, the rediscovery of poverty, and the civil rights movement. Suddenly, in the midst of affluence, it was widely recognized that there was an enormous health gap between the poor and the better-off—that the poor were likelier to be sick, that the sick were likelier to be poor, and that without intervention the poor grew sicker and the sick grew poorer.[6] And, while the majority of the sick and the poor were white, the association between poverty and race was so strong that to be black, Hispanic, or native American was, on the average, to pay a huge price in illness and early death.

Nationally, in 1960, the black infant mortality rate was 43 per 1,000 live births, roughly double the white rate. The national tuberculosis death rate was 11.5 per 100,000 for blacks, 4.2 for whites.[7] By every definition—self-assessment, limitation of activity, bed disability days, or length of hospitalization—the poor were sicker, lost twice as many days of work per year because of illness, and were five times likelier to be confined to their homes.[8]

While approximately 80 percent of Americans with annual incomes of $7,000 or more had some form of hospital or medical insurance in 1960, 60 percent of the poor had none.[9] In 1964, wealthier children made an average of 5.1 physician visits a year; the children of the poor, despite their greater burden of illness, saw a doctor 2.7 times.[10] Only 58 percent of low-income women saw a physician early in pregnancy.[11]

Of the first 600,000 poor children to attend Head Start centers[12] in 1964, a majority had never seen a physician, and 25 percent were found to have serious untreated health problems. A study of 162 poor families in rural Ohio found that only 18 of the 250 children had received smallpox, diphtheria, pertussis, and tetanus immunizations, and that only 15 had been immunized against polio.[13] In the rural South, hospitals were totally segregated—and they routinely denied admission, often even in emergencies, to blacks who could not pay. A handful of small black hospitals and a thin line of black physicians—in 1960, only 2 percent of the nation's 233,000 doctors were black—constituted the only reliable resource. In Mississippi, the ratio of black physicians to black population was 1 to 6,619, and more than half of all black births occurred at home—often without medical help—while 99 of 100 white births occurred in hospitals.[14]

In northern cities, the poor confronted a confusing, fragmented jumble of agencies, each providing a limited number of categorical services in its own style, at its own hours, on its own terms. By tradition, "public health" clinics and curative medicine were rigidly separated. A poor mother could take her infant to a health department well-baby clinic for immunization, but if the same child fell ill she had to go elsewhere, to a hospital outpatient clinic, an emergency room, or a private physician's office. A public health official documented the case of one "welfare" family with four children suffering serious chronic illnesses; in an average week, the children had eleven appointments at eight different outpatient clinics at five different public or voluntary hospitals. The response of the health department to this finding was to send an indignant letter to welfare officials demanding that the family's transportation allowance be increased.[15]

In the context of these problems, the proposal for community health centers reflected the belief that, while economic barriers to medical care had to be removed, access of the poor to medical care could not be accomplished by funding alone. The mere provision of tokens for the turnstiles of the existing medical care system would not lead to equity, so long as that system was remote, hospital centered, professionally controlled, fragmented, middle-class in its orientation, and unaware of (or unresponsive to) the social, physical, and biological environments in which both urban and rural poor lived. A new kind of institution, differently organized, locally based, and focused on primary care, would do better.

Furthermore—reflecting the central thrust of the civil rights movement for minority self-determination, and the commitment of the War on Poverty itself to the maximum feasible participation by the poor—such local health centers might be far more susceptible to community control than were complex hospital corporations or other entrepreneurial providers of care. Finally, an emphasis on the health of communities, beyond the traditional patient-by-patient focus of clinical medicine, might promote community development and permit intervention in social and environmental causes of ill health.

In many of these respects, community health center proposals represented a criticism of the entire mainstream medical system, not just the organization of medical care for the poor; and an unspoken goal—however grandiose—of some proponents was structural reform of that system for *all* its consumers, rich and poor alike. A political view was implicit in the definition of health problems as socioeconomic as well as biological in origin, and in the formulation of medical care as a social process rather than as a technical commodity. The goal was not an alternative health care system for the poor—that already existed, in effect, and was inevitably inferior—nor was it the inclusion of the poor in the existing medical-establishment model, with all its flaws. Meeting the health needs of the poor in a new way, some reformers hoped, might provide a base for change in the system itself.

THE ORIGINS OF COMMUNITY HEALTH CENTERS

Ambulatory care institutions called health centers have been intermittently present on the American scene since the early 1900s, and some observers—erroneously assuming that they were the precursors of the new initiative that was presented to the Office of Economic Opportunity in 1965—have written of "The First Neighborhood Health Center Movement—Its Rise and Fall,"[16] or of "The Neighborhood Health Center—Reform Ideas of Yesterday and Today."[17] It is true that these earlier ventures emphasized some of the same ideas: district location, a degree of community participation (though almost never a share in management or governance), and a formal administrative structure. But there were crucial ideological and practical differences that made them institutions of an entirely different kind.

Almost without exception, they were "public health" clinics, limited to a variety of preventive, social welfare, and nutritional services, and as a matter of deliberate policy they gave no medical care for illness. In accord with the implicit bargain struck between public health and organized medicine, the clinics were careful to avoid even the threat of competition with fee-for-service private practice or hospital "charity wards" and dispensaries. The published promise of the George White Health Units in Boston, the most famous of the 1920–40 era, was "no prescription given; no sickness treated."[18] Furthermore, they embodied no concept of entitlement, of a right to care; in most instances, they were proposed simply as a means of centralizing and increasing the efficiency of scattered voluntary social agencies and "public health" outposts. Only the recommendations of the Committee on the Costs of Medical Care in 1932[19]—never implemented and promptly renounced by organized medicine—and special projects such as the Navajo-Many-farms project[20] joined curative and preventive medicine in local centers serving defined populations.

The 1965 proposals were derived, instead, from models overseas: the Peckham Health Center, in England,[21] the work of John Grant (first at the Peking Union Medical College, in China, and later in Puerto Rico),[22] and in particular the work of Sidney Kark and his colleagues in establishing a network of community-based teaching health centers for African and Indian populations in South Africa.[23] With the exception of Peckham, all these centers served deprived populations with extreme poverty, high birth rates, high death rates, a heavy burden of both infectious and chronic disease, low levels of employment, low literacy, substandard housing and nutrition, and limited medical care resources.

When health workers in the United States who had studied or trained in these "international health" models[24] participated in the civil rights movement in the rural South in the early 1960s, it became clear that a whole series of identifiable populations in this country shared those characteristics to some degree: blacks in the rural South and northern urban ghettos, Puerto Ricans in the cities of the Northeast, poor whites in Appalachia, Mexican-Americans in the Southwest and West, and native Americans on reservations and in western cities. The overseas model (with particular emphasis on its epidemiological orientation) might, they thought, be adapted to the U.S. scene and added to the War on Poverty.

The first health center proposal to the Office of Economic Opportunity thus stated that its purpose was "to intervene . . . in the cycle of extreme poverty, ill health, unemployment and illiteracy by providing comprehensive health services, based in multi-disciplinary community health centers, oriented toward maximum participation of each community in meeting its own health needs and in social and economic changes related to health."[25] The proposed health services were to "include preventive, curative and health education programs in new patterns of medical care organization." They were to "emphasize the formation of community health associations . . . to stimulate change in family and community knowledge and behavior relating to the prevention of disease, the informed use of available health resources, and the improvement of environmental, economic and educational factors related to health."

Community health action was also defined as including "the training of local personnel" and "the conduct of both descriptive and analytic research on health levels and needs . . . and evaluation studies." The proposal was based on the following premise:

> Conventional approaches to health improvement . . . that deal only with narrow definitions of health and illness are unlikely to make major changes. The need is not merely for the provision of more preventive and curative health services, but also for the development of new organizational patterns to make the distribution of such services uniquely effective. . . . The need is not for the distribution of services to passive recipients, but for the active involvement of local populations in ways which will change their knowledge, attitudes and motivation. The central focus is . . . community-based health improvement.[26]

The initial proposals, for health centers at Columbia Point, a small but densely populated housing-project community of some 6,000 persons in Boston, and in northern Bolivar County, Mississippi, a 500-square-mile rural area whose center is the small town of Mound Bayou, were followed almost immediately by applications to the Office of Economic Opportunity for projects in the South Bronx (the Martin Luther King, Jr. Health Center), in Los Angeles (the Watts Health Center), in Chicago (the Mile Square Health Center), and in Denver. All of these proposals were funded by OEO as "research and demonstration" projects. The agency had no explicit funding authorization for health programs and had at first resisted venturing into health care. Significantly, although the projects were listed as Community Action Programs, all of these initial grantees were medical schools, teaching hospitals, or health departments. Though the commitments to community organization and community participation were sincere, health professionals and their institutions did the planning, wrote the proposals—and received the grants.

GROWTH AND DEVELOPMENT OF HEALTH CENTERS, 1965 – 1982

The Columbia Point Health Center, funded in June of 1965, opened in December of that year. Six months later, Sen. Edward Kennedy visited the center; subsequently he sponsored legislation for the creation of a national OEO health center network. The congressional mandate—passed in November 1966—for the OEO Comprehensive Health Services Program defined its purpose almost as broadly as did the initial health center proposals:

> . . . to assure that [health] services are made readily accessible to residents of such areas [of concentrated poverty], are furnished in a manner most responsive to their needs and with their participation, and whenever possible are combined with . . . arrangements for providing employment, education, social or other assistance needed by the families and individuals served. . . .[27]

In 1967, the Department of Health, Education, and Welfare joined the effort. An HEW program analysis issued in December 1967 identified comprehensive health centers, along with proposed changes in outpatient clinics and health manpower and financing programs, as a principal means for improving the delivery of health centers to the poor. The report estimated that 800 to 1,000 such centers might be needed.[28]

Between 1965 and 1971, more than 100 health centers were funded by OEO appropriations totaling $308 million, and another 50 were funded by $110 million in HEW funds.[29] The pattern of funding changed in an important respect. Of the early grants (1965–66), 50 percent went to hospitals, 37 percent to medical schools, and 13 percent to health departments. In 1971, 59 percent of the grants went to new health corporations as administering agencies for health centers—community groups in partnership with health providers, with assured community participation on boards and management structures—and only 10 percent went to hospitals and 7 percent to medical schools.[30]

The problems faced by these first 150 to 200 health centers stemmed more from the scope of their purposes and promises, the speed with which they were developed, and the difficulties of resource and manpower development than from external opposition. Though there were frequent fierce struggles with local medical and dental societies, the American Medical Association and organized medicine in general kept a low profile. The health centers—and the accompanying Medicaid and Medicare programs—enjoyed enormous public support. The National Medical Association, a generally conservative group of black physicians, was ambivalent. After a period of initial support, it perceived some of the projects as an invasion of black urban communities by colonizing white hospitals (health center sponsors) and professionals. In the South, where almost all OEO projects were correctly perceived as potential or actual vehicles for black autonomy, resistance to health centers by local and state governments and by professional societies was bitter and prolonged, though both OEO and HEW attempted to appease it by making occasional health center grants to white-controlled state and local health departments.

What drew much more attention, during the first decade of health center development, were the struggles—common to all OEO projects—over the meaning of community participation and/or control.[31] It was, more often than not, difficult to determine who represented the community—and participation in board elections was low. Even when personal political power and patronage were not at issue, community board members usually placed much higher priority on economic development (particularly the creation of health center jobs) than on health services. Conflict with health professionals, hardly prepared by experience and training to have to explain, justify, and defend their program and budget choices, was inevitable. In the numerous cases where grants had been made to hospitals and medical schools—which therefore had legal and fiscal control of the budgets, and were held accountable for them —community boards rapidly perceived that their role was only advisory and that their only leverage lay in organized community protest and confrontation. As Hatch and Eng point out elsewhere in this book, OEO policies favored the selection of community "representatives" who were skilled in the rhetoric of militancy but lacked both administrative experience and any true base of support in the target community. In other instances, professionals simply dominated boards with technical expertise. And in almost all cases, communities perceived that the traditional power relationships had not changed very much, because professionals (unlike the poor) could always leave and work somewhere else on their own terms. One frustrated community board member shouted at the professional staff: "I understand your idea of this partnership! I'll provide the illnesses and you'll run the services, just like always!"[32] If the shortage of physicians in poverty areas was acute, the shortage of skilled community organizers was even greater, and the failure to recognize that effective community organization required discipline, experience, and, above all, time was even more widespread.

A second major problem was the scarcity of physical facilities adequate to house high-quality health services in poverty areas. Project directors struggled to buy trailers and prefabricated modular units, or used health care funds to renovate warehouses, abandoned factories, stores, housing-project apartments, and, in one instance, a convent. Finally, an extraordinary arrangement was evolved that linked OEO, HEW, the Department of Housing and Urban Development, and the Office of Management and Budget with private mortgage and insurance companies to make FHA-guaranteed loans for health center construction.[33]

A third problem was professional staffing. By 1972, approximately 1,000 physicians were practicing at health centers, about 40 percent of them full-time.[34] The percentage of young physicians, black physicians, and female physicians working at health centers was substantially higher than the national norms. But the turnover was relatively high, with a "half-life" of about two years,[35] despite competitive salary levels, affiliations with medical schools and teaching hospitals, and the opportunity (as one analyst described it) to "practice modern medicine and social justice at the same time." He added:

> It is likely that a large percentage of these physicians would not have practiced at all in low-income areas under other conditions. . . . Further programs to increase the number of students in medical and other health professional schools from poverty neighborhoods are also critical.[36]

Finally, and overwhelmingly, there were problems of financing. Daniel Zwick, one of the OEO administrators most responsible for the development of the national health center network, wrote in 1972 that

> The initial OEO grant support of health centers assumed that long-term financial support would come largely from Medicaid, Medicare and other financing sources. The organization of the centers, in turn, would make it possible to achieve better use of the increased funds available for

health services. . . . It was estimated that funds from Medicaid and Medicare might finance 70–80 per cent of health center costs.

The nature of the growth of the Medicaid programs has frustrated the achievement of this goal. State programs have been restrictive with respect to both beneficiary eligibility and supported services. Benefits have been reduced rather than expanded. Some state administrators have resisted the completion of procedures to reimburse health centers. Even the most successful efforts by health centers to obtain Medicaid, Medicare and other private third-party funds has resulted in reimbursements for only 50 per cent or so of their budgets; in most cases, such payments have been in the range of 10–20 per cent. . . . Both Medicare and Medicaid have tended to treat hospital-sponsored projects more liberally.[37]

In short, trends that threaten the very survival of health care for the poor in 1982 were already evident a decade earlier, when Zwick concluded, "Sound long-term financing arrangements for the centers, and other health care programs for the poor, depend upon major changes in national health financing programs."[38]

As Medicaid and Medicare costs increased and competition intensified for the public health dollar (particularly by large hospitals, with the management resources and political clout to exploit and influence public funding), it was both tempting and easy to exploit rising public concern over health care costs with attacks on health centers. It was tempting because the national political mood had changed decisively and the Nixon administration had been reelected in part on the strength of a so-called southern strategy of opposition to civil rights and poverty efforts. It was easy to make health center costs look much larger than they were by comparing the cost of comprehensive care—a health center visit that might include transportation, a physician's examination, laboratory tests, time with a social worker, counseling by a family-planning worker, and other services—with the cost of a traditional limited visit to an outpatient clinic or a physician's office.

In fact, careful cost-accounting studies were revealing that the costs of providing clinical care in health centers compared favorably with comparable services in prepaid group practices, and data were already available to document an unprecedented—and enormously cost-saving—reduction in hospitalization among health center users.[39] But there was also evidence that centers were administratively top-heavy and that physician "productivity"—the number of patients seen per hour—was lower than in other settings.

Furthermore, there was criticism from the left.[40] The tail had failed to wag the dog; in the radical critique, health centers had failed to trigger broader social change, the poor were still locked in relative powerlessness in geographical or political ghettos, and even the health care system (particularly the university medical schools and the major teaching and voluntary hospitals associated with them) had remained essentially the same.

What all this overlooked was the amount of change—and successful effort—that had already occurred. The most extensive concerted public effort in the history of the United States to expand ambulatory health care resources in poverty communities on a nationwide basis had been launched, survived, and grown. The principle, if not the smoothly functioning mechanisms, of consumer participation had been firmly established. Outreach workers had been recruited from target populations, had been trained, and—in many centers—had demonstrated the predicted effectiveness of "nonprofessional" contributions to health care delivery. Physicians, social workers, dentists, family health workers, nurse practitioners, public health nurses, and, in some centers, sanitarians, community organizers and health educators, and psychologists were working together in health care teams. More than half of the nation's medical schools had been involved in one way or another. The wall between "public health" and "clinical medicine" had been breached; in some centers, health workers attacked environmental hazards, expanded community water and sanitation facilities, and launched new housing efforts.

Evaluation studies were beginning to assess the effectiveness of consumer-provider cooperation, health care teams, and training programs for new health careers for the poor.[41]

Though the answers to these questions were hardly complete, these tests of accessibility, availability, and acceptability had become commonly applied standards for community health services. One observer concluded that "the bold rhetoric of the 1960s is the common talk of the 1970s."[42] Most important of all, more than 2 million people were being served. In some poverty-stricken communities, health centers had become the dominant source of primary care, sharply lowering the use of emergency rooms, and they were competitive or significantly lower in cost than hospital outpatient departments, clinics, and large prepaid group practices. At the Bunker Hill Health Center in Charlestown, Massachusetts, for example, in a single year services were used by 52 percent of the 16,800 people in the target population, including 75 percent of the children and adolescents. Most were regular and continuing users of the center.[43]

During this first decade of health center development, an extraor-

dinary diversity of health center projects developed. Two brief examples may illustrate this range of variation. In one case, a health
center was organized with the specific goal of meeting a community's needs for primary health care and at the same time developing
an epidemiological research program for studying high-prevalence
chronic disease in the total community. In the other case, a health
center accomplished less in the way of continuing community surveillance and epidemiology but made major efforts at community-
oriented environmental, health education, community organization,
and training programs linked to primary care delivery.

The East Boston (Massachusetts) Neighborhood Health Center
developed as a specific partnership between the community, which
badly needed accessible primary care services, and the Channing
Laboratory, Affiliated Hospitals Center, Inc., of Harvard Medical
School, one of the nation's most productive centers for epidemiological research.

In the first ten years of the center's work, its staff and their
colleagues at the Channing Laboratory (many have joint appointments) have published more than sixty scientific papers on the East
Boston community: studies of hypertension; bacteriuria in women;
oral contraceptive use, bacteriuria, and fasting triglycerides; plasma
cholesterol and HDL cholesterol; household aggregation and household risk factors in chronic nonspecific lung disease; surveillance
techniques for respiratory illness, and familial aggregation of
chronic bronchitis. At the same time, the health center has offered
services in internal medicine, pediatrics, adolescent medicine, ob-
stetrics/gynecology/family planning, emergency service, home
care, dental service, social service, nutrition and public health nursing, together with the usual support services. Its "market penetration" of the community is extraordinary; there are only two other
primary care providers in the community, and in one recent year the
center provided 111,000 visits to 27,000 persons out of the total
East Boston population of 32,000 people.[44]

The center conducts a total household-by-household census of
the community every two years. Some of the center staff provide
only direct primary care services, others are exclusively involved in
epidemiological research and analysis, and still others do both. A
major part of the funding for the census, the surveys, and the
epidemiological analyses comes from research grants rather than
from the medical services budget drawn from federal health center
grants and third-party reimbursement.

The Delta Health Center, in contrast, was designed to serve a
population of some 14,000 rural black residents in a 500-square-
mile area of northern Bolivar County, Mississippi.[45] More than half
of them were clustered around the base town of Mound Bayou and

nine other small communities; the rest were scattered in rural areas. The population was characterized by extreme poverty, high unemployment as a consequence of the mechanization of cotton agriculture, low educational levels, an extremely high infant mortality rate, and heavy burdens of both infectious and chronic illness. There was a high dependency ratio: a large and relatively stable population of young children and the elderly, and a shifting population of young and middle-aged adults, particularly men, moving back and forth (to places as far away as Chicago) in search of work. The environmental hazards were extreme. More than 75 percent of the dwellings were unfit for habitation, lacking protected water supplies and relying on surface privies for sanitation and unshielded small stoves for heat.[46] Many had no electricity. The prevalence of cotton agriculture meant that exposure to pesticides was frequent. Malnutrition was a major problem, and support services (welfare, food stamps, and so on) were minimal to nonexistent. The physician-to-population ratio was very low, and access to care was severely limited by fiscal barriers and lack of transportation.

The center had a strong affiliation with the Tufts medical school, but the school was 1,500 miles away. No special funding was available for demography or epidemiological research. A total community census was accomplished once, early in the center's development, but never repeated; a community-based epidemiological survey of malnutrition in children was completed, but did not lead to ongoing surveillance. Studies of medical care utilization and of environmental hazards were conducted regularly in the three sectors into which the target area was divided.

From the very start, the center's plan was to reach beyond the provision of personal health services to individuals and families, to stimulate community development and economic growth, and to make the social and political investments necessary for community health autonomy and self-management. Therefore, in addition to the core *clinical services*—preventive and therapeutic pediatric, medical, obstetric-gynecologic and minor surgical care, emergency services, mental health services, nurse-midwifery, community health nursing, homemaker and school health services—four other major programs were undertaken.

Each of these was shaped by the needs of the community rather than by traditional public health concerns. Thus, *nutrition services* moved beyond emergency food and food-stamp programs to the organization of a cooperative farm to grow vegetables and high-protein corn. *Environmental services* focused on digging protected wells, constructing sanitary privies, housing repair, and vector control. *Social services,* in addition to traditional casework, welfare, and food stamp assistance, targeted high-risk groups through community services for the isolated elderly and family services for youthful offenders.

Community health action programs were the most varied. They included the development of ten local health associations, the organization and operation of a bus transportation system, the provision of legal services, the provision of technical assistance for community development projects, and the organization of a network of day-care and pre-Head Start centers for young children.[47]

Many of these services included activities of wider social and political significance. The local health associations, for example, were helped to obtain mortgages so that each could develop a community or "contact" center. In the process, the health center and community board used the substantial leverage of their million-dollar annual budget to end (or at least limit) racial discrimination in lending practices by local banks, so that black local residents— particularly those employed by the health center—could obtain loans for home improvements or purchases. The community "contact" centers, in turn, were rented to the health center during the day for OEO-funded health care activities, thus repaying the mortgages on those buildings. During the evenings, they were free to serve as focal points for voter registration drives, civil rights, and other activities.

Similarly, the legal services program was instrumental in the development of a lawsuit demanding that local towns and the county government provide paved roads, lighting, sewers, and other municipal services on an equal basis to black residential areas. By the time the suit was won, this health-related work had already begun in some of the target areas—because voter registration had resulted in the election of a black majority to the county commission and black mayors in several of the towns.

In like fashion, the cooperative farm became the North Bolivar County Farm Cooperative, Inc., a 600-acre irrigated farm, collectively worked—and owned—by members of some 1,000 families. It had begun as a nutrition demonstration project to supplement the inadequate diets of unemployed local residents and their families.

Visits to the health center for personal health services during any one time period were usually exceeded by individual participation in local community health association activities. On the average, some 3,000 individuals each month had contact outside the health center, in the community, with field staff. Since the primary health care teams that served each sector included not only clinicians but also sanitarians, social workers, health educators, and other field staff, there was a fairly regular and accurate transfer of information between clinical and community programs.

Perhaps the most important of the center's activities, in the longer run, was the least conventional. On the premise that the community's own human resources were its most important asset for long-term change in health status, the health center provided, facilitated, or arranged for the health vocational, preprofessional, or professional training of community residents. These programs ranged from high school equivalency certification and college preparatory courses at the center to arrangements that sent thirteen area residents (including six from Bolivar County) to medical school, others to nursing, social work, and public health schools, and enabled many more to obtain certification as sanitarians, physical therapists, medical records librarians, X-ray technicians, and the like. Altogether, more than 100 people participated, of whom more than half are back in Mississippi—including a former local high school teacher, now a board-certified internist, who is the center's clinical director.

By the mid-1970s, however, the diversity and scope of these and many similar programs was no longer being encouraged. The Nixon and Ford administrations had effectively disassembled OEO. All health centers were turned over to HEW, which in turn grouped them under the new Bureau of Community Health Services. Faced with explosively rising health care costs, the bureau rigidly pushed for increased physician productivity, intensive third-party billing, tight administrative and fiscal controls, reduction in outreach, transportation, and other nontraditional health services, and sharp reductions in funding for community boards. Health center staffs complained that their programs were being turned into federally funded Medicaid mills, grinding patients through as fast as possible in order to maximize reimbursements, and that much of the innovative character of the program was being destroyed. The bureau maintained that personal health services were the real basis of the centers' continuing public and congressional support, and that the centers had to be economically competitive in the "marketplace" of primary health care if they were to survive.

No sooner had an uneasy stability been reached in this new mold, however, than growth began again. New legislative authorizations for a new generation of smaller centers—migrant health centers, Rural Health Initiative and Urban Health Initiative projects—rapidly swelled the total. By 1982 there were 872 centers in all, serving 4.2 million people. Of these, according to a 1976 survey, 71 percent were poor, 80 percent belonged to a minority, 49 percent had no employed family member, and 41 percent were under eighteen—in sum, the population that has the highest health risks, the greatest burden of illness, disability, and preventable death, the least access to primary care, and the highest rates of hospitalization.[48] At the same time, the development of the National Health Service Corps offered the promise, at last, of a steady pool of physicians, dentists, and nurse-practitioners for health center staffing.

EVALUATION: SOME OUTCOMES

Close to a hundred studies have examined various aspects of health center performance since the beginning of the movement. They constitute, by now, a substantial body of evaluative work. Perhaps the best- and longest-documented effect of health centers—one that was reported in the very first evaluations from Columbia Point,[49] Chicago,[50] and Portland, Oregon[51]—is in lowering the rate of hospital admissions from the target populations, achieving hospitalization at earlier stages of disease, reducing the lengths of hospital stay, and lowering the number of hospital days per capita. Altogether, more than thirty studies show reductions in admission rates as high as 44 percent, and reductions in hospital days per capita ranging from 25 percent to as high as 62 percent.[52]

One recent analysis,[53] based on surveys in five communities (Atlanta, Boston, Charleston, South Carolina, Kansas City, Missouri, and East Palo Alto) involving 20,863 persons, showed that the number of annual days of hospitalization per capita was 50 percent lower for community health center users than for those using outpatient departments and emergency rooms as their primary source of care, and 31 percent lower than for those who used private physicians as their primary source—holding constant the effects of age, sex, race, education, income, insurance coverage, and health status. Another recent study[54] compared Medicaid beneficiaries (AFDC recipients) using community health centers as their primary source of care with similar Medicaid recipients using other sources of care, in each of three communities. The hospitalization rates of health center users were only 52 percent of those of non-users; their patient days per capita were only 60 percent as high. Outpatient department and emergency room use was dramatically lower among the health center users.

As one might expect, given these patterns, the total per capita costs to Medicaid of community health center users were significantly lower for ambulatory care, for hospitalization, and for all medical care. The total costs per person per year were 6 percent, 31 percent, and 45 percent lower in the three communities.

There is no reason to believe that these cost savings were the result of reductions in the scope or quality of services. On the contrary, the range of services of the community health centers was usually broader than that of the more traditional providers, and repeated quality-of-care audits have shown the quality of health center services nationally to be equal to those of outpatient clinics, private physicians, and prepaid group practices.[55]

Perhaps the most important studies, although they are methodologically the most difficult, are those that demonstrate a significant effect of health centers on the health status of their target populations. One recent multiple-regression analysis[56] of data from comparable counties, comparing those with and those without a community health center, suggested that the health centers had accomplished a significant reduction in infant mortality, particularly among blacks, and in neonatal mortality. Overall, the reduction attributed to health centers was 2 deaths per 1,000 live births for blacks—or 10 percent of the black infant mortality rate in these counties. "The excess mortality rate of black babies has been identified as a goal of public health policy for a number of years," the study noted; "our results suggest that community health centers have the potential to make a substantial contribution to the achievement of this goal," and at a very favorable cost-benefit ratio in comparison with other programs to reduce infant mortality, such as the construction and subsidization of neonatal intensive care units.[57]

Other studies have indicated striking reductions in infant mortality in rural southern counties served by community health centers,[58] in a health center population in Denver,[59] and in Dade County, Florida.[60] A New York study reported a 41 percent decrease in the perinatal mortality rate over four years, a 29 percent decrease in the prematurity rate, and an accompanying decrease in neonatal mortality.[61] Finally, a survey of low-income census tracts in Baltimore over a ten-year period showed a 60 percent reduction in the incidence of rheumatic fever—a change attributed to the early detection and treatment of streptococcal infection—in those tracts served by health centers; it showed no similar reduction in comparable areas without health centers.[62]

Karen Davis, until recently a deputy assistant secretary of Health, Education, and Welfare and a co-author of a ten-year appraisal of health and the War on Poverty, concluded on the basis of these and other findings that health centers have been highly effective in increasing access to primary care, have reduced hospitalization and reduced costs, have maintained quality of care, have achieved good "market penetration" and continuous coverage of their target communities, and have made measurable (and sometimes striking) improvements in the health status of populations at very high risk of illness.[63]

By the traditional yardsticks of efficacy, efficiency, and cost-effectiveness, then, health centers have proved themselves to be superior instruments of primary health care delivery to impoverished high-risk populations, as compared with the traditional medical care providers to the poor. In these respects they have amply fulfilled the original hopes held out for them. They represent a social saving of two kinds: they reduce the society's health care expenditures and, more important, they improve health status. Those are no mean successes for relatively new institutions that have had to struggle every year for their funding and their survival.

What we do *not* know, so far at least, is the relative contribution of the different elements of the health center model to these achievements. How much is due to easier geographical access, and how much to the partial removal of fiscal barriers? What is the impact of health care teams, of outreach workers, of community boards, of the target population's sense that they have a community-responsive institution that "belongs," more or less, to them?

And beyond this, have there been effects outside the realm of health care? We know that health center ideas have diffused widely within the health care system. Community representation, health care teams, and outreach attempts are now routine in many health care organizations, although "community organization" has been replaced by "marketing" in some. What we do *not* know—beyond anecdotal evidence from a scattering of centers—is whether any broader processes of social change have been catalyzed in poverty communities by health center programs, albeit far more slowly than was initially hoped.

We can conclude that the nation's health care system has been modified—but that its essential structure is unchanged: it remains hospital centered, technology oriented, tertiary-care focused, and entrepreneurial, though power within that system has shifted steadily from physicians to corporate hospital and insurance structures.

IMPLICATIONS FOR THE FUTURE

In the face of Reaganomics and the current administration's social (or antisocial?) policy, one must first question whether health centers even have a future. Not if the administration has its way, surely, for the attempt now is to abandon the very social commitments that constitute their foundation, to deny that health care is a right, to refuse the special needs of the poor by excluding them from the roster of the "truly needy," and to substitute the economic fiction that health care is a rational marketplace that will respond to classic market forces.

The assault is both financial and organizational: cut direct health center funding, cut Medicaid and other reimbursement sources, cut categorical funding for preventive programs that health centers can help implement, and return the management (and ultimately the funding) of the whole program to the tender mercies of the states, whose failures and inabilities created the need in the first place. The cuts have already occurred; more than 200 health centers have been closed, and most of the others are struggling desperately to maintain services for their patients despite severe budget reductions. But the attempt to include health centers in state-run block grants has, at least for the present, been fought off.

And that victory is significant, for it demonstrated that health centers have an active and potentially powerful constituency, one that will most likely have to be mobilized again and again during the next few years. During that time, there will be only one political agenda for health centers: mustering the political support to stay alive and relatively independent, even if both the numbers of centers and the size of their budgets is reduced.

In that effort, friends will have to be found beyond the 4.2 million health center users and their families, supporters in the middle-of-the-road middle class that makes up most of the electorate (but less of the political funding and political power). There are, I believe, two strategies for mustering that support. The first rests on the evidence that most Americans are profoundly concerned about health care costs and about the level of governmental spending for health and other social programs. To this constituency, the case must be made that health centers are cost-effective. As we have seen, the evidence exists.

The second strategy rests on the conviction that most Americans gave no mandate in 1980 to allow children and the elderly poor to go hungry, the sick poor to suffer, or infant mortality rates to rise —all the inevitable consequences of current policy. What will be needed to reverse the trend of cuts and abandonment is evidence that these things are beginning to happen. Health centers themselves, however constrained by current budget cuts, are among the institutions closest to the affected populations, and they can have no more urgent priority than the careful documentation and demonstration of these consequences.

Coupled with this, and of greater consequence for the longer term, is evidence that the majority of Americans are fiercely protective of the more general (if not universal) entitlement programs— Medicare, Social Security, student loans—those that benefit the middle class and are not categorically restricted to the poor. The realities of race and class in American life make it unlikely that health centers will be able to enlarge their service populations to attract additional middle-class patients, but to the extent that they can identify their needs with these general social interests, they will gain political strength.

For the middle term, the appeal to universal entitlement, rather than categorical programs, may be the most useful way to approach the restructuring of the health care system. The Reagan administration has taken a risk by making ideology a central issue: supply-side economics, corporate power, regressive taxation disguised as "tax reductions," reduction in governmental responsibility, militarism, and huge military budgets. If the immediate consequences—massive unemployment, depression, huge deficits, and high interest rates, with the simultaneous erosion of social supports—continue, then the way has been opened for ideological challenge. Rather than joining dreary arguments about categorical programs, reformers may then be able to present arguments for national health insurance *and* a national health service as explicit examples of an alternative ideology—one that might work!

At the least, and short of such optimistic hopes, we can anticipate another and early "rediscovery" of poverty, precisely because poverty is now growing so rapidly. If that happens, we can push for a third wave of expansion in the health center network, keeping very much in mind the advice of some friendly critics of early health center work, offered in 1974 but as useful now as it was then.

"Invest heavily early on," they wrote, "in evaluation systems that will generate information in time to wage a more effective fight for survival a few years later. Sit hard on the coat-tails of colleagues eager to preach the myriad virtues of the new approach and to promise quick rewards from the requested public investments. Build in incentives for efficiency. Watch out for faint-hearted friends. Know the opposition."[64]

2.

the urban hospital:

INEQUITY, HIGH TECH, AND LOW PERFORMANCE

Quentin Young

The end of World War II marks the end of a medical era. The transformation of the medical care system was heralded by two "casualties": by the decline of the general practitioner and the rise of specialization; and by the shift of medical service from the physician's office to the hospital. These changes had irreversible effects on hospitals, which underwent more thoroughgoing changes than any other portion of the health care system.

Thousands of demobilized American physicians sought training in a specialty before taking up their interrupted private medical careers. The military service had vividly demonstrated to these fledgling physicians the advantages of specialization with respect to rank, privilege, and opportunity for advancement. At the same time the growth of medical knowledge and skills since the turn of the century undermined the general practitioner as a professional model. The move to specialty training was facilitated by the GI Bill of Rights benefits, which supported the returning veteran's postgraduate work. Federal support for specialized medical training through the enlargement of existing medical schools, the creation of new medical schools, and research grants laid the material basis for the emergence of a highly specialized medical work force.

As doctors became more specialized, the hospital increasingly became "the physician's workplace." As the types and the quantity of services deliverable only in the hospital rapidly expanded, costs immediately reflected the high capital investment in high technology. In this milieu of specialism and federal largesse, the urban teaching hospitals, both public and private, inevitably developed two powerful superstructures: a "full-time" geographically fixed medical staff and a bureaucracy of hospital administrators to handle the complicated fiscal and managerial aspects.

Postwar health care economics was most affected by the growth of prepaid hospital insurance. In the mid-1960s the federal government enacted Medicare (for the aged) and Medicaid (for the indigent) to fill deficiencies in the booming private insurance sector. The overall impact of the growth of insurance was to create powerful incentives to hospitalize more often and to render more service there, all costs to be paid from a seemingly infinite insurance base. The cost of hospitalization constituted the most important inflator of health care system costs.

What was the source of the rapid surge in insurance against hospital costs? During World War II, wage controls, imposed to mitigate the distorting effects of the armaments economy, left a loophole for certain kinds of nonwage benefits. The ability to negotiate health insurance benefits was exploited eagerly by the industrial trade unions. As a result, literally millions of workers and their families in basic industries—steel, auto, meat packing, to name a few—became beneficiaries of more and more comprehensive health care coverage. Union and company negotiators in the 1940s and 1950s were completely unaware that they were sowing the seeds of the gravest problems within health services for the 1970s and 1980s: the overwhelming rise in costs, the concentration of services in the hospital, and the rapid growth of the health care work force, particularly the hospital-based workers.

This period witnessed the proliferation of health workers— nurses, dietitians, and essential hospital workers—augmented by hundreds of thousands of clinical and research technicians, social workers, pharmacists, radiology technicians, physical therapists, occupational therapists, venipuncturists, and so on. The nursing profession was differentiated into new specialties such as neonatology, intensive care, physician's assistants, and emergency care.

The period was also characterized by huge governmental expenditures on hospital renovation and, to a much larger degree, the building of new hospitals. The Hill-Burton Act of 1948 changed the face of the nation's hospital system. In rural or semirural America, it brought small- to medium-sized hospitals to communities that had previously had none. In 1974, in 600 of the 3,400 counties of this nation, the public general hospital, typically run by the county government, served as the only hospital resource for private and public sectors alike.

The urban hospital, however, evolved in a much more highly developed fashion into the "medical-industrial complex." These giant complexes were tied, moreover, to the process of "urban renewal."

Particularly in the cities of the northern and central states, the original "central city" indigenous population has been regularly replaced by black, brown, and white lower-class immigrants seeking better opportunities. The industrial concentration of World War II greatly accelerated this process. Established urban hospitals, those with long service and teaching traditions, found themselves surrounded by new neighbors who were perceived as alien to the hospital, its historic service group, and even its mission. These hospitals' plants were often superannuated and ill prepared for the bright new technological vistas that were rapidly emerging.

Ambitious "urban renewal" plans created enclaves of modern structures that swept clean acres of lower-class housing surrounding the hospitals. The schemes captured billions of urban-renewal dollars augmented by such local matching subsidies as the development of services and tax relief. In city after city, this vast shift in land use from lower-class dwellings and communities to grand expanses of brave new hospital complexes became the characteristic of the past thirty years.

This highly dynamic system of money, building technology, and human resources developed primarily under the aegis of private initiatives. While public hospitals in the urban setting were occasionally replaced with more modern facilities, the process was overwhelmingly a feature of private medicine. The ruling elite in this country have historically chosen to fulfill civic obligation by service on local hospital boards. The fact that hospital board activity has evolved from a marginal charitable obligation into a distinctly big-business event has not discouraged ever more active participation of the bankers, realtors, and merchants on financially potent hospital boards of governors.

The problems that emerged from this mélange created the health politics of the 1960s. Skyrocketing costs posed impossible obstacles to the huge portion of citizens outside the hospital insurance family. This was particularly serious, even scandalous, as it affected citizens over sixty-five years of age. Quite prudently, the private insurers either refused coverage to the elderly or required confiscatory premiums. Equally cruel, but perhaps less dramatic, was the plight of the sick poor. The dynamic of the postwar economy made the black and brown fraction of the poverty sector ever larger, so that

the racist implications of denying health care access became a burning issue at a time when the civil rights movement was gaining
political momentum.

In like fashion the expanded hospital work force formed a pyra-
mid of inequality based on sex and race. In terms of financial gains
and status, the apex was the province of physicians, who constituted the nation's most highly rewarded profession, mostly white
and male. Each succeeding stratum of workers was composed in
larger proportion of nonunionized, grossly underpaid, highly exploited, nonwhite women.

Yet if the purpose of the health care system is to defend and
improve the health status of the people, this country's incomparable
expenditure for services and capital investment for health yielded
a disappointingly inferior rank for the United States measured by
these traditional international standards: infant and maternal mortality, life expectancy by race and sex, and incidence and rates of
death from preventable or treatable diseases. These disparities in
the health of the American people, moreover, were clearly linked to
class, race, and age.

THE REFORM EFFORT

With growing expectations for improved health services, the public
soon found both the private and the public urban hospitals wanting. While the shortfalls affected different sectors unevenly (the
traditionally denied were still the most denied), it was a rare citizen
who did not have a story of neglect, indifference, or costly encounter stemming from illness in the urban hospital.

. Expressions of organized and individual protest soon developed.
An early example was the Committee to End Discrimination in
Chicago Medical Institutions (CEDCMI), which was born in 1951.
This interracial group of health professionals and members from the
general public documented the pattern of racial exclusion in Chicago's seven medical schools and sixty-eight hospitals. After an
initial encounter with the deans of the medical schools, who assured
them that "qualified minority students" would be welcome, the
committee turned its attention to the city hospitals. Despite the
McCarthyite mood in the country and Mayor Richard Daley's ma-
chine-dominated grip on Chicago, the committee achieved landmark victories a decade before the enactment and enforcement of
the national Civil Rights Act. In 1955, following hearings wherein
the CEDCMI, using official birth and death data, proved that blacks
were barred from almost all of Chicago's hospitals, the city council
of Chicago passed the Harvey-Campbell Ordinance. Appropriately,
this legislation amended the licensure provisions maintaining

health standards; it was not a civil rights law. This law prohibited any licensed hospital from denying a patient admission because of race.

In 1957, in the same legislative body, the law was changed to penalize the denial of staff appointments to physicians on the basis of race. These two laws, well in advance of the national readiness for civil rights reform, achieved modest changes in the practices of Chicago's private hospitals. They represented an important statement of public policy and were a harbinger of the changes to come.

Part of the information that persuaded the city council to act was the statistics for black deaths in 1953. Seventy-one percent of all black hospital deaths occurred at Cook County Hospital. Indeed, a black person dying anywhere in Chicago in 1953 had a 42 percent chance of breathing his last at County. Similarly, 52 percent of all black births took place at Cook County Hospital (compared with only 2 percent of the white total). These numbers suggest what was becoming the dominant function of the public general hospital in American cities—service to minority patients. This role carried with it large political and social implications, which influenced tremendously the fortunes of the public hospitals with the ebb and flow of the movement for equity and equality in the 1960s and 1970s.

Building on the 1950s local prototypes like the CEDCMI, the Medical Committee for Human Rights (MCHR) emerged in 1963. Its basic membership was professional—liberal physicians augmented by nurses and other health workers, drawn mainly from northern cities. The MCHR flourished in the gathering national consensus for the civil rights of blacks. Chapters sprang up in the major cities (over forty by 1966), supported financially by the contributions of the membership and friends of this effort to establish a medical presence in the nonviolent demonstrations.

The initial thrust of MCHR was to support on site the marches and acts of civil disobedience developing throughout the South under the leadership of Dr. Martin Luther King, Jr., the Student Nonviolent Coordinating Committee, the Committee on Racial Equality, and others. This initial commitment saw the Medical Committee cadre gathering data for enforcement of the provisions of the Civil Rights Act dealing with discrimination in hospital services. Frequently at some risk, white and black MCHR activists surveyed hospitals in small and large communities in the South. Their accumulated information documented pervasive racial segregation and exclusion, thereby enhancing the national consensus for reform.

By 1966, the dynamics of the black-liberation movement made redundant if not archaic the presence of predominantly white professional groups, regardless of the high level of regard the MCHR had earned from that movement. Thus, in its 1966 convention MCHR had to make an organizational decision. Should it disband, its "mission" to the South having become outdated, or should it undertake the much more difficult commitment to work long-term for social justice in the cities where its membership resided? The MCHR voted overwhelmingly to undertake the local struggle. Among the immediate results was a significant drop in membership and funding. Nevertheless, the committee flourished, unfolding an array of strategies for health care reform, many of which affected the urban hospital.

The MCHR firmly supported the unionization of hospital workers. It called for an end to discrimination, both in staff appointments and employment opportunities, as well as in the delivery of services. It supported and facilitated the growing consciousness of the women's health movement, with particular emphasis on reproductive rights, many years before the historic Supreme Court decision. It developed a vision of a national health service including public control of hospitals, which would radically reform the health care system, from an essentially private profit-seeking enterprise to a public service. It called for a much higher level of quality of care and commitment to the health issues in America's workplace, a notoriously shameful arena. It challenged, finally, the establishment health professional organizations, notably the American Medical Association, from every forum; it even invaded the meetings of the AMA on several occasions in order to offer alternative messages to the profession and to the public.

Coincident with the upsurge of mass civil rights and antiwar political action in the 1960s, there emerged a remarkable phalanx of highly dedicated health science students, including medical students. The major expression of this new development was the Student Health Organization (SHO), a national effort facilitated by funding from private foundations and the federal government. In many locales the leadership was influenced by the achievements and program of the Medical Committee for Human Rights in the preceding half decade.

The emergence of SHO invigorated the Student American Medical Association. SAMA had been created by the AMA to displace the progressive Association for Interns and Medical Students, destroyed in the McCarthyite hysteria of the 1950s. SAMA was a thoroughly docile and inactive offspring until the SHO catalyst incited it to unprecedented activism. Symbolic of its latter-day conversion to social concerns was its changing its name to AMSA (American Medical Student Association) to make certain that the student group would not be confused with its progenitor. SHO and

AMSA undertook a variety of local, institutionally based projects, which did much to sensitize hospitals, particularly those engaged in teaching, to a higher level of social responsibility.

Even before the emergence of the Student Health Organization, the influence of the student movement of the 1960s was by the end of the decade already manifest in house staff activism. At Cook County Hospital, a center of patronage hiring, political exploitation collided with the militant conscience of the civil rights movement and with the young doctors who came there for residency training. The confrontation climaxed in 1969, when the Illinois legislature unanimously enacted a reform bill that transferred control of the hospital from the Cook County Board of Commissioners to an independent governing commission. This legislative rebuff to the powerful Cook County political machine was critically facilitated by an intensive lobbying effort by some 200 interns and residents from the hospital, in whites with stethoscopes dangling, visiting every available lawmaker.

In the early 1970s, the Patients' Bill of Rights was developed by consumer groups such as the National Welfare Rights Organization and the Gray Panthers. It was subsequently adopted by the American Hospital Association as a credo that was made available to the public and patients in many hospitals. This document enumerates a variety of important rights to which patients are entitled, both under law and under the standards of ethical medical practice. As often happens, rights are worth little unless they are understood and exercised. The gap between the promise of the Patients' Bill of Rights and its execution is large, but it is nonetheless a landmark document.

By the early 1970s, hospital workers constituted the largest group of unorganized employees in the nation. Though the trend has been slow and steady, grass-roots initiatives to secure union recognition were uneven and remain so to this day. Among the pioneer organizers in the private hospital sector was Local 1199, in New York City, which undertook heavy organizational efforts in the New York City area with considerable success in several different realms. Thereafter it sought to organize workers along the eastern seaboard in the immediately adjacent states, with mixed success. Similarly, the public hospital workers in New York City were unionized by the American Federation of State, County, and Municipal Workers, Local 37.

Since the basic hospital work force was grossly exploited, with wage rates at or barely above the legal minimum wage, extremely limited benefits, and little job security, the turn to union representation, particularly in those areas where unionization is the rule, was probably inevitable. These unions regularly succeeded in breaking down barriers for advancement in the ranks, particularly for minority workers.

The growth of hospital unions on a national basis has been very uneven. A variety of established and some newly created unions have competed to represent the workers and frequently jeopardized a united struggle for representation. In the public sector, efforts at unionization were about as successful despite the extra impediment of traditional resistance to unions of public employees and especially to their right to strike.

Support for both unionization and reform of the hospital system came from an unexpected source—the house staff. These doctors in training began to look to union representation to replace the associations and councils through which they related to the hospitals' governance. Early on, the question of whether they were employees or students was raised, primarily by the hospitals and hospital associations. This matter was legally resolved in 1980, when an appeal of a National Labor Relations Board decision that house staff were indeed primarily students, and therefore not eligible for the benefits of the National Labor Relations Act, was denied by the Supreme Court.

Although this decision did not preclude the organization of house staff into unions or the recognition of them by hospitals, objectively it was a severe blow. House staff unionization suffered another major setback when, in 1980, despite broad bipartisan support (including that of the American Medical Association), Congress narrowly declined to amend the National Labor Relations Act specifically to include doctors in training.

However, the decade of the 1970s had witnessed important contributions to hospital improvement by the residents in unions. These young doctors in the 1970s had significant economic hardships to face, given their 80- to 100-hour work week, and the fact that many had family responsibilities and had incurred substantial debts while preparing for medical practice; nevertheless, house staff demands invariably stressed improvements in patient care above all else.

Important strikes over such issues took place in New York City public hospitals, led by the Committee of Interns and Residents, and in Chicago, at Cook County Hospital, led by the Interns and Residents Association. Their main demands were characterized by the Hospital Governing Commission as "encroachments of management prerogatives." They called for some elementary apparatus like the installation of a patient-to-nurse call system, curtains around beds in the twenty- to thirty-five-unit open wards, modern hospital beds (lack of side rails on the beds in use required that confused or feeble patients be placed in restraints), lights at each bed (throughout the night the whole ward had to be illuminated when staff attended to individual patient needs), screens on the windows to keep out flies, and air conditioning in the operating rooms.

The strike stretched out over two weeks. The Governing Commission's tactic of "business as usual" in the absence of 500 residents who were on strike placed a huge physical strain on the nonstriking attending-physician staff. Some felt that the attending staff would soon break the strike by threatening the house staff with noncertification of their training. Instead, as the attending staff seemed at the breaking point, they demanded and won from a reluctant administration a place on the negotiating team. The strike was settled in forty-eight hours, with the patient care issues agreed to in the contract.

More and more house officers in public hospitals came to view themselves as the advocates of their poor patients against an unyielding, cumbersome, and insensitive administration that, from the vantage point of the beleaguered residents, was fronting for an often heartless establishment.

During this period, extant federal law offered opportunities to reform hospital practices. The Civil Rights Act, Title VI, rapidly brought an end to many of the practices of racial exclusion or segregation. The Hill-Burton Act, which had done so much to transform the size and shape of the American hospital system, contained a requirement for charitable service that was honored in the breach until relatively recently. Despite many years of pressure on the Department of Health, Education, and Welfare, only recently were regulations elaborated defining charitable obligations of hospitals that had received Hill-Burton subsidy. Potentially these rules offered an opportunity to secure hospital service for many medically needy people. These important regulations were a long time in coming, however, and not at all in harmony with the new federal mood. Indeed, recent modifications of the regulations by the Reagan administration have virtually relieved the affected hospitals of future charity obligations.

Other federal strategies had a profound impact on the hospitals, not least on those in an urban setting. The enactment in 1966 of Medicare and of Medicaid moved tens of billions of federal dollars into the health systems of the nation. They provided entry to the hospital to those in need whose poverty had earlier precluded admission. For that reason it was a humane and noble undertaking. But by permitting a private system of fee-rewarded medicine to avail itself of the federal and state treasuries, it opened wide a Pandora's box of fiscal cost. It became evident early on that the incentive arrangements for the providers in these new programs would become huge and growing drains on state and national treasuries.

Since there were very few provisions for basic quality control, let alone broad fiscal control, these programs were mercilessly exploited both by criminal elements with Medicaid mills and by those who saw a splendid opportunity to expand income and services on pickings from the federal money tree. It is an irony that this ridiculous arrangement, with its enormous cost and not infrequent felonies, earned "government medicine" a bad name among a bewildered public. In fact, the fiscal problems in care for the indigent and elderly derived in very small part from the alleged culprits, government red tape and bureaucracy, and in very large part from the exuberant enterprise of both the criminal and ethical providers of the health services.

These government dollars have been available to practitioners for "doing things to people" (for example, surgery, necessary and unnecessary), but not for preventive health and health maintenance endeavors.

To the concerns about costs was added the growing national disinclination to help the needy. As a result, defensive strategies (most of which failed) were elaborated to control costs of these federal programs. Reduced appropriations, the exclusion of particular services, and the lowering of the income threshold for the entry of the medically indigent were the often heartless ploys used to solve problems that could be remedied only by systemic reform. However, that basic recourse was never a viable alternative, given the resolute determination of the medical establishment to defend the status quo. The federal costs of the operation of Medicare and Medicaid had become threatening.

Far outstripping the burdensome rate of inflation throughout this period, all health costs, principally hospital costs, approached 10 percent of the gross national product, more than a quarter of a trillion dollars, in 1980. While government at all levels underwrote more than 40 percent of these costs, the industrial empire, with hospital and health insurance an intrinsic part of its employees' benefit package, felt this economic crunch very acutely. In a world where America's preeminence in international and domestic markets was being challenged and toppled by rivals such as Japan and Germany, the costs of hospital insurance seriously aggravated the economic difficulties of the stagnating economy. Containment of hospital costs became a national imperative.

The response of the hospital industry was "voluntary effort." President Carter's modest legislative proposal sought only to limit the *rate* of inflation of the hospital industry. Its decisive defeat at the committee level is a tribute to the power of the health establish-

ment lobby, which had generously contributed to the campaigns of
most of the members of the Appropriations Committee.

Over the years, more sweeping proposals for federal remedies
came in the form of national health insurance bills, modified (usually diminished) by the fickle political winds of the decade. Although organized labor and other sectors of the liberal
establishment placed these measures high on their legislative wish
list and although Sen. Edward Kennedy sought to make this his
most important senatorial achievement, the bills never really had a
chance.

A radical alternative proposed by Congressman Ronald Dellums,
from Oakland, California, enjoyed sponsorship by less than a score
of intrepid representatives and not a single senator. Nevertheless it
was a prototype of a transformation of the system into a national
health service with government operation of the entire process,
providing, however, for very strong local control in decision making. Its most ardent advocates would have to concede that as the
1980s began the bill served only as a rallying point for thoroughgoing reform at some indeterminate date.

OUTCOMES

An evaluation of two decades of hospital expansion and of the
struggles for alternatives provides pessimistic, if not absolutely negative, conclusions. Several important victories can be expected to
have a continuing positive imprint on health services. The adjacent
terrain is littered with the debris of visions unrealized or unrealiza-
ble.

A powerfully entrenched health care establishment dominates
policy formation by government and community. As medical care
and the hospital empires evolved from a cottage industry into the
biggest of businesses, the "old boys" domination by the American
Medical Association and the drug industry was superseded by even
more powerful corporate interests. Thus the hospital community,
hitherto composed of "not-for-profit" private institutions and a
smaller but vigorous public sector, is experiencing encroachment by
for-profit corporations that are building new hospitals or capturing
financially failing or abandoned not-for-profit institutions. By
1980, 15 percent of the nation's hospital beds were owned by these
free-enterprise ventures dedicated to and successful at bringing the
"marketplace" to health care services.

Among the lasting accomplishments of the liberal reform, the
solid blows struck against racial segregation and exclusion are the
most noteworthy and unequivocal. The unrelenting and often he-
roic struggles of the black people, joined later by the Hispanic

community, ended the institutional apartheid that had been enshrined in American law and custom. Powerful legislative victories at the local, state, and federal levels have undermined institutional racism in a fundamental way.

The distributive endeavors, including Medicare and Medicaid and a variety of other special programs, must be viewed as qualified victories that are attenuating with the passage of time. The contradictions of attempting to offer broad, universal quality health services to previously excluded millions foundered on the realities of profit seeking. By the end of the 1970s, the American people were sensitized to appeals for reduced government responsibility and expenditure skillfully broadcast by the resurgent ideological Right. This movement exploited persisting racism, the widespread discontent with oppressive taxes, and a new awareness that the hemorrhage of the public treasury into a bottomless pit of "medical services" could not be endlessly sustained. Such ideological ferment fostered a political climate favorable to the attrition and dismemberment of federal support for hospital services like Medicaid and many of the special efforts to help children, the handicapped, and the blind. The measures undertaken to stem Medicare costs have savaged that program to the point that co-insurance, deductibles, and other limitations threaten to price the bulk of the aged sick out of the health care market, the national phenomenon that created the Medicare system in the first place.

Similarly, as the 1980s began, the drive of trade unions to represent the three million unorganized hospital workers was idling. As with the union movement nationwide, the hospital worker sector encountered sophisticated and effective union blocking aggressively adopted by hospital administrations. This resistance was undoubtedly facilitated by the fragmented, multi-union competition in the drive to organize hospital workers. The constricting economy raised the specter of job insecurity with a work force that had not yet developed a militant unity. In addition, the small but significant surge toward union formation by residents and interns was hobbled by adverse court rulings and legislative failures.

Since the hospitals were now mired in unprecedented capital investment, which proliferated new facilities emphasizing superspecialized high technology, the liberal reforms proved impotent as alternatives for stemming these costly and often antihuman developments. From another quarter the critique mounted by antitechnologists, most vividly by Ivan Illich, was a systemic one; it argued that the massive growth of the health professions and the associated institutions, especially hospitals, was per se health denying. This overarching criticism was never fully embraced by liberal reformers. However, the concept that "small is beautiful," and demands for decentralization of services with consumer control, represented a partial acceptance of this ideology.

The reality of the matter is, regardless of the validity of the Illich critique, that hospitals as institutions are enormous centers of power within the urban community. The boards of the private hospitals regularly include the elite of the city. The public hospitals have in their way become political prizes of the first order, commanding, as they do, armies of potential patronage workers and those huge monetary transactions so appealing to urban political machines. In sum, hospitals in the urban center became even more remote from democratic control or popular influence precisely because they became far too important to the dominant political and industrial corporate interests. From time to time, strong fights developed, notably in defense of public hospitals, but at the end of the day more power was lost than was gained by those who entered the struggle.

A continuing theme in the public-hospital reform movement has been the call for involvement of the patient constituency in the decision making. Various formulas were recommended, such as constituting advisory boards from the community and appointment to the governing body. To facilitate such participation, coalitions in support of the local public hospital appeared in affected cities, particularly in regard to fiscal issues. In Chicago, an extremely broad coalition, the Committee to Save Cook County Hospital, emerged at about the time of the house staff strike.

The committee's work extended the public's awareness of and knowledge about the hospital. The committee's organizing vigor recruited standing-room-only crowds at the annual budget hearings, where as many as eighty to ninety citizens representing extremely diverse constituencies testified in support of the hospital's needs. This doubtless helped to bring about the paradoxical result that, in a decade of deficits and cutbacks, Cook County Hospital has so far experienced substantial annual increases in local county funding.

But failing a breakthrough to actual democratic control of such an institution, an inevitable battle weariness engulfs even highly dedicated movements; as in military clashes, popular movements must not only prevail in skirmishes but must occasionally win a battle.

IMPLICATIONS FOR THE FUTURE

The dominant theme of the liberal critique of the hospital system for the past twenty years has been the issues of access and equity, with a wholesome concern about racial discrimination and the plight of especially burdened groups, notably the very poor, the physically handicapped, and women. The dominant features of the contemporary hospital industry—capital-intensive high technology, corporate control, profit motivation—are inimical to these reform goals. In the absence of a program addressing this central contradiction, the reform movement victories have inevitably been limited and transient. The functional and fiscal collapse of its model of public support for health care by private entrepreneurs, likewise inevitable, is being aggressively implemented by the Reagan government.

This score of years saw some important gains in urban hospitals: irreversible victories were won against racial exclusion in hospital care, employment, and professional opportunities; the public demanded, and on occasion secured, vital health services, including abortion services, outpatient clinics, primary care training programs, and an overall increase in available services; health workers and consumers in general experienced a heightened awareness of hospital matters (aided by the impressive achievement in public education by the linear and visual media); moderate gains in trade union organization improved the lot of some of the millions of hospital workers; and, not least important, the ideological concept that "health care is a human right" achieved wide popular acceptance and support, however shallow the political and economic underpinnings of this idea.

This work, the product of some twenty-five years of struggle, represents modest, vulnerable achievements at best. In ironic contrast, the professional and corporate power groups that fashioned the hospital system emerged from the 1970s politically triumphant and wealthier, attracting new investors seeking to partake of the multibillion-dollar riches of the health industry, which, it must be remembered, thrived and expanded as the rest of the economy decayed and declined.

It is often forgotten that the United States is unique in its failure to have a highly developed public health and hospital system. This failure derives in part from the strength and political skill of organized medicine in the past. But it derives also from the absence of a political force campaigning consistently and effectively to achieve this popular goal—the nationalization of health services. In other Western industrial countries the originators of such reform legislation have been the labor and socialist parties. But so popular and successful have these programs been that the conservative parties have invariably had to support them in principle, even if in practice they sought to limit the benefits.

In the United States, the most advanced legislative proposal promulgated by the trade union movement, and sponsored by Senator

Kennedy, was universal health insurance. It is not practical to re-count here the basic concessions, even in this modest legislation, that were offered up at every session of Congress in the futile effort to achieve a parliamentary majority. However, it is important to note that all these insurance proposals, like Medicare and Medicaid before them, linked federal dollars with the enterprising response of a fee-motivated health care system. Given the national percep-tion of how government-funded health services evolved, the con-servatives could ask the public, with increasing effectiveness, to reject "government medicine."

The failure of the liberal reform movement to develop a continu-ing political effort to establish a national health service accounts for the limited achievements of the past period and for the basically defensive position of health reformers at this time. This generaliza-tion is particularly true when applied to the hospitals of the nation. However "private" our system was, it could be argued that the individual hospitals were traditionally not-for-profit services for the public. They were relatively free of the tooth-and-claw com-petitiveness of business enterprise and of the concern with market-ing, profitability, the bottom line, and growth. In contrast, we enter the 1980s with a strong movement of private capital seeking "for-profit" hospitals as investments and bases for political power.

Clearly, this is a time for new approaches. It is a major premise of the strategies for the next period that the current economy binge, which dismembers the protective and nurturing functions of gov-ernment, ranging from occupational safety to school lunches for children, will fail. While failing, the policy will aggravate the inequities and oppressions already well established in our society. Widespread unemployment, living standards of the middle class eroded by inflation, and health services rationed to exclude the poor will in time create a readiness for something better. As the protec-tions in federal (and state) support systems are undermined or eliminated, social health will be jeopardized: malnutrition, infant mortality, maternal mortality, preventable infections, tuberculosis, venereal disease, and occupational and environmental illness will all increase. "Horror stories" of the denial of care at risk of life or suffering in acute situations will multiply. The rising expectations of the last half century, denied by the current federal policy, will seek new political expression.

Therefore, every effort must be made to define and to win support for a thoroughgoing transformation of the health and hospital sys-tem, consonant with public concerns. For example, the sarcastic characterization of liberal reform as "throwing money at our prob-lems" has a core of truth that must be addressed. There is no question that the billions spent by the government for health services (now 42 percent of the total) and the other billions paid by "private" sources did not produce the health system that these expenditures could (and should) command; the general public senses this. Despite the lack of real debate, the American people are to a remarkable degree prepared for basic changes in their health services. When they can voice preferences, whether in surveys by the national pollsters or in the occasional local referenda, they support, in surprisingly high percentages, the essential principles of a national health service.

There is an immediate need for a sector-by-sector analysis of health status for such groups as the aged, women, minorities, and the beleaguered middle class and workers. Then the benefits of an alternative system, a national health service, could be delineated for each constituency. In the realm of occupational-health protection, for example, the present system of company doctors working for company employee health services (regulated by a politicized Occupational Safety and Health Administration) would be replaced by a service dedicated to defending the health of workers above all else, in stark contrast to the present arrangement.

Public dissatisfaction with callous federal and state bureaucracies, which the ideologues of the Right have skillfully exploited ("Get the government off our backs"), is a valid concern about a serious blight afflicting every advanced nation-state. The remedy the Left can offer is the development of local democratic control by consumers and health workers. This wholesome approach, whether it is called holding town hall meetings or going to the grass roots, is as American as apple pie.

An unanticipated development is the imminent change in status of America's physicians, from "cottage industry" entrepreneurs to salaried minions of the government, medical institutions, or private corporations. However well paid they are and however much they identify with the corporation, the salaried doctors are objectively in a worker relationship to their employers, leading to the eventual development of confrontation over the same issues that employees have always faced—wages, hours, and conditions of employment.

The main expression of organized physicians, the American Medical Association (and its state subsidiaries), has already sought to represent doctors as a union bargaining agent. If this trend accelerates because of the shift to salaried posts, it may have the result of breaking the AMA into a salaried physician sector, in contradiction to another, smaller but more powerful group of physicians who employ their own colleagues. Under these conditions of diminishing opportunities to practice solo, it is not unlikely that many physicians—particularly those newly entering the system while heavily in debt—will be more amenable to a progressive restructuring of their field of employment on a basis of public service rather than of private gain.

The alternatives to the Reagan program will not be found in fragmented strategies for, say, hospital services as juxtaposed to women's health needs or union rights of health workers. Since the entitlement programs being dismembered were already faltering and highly vulnerable to liquidation precisely because of their patchwork nature and their fatal reliance on funding rather than on structural change, not only did these reforms fail to garner the energies of the people, but to no small degree they impoverished them through dependency-inducing welfarism.

As always, the issue is transfer of power. To succeed, the next strategies must propose popular control and an end to privatized, corporate control; enable people to do rather than have done to or for them; and supplant the hopelessly expensive centralized technological system with local, prevention-oriented centers emphasizing social, economic, and political roots (and treatment) of the major maladies of our society.

EPILOGUE

There is a large area of policy that no group or movement has addressed comprehensively. It derives from the confounding reality that contemporary health problems are proving increasingly resistant to resolution by the prevailing scientific, technological approaches. Ever larger inputs yield poor, sometimes grotesque, results (for example, intensive care life support to the comatose terminally ill).

The truism that the major health problems, from highway- and weapon-inflicted trauma to cancer due to ambient pollution, from the high risk associated with teenage pregnancy to the epidemic of diseases resulting from substance abuse, the truism that these are "life-style" problems actually obscures the reality that these are social problems reflecting inequities, tensions, planlessness, and the preeminence of property and production values over human ones.

Seriously to confront this reality and developing the policies that can prevail over these ubiquitous miseries is an unfulfilled task internationally. The best (still meager) wisdom suggests that the greatest promise lies in local initiative, widespread citizen participation, and emphasis on improving prevention, nutrition, and social conditions and on diminishing the damage to society as a whole and to the environment by the industrial process.

3.

medicare
and medicaid:

BAND-AIDS FOR THE OLD AND POOR

E. Richard Brown

When President Johnson signed the Medicare and Medicaid legislation into law on July 30, 1965, a great many Americans believed that the elderly would no longer be impoverished by medical care costs and that the poor would get the care they needed from essentially the same sources as the middle class. Under the Medicare program, the federal government would pay for most of the costs of hospitalization for the elderly and would insure them for physicians' services and related care—coverage the elderly were unable to obtain at a price they could afford from the private insurance industry. Under the Medicaid program, the federal government would provide grants to the states to greatly expand medical care for the poor, subsidizing those on public assistance and several related categories of low-income persons not receiving public assistance, to enable them to get their care from the private medical market.

These legislative reforms culminated half a century of intermittent struggle for compulsory health insurance. They represented a substantial compromise of the goal of national health insurance, vigorously pursued in the 1940s. Medicare and Medicaid partially succeeded in fulfilling their more limited objectives of improving the access of the poor and the elderly to medical care and preventing the pauperization of the elderly due to medical expenses. But even these more limited objectives have been compromised by political and fiscal pressures on federal, state, and local governments. The programs proved far more costly than almost anyone had imagined, and within a year of their implementation in 1966, cost containment competed with and then replaced the original legislative goal of equity as the dominant concern of state legislatures as well as of the Congress.

BACKGROUND: 1930 – 1965

Inequities and Instability

Half a century ago, the Committee on the Costs of Medical Care[1] documented the great disparities in access to health services due to the unequal distribution of income in our society. In a study conducted between 1928 and 1931, the committee found that persons in upper-income families averaged one and a half times as many hospital admissions and twice as many physician visits each year as members of low- and moderate-income families.[2] The lesson from these research findings and ordinary experience was simple: when medical care is produced and sold in a market system, its distribution parallels the class structure of society. Economic demand becomes the basis for use, creating inequities in access to health care, whereas equity would require that health must be the primary determinant of use.

Adding to such inequalities, many working-class and middle-class persons who could afford ordinary medical expenses—physicians' fees, prescription drugs, simple laboratory tests—were either totally impoverished by extraordinary expenses related to hospitalization or were forced to forego such care when it was really needed. These financial and medical problems increased the personal and social burdens of illness and were borne individually by those afflicted unless relieved by charity, a partial solution that always carried with it a humiliating means test.

In addition to the deprivations suffered by the public, hospitals and physicians felt the pinch of frequent downward business cycles. Unstable and declining incomes, particularly during the Great Depression, were a source of bitterness for doctors. Some hospitals were forced to close their doors. These problems of inequities in access, impoverishment due to large medical expenses, and unstable hospital and physician revenues called forth two distinctly different strategies, one focused on public health insurance and the other on private insurance.

Public Insurance: Defeats

For decades, American social reformers, socialists, and even a worried medical profession had been watching the development of compulsory public health insurance in Europe. In 1883, Bismarck established the Sickness Insurance Act to help stem growing support for socialism among the German working class. In 1911, Lloyd George and the Liberal party enacted the National Health Insurance Act to win English workers' votes from the socialistic Labour party.

Efforts to establish some kind of public health insurance system in the United States date back to the 1915–18 campaign of the American Association for Labor Legislation, but it was the effort to link health insurance to the 1935 Social Security Act that was the most important antecedent of the Medicare and Medicaid bill passed three decades later. Although the original bill to create a system of social insurance for the aged, the unemployed, the blind, the widowed, and their children included only a suggestion that the new Social Security Board study the need for a government health insurance program, opposition from the powerful medical profession was so swift and formidable that President Roosevelt abandoned the issue, fearing it might sink the whole Social Security bill.[3]

In the 1940s, bills to establish a compulsory national health insurance program were regularly introduced into the Congress, and just as regularly defeated by the AMA's well-funded political campaigns. The annual battles over the Wagner-Murray-Dingell national health insurance bills culminated in President Truman's strong personal endorsement of the 1949 version of the bill. The bill would have covered all medical, dental, hospital, and nursing services; been financed by a payroll tax; included all contributors and their dependents and subsidized the poor; been administered by a federal agency; and included freedom of participation by doctors and hospitals and freedom of choice for patients and doctors alike. The Wagner-Murray-Dingell bills embodied the view— supported by Truman's advisers, the labor movement, and public opinion polls—that financial means should not determine a person's access to health care. But the AMA's massive public-relations and lobbying campaign, caricaturing the proposal as being one step away from a socialist America, stopped the proposal at its congressional starting gate. With this defeat, proponents of national health insurance gave up any serious prospects of enacting a proposal, although bills were ritualistically introduced through 1952.[4]

Private Insurance: Success and Limitations

Partly in response to the "threat" of government health insurance and more fundamentally in response to hospitals' needs for greater financial stability, the American Hospital Association actively expanded its Blue Cross hospital insurance plans, introduced in 1929 by Baylor University Hospital, in Dallas, Texas. Medical societies followed suit with Blue Shield plans covering mainly physicians' fees and related services. After the threat of compulsory national health insurance, the AMA found voluntary private insurance an attractive alternative and praised it as "the American way."[5] By 1940, some 12 million people (less than 10 percent of the population) were insured for hospital expenses and far fewer for surgical expenses or physicians' fees.[6]

But private health insurance proved very popular. The risk of medical misfortune was spread among many individuals and families, enabling them to obtain more expensive kinds of care without necessarily devastating their finances. The demands of labor unions for greater economic security and more benefits encouraged the spread of work-related group plans. In 1945, after several years of cost-plus government war contracts and labor pressure on employers, enrollment in hospital insurance plans provided coverage for 32 million persons, 24 percent of the population.[7] After the war, commercial insurance companies, following the Blue Cross lead, pushed energetically into the health insurance market they had previously considered unprofitable.

Although private health insurance coverage was growing rapidly, it left out many services and important population sectors. In 1950, private health insurance paid for only 37 percent of total hospital costs and for only 12 percent of physicians' services.[8] Perhaps more important, private health insurance was available mainly to the middle and the upper-working classes, that is, those covered by union- or employer-sponsored plans and those affluent enough to buy individual insurance policies. It was becoming apparent that private health insurance would not meet the needs of the poorly paid, nonunionized working population or their families, or those who were very poor and unable to work—single-parent households with very young children, the blind and disabled, and the aged.

The Legacy of Social Security

The Social Security Act of 1935 and the defeat of the Wagner-Murray-Dingell bills throughout the 1940s reinforced and codified in federal law two levels of distinctions in social welfare programs. The Social Security Act was intended to provide federal support only for the "deserving poor," those who are poor through some misfortune that is beyond their control—persons who are too old to work, the blind and disabled who are unable to work, dependent widows and children, and those who truly cannot find work. All others who might be indigent, including the working poor and persons who do not work for reasons other than those included in the act, were considered "undeserving" of federal relief and were left to the resources and charity of the state and local governments and the private agencies. This distinction had a long tradition in Anglo-American social philosophy.[9]

But the Social Security Act added another important distinction *among* the "deserving" poor—the distinction between social insurance and public assistance. As Robert and Rosemary Stevens have noted,

> Benefits made available under social insurance were contributory, work-related, available to beneficiaries as a right, and determined by Congress. Public assistance, on the other hand, was a matter for administrative discretion at the lowest levels of government.[10]

Workers *earn* their rights to benefits from social insurance programs by their contributions. Public assistance involves no direct contributions by individuals into programs from which they might later draw benefits. The Social Security Act provided contributory social insurance programs for the aged, and grants to the states for "categorical" public assistance to the elderly, to dependent children, and to the blind. In addition it created a hybrid program of unemployment compensation that was not contributory on the part of workers but in other respects was very much like social insurance. As the Stevenses observe, the distinction between social insurance and public assistance, codified in the Social Security Act, has dominated social welfare legislation in the United States ever since, including the strategies leading up to the enactment of Medicare (a social insurance program) and Medicaid (a public assistance program) and their history since 1965.

Three Steps Back, Two Steps Forward

The defeat of the Wagner-Murray-Dingell bills to create a compulsory national health insurance system for all Americans was a major setback in the efforts to develop health insurance along social insurance lines. To the federal strategists leading the efforts to create a government health insurance plan, there seemed only one way to salvage victory from retreat. But even then they faced stiff competition from the successes of private insurance and from the advocates of public assistance medicine.

Following the defeat of Truman's national health insurance proposal in 1949, his chief advisers on Social Security proposed a federal plan that would limit health insurance to the beneficiaries of the Old Age and Survivors Insurance program, the social insurance part of the Social Security Act. Tying the plan to the Social Security program would avoid the stigma of welfare, and it would let the plan bask in the legitimacy and popularity achieved by Social Security. Backing away from any general insurance plan for the entire population, Truman's advisers believed they could side-step the opposition of the AMA and its allies by restricting the program to Social Security beneficiaries, excluding physician services, and limiting benefits to sixty days of hospital care.[11]

Indeed their plan seemed to have political merit. By 1950, private hospitalization insurance plans covered 51 percent of the population, more than double the proportion covered just five years earlier.[12] The spread of private health insurance, especially to workers in unionized industries, undercut the labor movement's political support for national health insurance. Liberal political programs that had seemed to have a broad base of popular support a few years earlier were under attack in 1951, undermined by the Korean War and the rise of McCarthyism.

Furthermore, the Social Security Amendments of 1950 also undercut the demands for national health insurance. The amendments expanded categorical public assistance programs to include federal cost-sharing grants to the states to cover hospital and other medical care for public assistance recipients, with bills paid directly by welfare agencies (known as "vendor payments"). Despite its meager funding, this program provided opponents of national health insurance with the hope that medical care for the poor could be kept isolated from the health care needs of the rest of the population and kept narrow in its impact. Even by 1960, medical vendor payments under all public assistance programs totaled only $514 million nationally, more than half the amount going for hospital and nursing home care.[13]

The Eisenhower years drained any remaining vitality from efforts to pass even more limited insurance plans. Eisenhower had campaigned for the presidency in 1952 against "socialized medicine," a rubric under which he included both the Truman general health insurance proposal and a limited Social Security–based hospitalization insurance plan for the aged, introduced into the House of Representatives by Rep. Aime Forand. The AMA spent a quarter of a million dollars lobbying against the bill, which was defeated in 1959 in the Ways and Means Committee, chaired by Rep. Wilbur Mills.

Despite the apparent demise of the Forand bill, the hearings and the AMA's campaign against it dramatized the medical-financial needs of a large segment of the elderly and vividly reflected the dichotomized approach to social welfare legislation in the United States. The proponents of the Forand bill pointed out that among persons sixty-five years old and over, about three-fifths had annual incomes of less than $1,000, more than half had no hospital insurance, and even those with insurance found it inadequate. Moreover, the elderly were more than twice as likely as those under sixty-five to need medical care. The bill's opponents had to concede the great need of many of the aged—though they disputed many of the statistics—but they favored a welfare approach over the Forand bill's social insurance approach. They argued that a welfare program, which would include a means test and be administered by state and local governments, would be directed only to those really in need and that it *should* provide for broader medical needs of the aged than the Forand bill's hospitalization benefits did. Theodore Marmor notes the irony of the conflict: the more liberal supporters of the social insurance-based Forand bill proposing a limited hospital-surgical insurance bill for all the aged, to be financed by the inherently regressive Social Security taxes; the more conservative opponents of the bill favoring broader benefits only for the destitute aged, to be financed from the more progressive federal tax revenues through a welfare-based program.[14]

Kerr-Mills

By 1960 it was widely accepted, in and out of the Congress, that some federal program was necessary to help the elderly meet the high cost of getting sick. Although the House Ways and Means Committee again defeated the Forand proposal, public sentiment continued so strongly in favor of it that the committee had to come up with an alternative. That political necessity opened the door to the basic welfare approach favored by the opponents of the original Forand bill. Sponsored by Representative Mills and Sen. Robert Kerr and enacted in 1960, the Kerr-Mills Act expanded the existing system of federal grants to states for vendor payments for medical care provided to welfare recipients under old-age assistance. The program provided more generous federal matching grants to the states in the hope that every state would develop its own program of adequate care, and it added a new category of vendor payments to cover elderly persons (in 1962, the blind were included) who were not receiving cash assistance but were too poor to pay their own medical bills. (This group was labeled "medically needy," and the concept of "medical indigency" was carried over to the Medicaid program.)[15]

As had been predicted by Forand and supporters of his bill, the states moved slowly, and most of them haltingly, in implementing Kerr-Mills. The more affluent states that already had substantial vendor payment programs expanded their benefits and coverage, while the poorer states participated only marginally, if at all. By the end of 1962, only twenty-eight states had Kerr-Mills programs. By 1965, forty-four of the fifty-four states and territories had some program in effect, but five large and relatively affluent states—New York, California, Massachusetts, Minnesota, and Pennsylvania— which together included 31 percent of the aged in the country, were receiving 62 percent of the federal funds for the medically needy program. The program increased the flow of funds to hospitals and nursing homes, encouraging the rapid expansion of the latter industry. Of total vendor payments of $1.4 billion in the fiscal year 1965–66, two-thirds went to hospitals and nursing homes.[16]

Kerr-Mills satisfied few interest groups. Senior-citizens groups continued to campaign for Social Security–based health insurance to meet the ever rising costs of medical care without the indignities of a means test. The rising costs of welfare medical care remained a burden on the states, even with the additional federal aid.

The Momentum for Medicare

In his first few weeks in office in 1961, President Kennedy sent a proposal to Congress calling for the extension of Social Security benefits to cover hospital and nursing home care, but not including surgical benefits that had been a part of the Forand bill. The administration back-stepped from the Forand and earlier proposals in order to widen the base of support for its bill, anticipating an uphill struggle despite the Democratic majority in both houses and the two-to-one public-opinion support for the idea. The bill, introduced by Sen. Clinton Anderson and Rep. Cecil King, was a competitor to the Kerr-Mills program, a severe disadvantage since Mills chaired the powerful House Ways and Means Committee, which had to approve the bill. Between Mills's commitment to the program that bore his name, the political opposition of Republicans and southern Democrats (including Mills), and the vocal opposition of the AMA and the Health Insurance Institute (representing the private insurance industry), the bill was firmly defeated in the House Ways and Means Committee. A similar proposal by Senator Anderson in 1962 also met its demise.[17]

But pressure continued to build—as medical costs for the elderly continued to rise, as senior-citizen groups and the AFL-CIO grew more vocal in their support, as the civil rights movement grew larger and more insistent, and as the Kerr-Mills program remained ineffective. In 1963, Kennedy again urged the Congress to approve his proposals for hospital insurance, the King-Anderson bill was reintroduced, and the House Ways and Means Committee once again held hearings. The next year, the Senate for the first time approved a proposal for hospital insurance as an amendment to the Social Security bill, and Mills's committee was within one vote of a pro-health-insurance majority. But in October 1964, Mills was able to kill the bill in a House-Senate conference committee.[18]

The Democratic sweep of the November 1964 elections assured that health insurance would finally be enacted. The defeat of the Goldwater Republican platform of opposition to social programs was taken as a popular mandate. The Democrats gained a two-to-one majority in the House, and the composition of the Ways and Means Committee was altered in favor of compulsory hospital insurance. President Johnson called for immediate action on the King-Anderson "Medicare" bill. However, while Congress was certain to pass some health insurance bill, its substance was not certain. Republicans and AMA spokespersons shifted from simple opposition to Medicare to an endorsement of what one AMA official called "more positive programs."[19]

As the Ways and Means Committee began its work under Mills's firm hand, it had before it several different proposals, all of which were regarded by their proponents as mutually exclusive. Unexpectedly, however, Mills suggested a compromise incorporating elements of all three bills. The administration's King-Anderson proposal would be included as hospital insurance financed through additional Social Security taxes, providing inpatient hospital and nursing home care benefits to all persons eligible for Social Security retirement benefits. (The hospital insurance plan became part A of the Medicare program.) The essence of the AMA proposal, introduced by Republican John Byrnes, was incorporated as a separate, voluntary insurance plan covering physicians' services for the elderly, paid for by premiums from those who chose to enroll and by federal subsidies, and administered by private insurance carriers. (The physicians insurance became part B, or Supplemental Medical Insurance.) The committee also added an expanded and liberalized program of federal assistance to the states for the medically indigent and needy, which the AMA had supported as a substitute for the other proposals. (This expansion of the Kerr-Mills concept became known as Medicaid.)

Mills's compromise undermined the AMA opposition, played to the Republicans, and gave the administration more than it had ever hoped to get in one legislative session. Wilbur Cohen, then HEW assistant secretary for legislation, called it "the most brilliant legislative move I'd seen in thirty years."[20] For Mills, the compromise proposal apparently represented his desire to be the "architect of victory" rather than a defeated obstructionist. Mills also explained that including the voluntary premium-supported physicians insurance program would "build a fence around the Medicare program" and undermine later demands for liberalization, such as the inclusion of physician coverage under Social Security, which "might be a burden on the economy and the social security program."[21]

Once the administration was convinced that Mills was not just trying to scuttle the King-Anderson bill, they delightedly endorsed the compromise. The new bill passed the House, was supported with some changes in the Senate Finance Committee, was approved by the Senate, and was further revised in conference committee. It was finally approved by both houses as Public Law 89-97, including Medicare as Title XVIII and Medicaid as Title XIX of the Social Security Amendments of 1965. On July 30, 1965, President Johnson flew to Independence, Missouri, and signed the bill into law in the presence of Harry Truman, who had vigorously supported a broader, compulsory health insurance plan for the entire population some sixteen years earlier. Johnson observed that the marvel was not "the passage of this bill but . . . that it took so many years to pass it."[22]

FROM VICTORY TO IMPLEMENTATION

The flourish with which Johnson signed the Medicare and Medicaid legislation into law marked the end of victory and the beginning of implementation. The programs quickly involved many millions of people, required massive administrative machinery and enormous amounts of federal funds, and met drastically different political responses.

Medicare

Part A, the hospital insurance (HI) portion of the Medicare program, covers the major portion of inpatient hospital care, 100 days of nursing home care following hospitalization, and 100 home health care visits, also following hospitalization. This part of the program is financed by an increase in the Social Security tax paid into a special trust fund; anyone who is eligible for Social Security retirement benefits is also covered by HI benefits. Because it is paid for by all working persons in the country, it is considered "compulsory."

Part B, the Supplementary Medical Insurance (SMI), covers physicians' and surgeons' services (whether in the hospital, office, clinic, or home), home health services not necessarily following hospitalization, diagnostic tests and procedures, and the like. Unlike part A, SMI is a voluntary program in which anyone eligible for part A benefits may enroll. It is supported by monthly premiums paid by enrollees into another special trust fund and matched by federal general tax revenues.

Medicare began in 1966 with an enrollment of 19 million aged persons in part A and nearly 18 million in part B, a testament to the successful campaign conducted by the Social Security Administration to inform the nation's elderly about the program. By 1978, enrollment in HI and SMI had both surpassed 26 million, including nearly 24 million persons sixty-five and over (the remainder are disabled persons under sixty-five and kidney disease patients who qualify for the End-Stage Renal Disease program, both added to Medicare in 1973).[23] Thus, very nearly all persons over sixty-five in the United States, with the main exception of undocumented immigrants, were covered by Medicare.

Following the pattern in private insurance programs, Congress included substantial "deductibles" (paid by the patient before the plan pays anything) and "co-insurance" (a portion of the remaining charges for which the patient is responsible). Under part A, the patient had to pay, as a deductible, the first $40 of a hospital bill (increased to $264 by 1982) and, as copayments, $10 a day for the sixty-first through ninetieth days of hospitalization (raised to $75 a day by 1982). Part B, the SMI, required a monthly premium from each enrollee of $3 per month (up to $12 in 1982), a deductible of $50 (raised to $75 by 1981), and copayments equal to 20 percent of the remaining bill.

Elderly patients would have to keep proper records and submit their bills to Medicare so that they could be credited with the deductible and begin obtaining their benefits. In addition, physicians could bill Medicare patients more than the "reasonable charges" set and reimbursed by Medicare, with the patient paying the difference.[24] For most elderly persons these deductibles, co-insurance, and added charges could quickly climb beyond their financial resources. They would then have to turn to supplementary private insurance or Medicaid.

Medicaid

Medicaid was intended to "pick up the pieces" left over by Medicare—to cover the deductibles and co-insurance for indigent Medicare patients, to pay for services not covered or covered only inadequately by Medicare (that is, outpatient and nursing home care), and to pay the costs of medical care for indigent persons other than the elderly. Unlike Medicare, which is primarily a social insurance program administered by the federal government as an earned right to "entitled" persons, Medicaid is a public assistance program following the well-established pattern of other welfare measures.

Medicaid provides federal contributions to the states' approved programs of medical assistance; the federal share ranges from 50 percent, for states with higher per capita incomes, up to 83 percent for the poorer states. The generous matching formula was intended to encourage all states, including the poorest, to develop Medicaid programs. Alabama, Arkansas, and Mississippi finally began their programs in 1970. Both Alaska and Arizona complained that, because nearly all Eskimos and Indians would be eligible, the costs would be more than they could bear. Nevertheless, Alaska implemented a Medicaid program in 1972; Arizona remained the only state without one until it adopted a very restricted one in 1982.[25]

By 1972, when all the current state Medicaid programs (except Arizona's) were operating, 17.6 million poor people in the United States were enrolled in Medicaid. Enrollment reached nearly 23 million in 1977 and has been gradually declining since.[26] Although the size of the Medicaid program may seem impressive, restrictions on eligibility have kept many of the nation's poor off the Medicaid rolls.

Title XIX required state Medicaid programs to include all "categorically needy" persons—those receiving cash grants under Old Age Assistance, Aid to the Blind, Aid to Families with Dependent Children (AFDC), and Aid to the Permanently and Totally Disabled. In addition, the states were required to cover the "categorically related needy," persons not receiving cash grants because of certain eligibility restrictions imposed by the states. Besides these mandated groups, states could opt to include additional "categorically related needy" groups and the "categorically related *medically* needy"—that is, persons who would be eligible for public assistance (children, the aged, blind, and disabled) but whose incomes are above the state's standard set for cash grants.

California and New York quickly established the most liberal eligibility standards and most generous benefits of all state Medicaid programs. In 1977, each of them spent more than $1.5 billion in state and local funds (in addition to the federal contributions) on their Medicaid programs.[27] California's program, known as Medi-Cal, in 1971 even added coverage for "medically indigent adults," a category that, unlike "medically indigent children," is not matched with any federal contribution and absorbed 41 percent of the state's Medi-Cal costs.[28] California and New York together account for 27 percent of all Medicaid recipients in the United States.[29] Although California and New York were very generous in setting eligibility levels, many states were very restrictive. In 1977, twenty state programs excluded the medically needy or indigent.[30] And the states are free to set income levels for public assistance cash grants, and therefore Medicaid eligibility, far above or far below the federal government's official poverty level.

The confusing array of "categorical" groups and income levels that had to be or could be included in state Medicaid programs suggests that many categories and numbers of persons, although poor, were excluded from the programs. Somewhere between 40 percent and two-thirds of all poor persons in the United States are ineligible for Medicaid because of categorical or income requirements.[31] In eight states, Medicaid recipients totaled less than 20 percent of the poverty population in 1970.[32] To be eligible for Medicaid, "one had to wear the appropriate label," as Robert and Rosemary Stevens observe. "To be just 'poor' was not sufficient."[33]

Impact on Access and Equity

The poor have greatly increased their use of health services since the large disparities found by the Committee on the Costs of Medical Care half a century ago. Whereas the committee found that upper-income groups had far more physician visits and hospital admissions than low-income groups, the National Health Interview surveys in the late 1970s found that poor adults actually had more physician visits, and poor persons of all ages averaged more hospitalizations than the nonpoor.[34]

These very substantial improvements are clearly attributable to the effects of Medicare, Medicaid, community health centers for the poor, and public hospitals and clinics. For example, in 1976, poor children averaged 65 percent more physician visits than in 1964, poor adults averaged between 27 and 33 percent more visits, and the elderly poor, 18 percent more visits. In each age group, the poor registered a much greater increase over this period than did the nonpoor.[35]

However, some very important gaps remain. Children in upper-income families still average considerably more visits to physicians than do children below the poverty line. And the nonpoor of all ages are far more likely than the poor to receive dental care or preventive medical care.[36]

In addition, when people are grouped according to their health status, the nonpoor are found to use health services much more than the poor do. Among those who report they are in fair or poor health, a measure of health status that correlates well with clinical symptoms and other indicators, persons with incomes twice the poverty level make 24 percent more physician visits than those with incomes below the poverty line. The differences are especially marked for children. When people are grouped according to the number of days of bed disability, upper-income groups make three-fourths more physician visits each year than lower-income groups of comparable health status.[37]

The differences that are noted between income groups are also apparent between nonelderly blacks and whites. Even when one controls for income, one finds that poor blacks tend to be in poorer health and have less access to physician and dental care and preventive medical care of all kinds.[38]

Despite the large inequities that remain between the poor and nonpoor, Medicaid has demonstrably contributed to the improvements that have occurred since its inception. Poor persons with Medicaid make substantially more physician visits than the poor who have no insurance coverage.[39] The poor who do not wear a "label" that qualifies them for Medicaid are left far behind the Medicaid-eligible poor and nonpoor groups.

Medicare—which, together with supplementary Medicaid or private health insurance, provides more universal coverage and more financial incentives for provider participation than Medicaid alone does—has effectively reduced the gap in the use of health services between the poor and the nonpoor elderly populations. In 1964, nonpoor elderly persons averaged substantially more physician visits. By 1978, the gap had been reduced by half, from 22 percent to 10 percent. It also appears that income differences in usage have virtually disappeared among elderly persons who have chronic health problems. Even utilization differences between elderly blacks and elderly whites have been greatly reduced and, in many areas, been essentially eliminated.[40]

Thus, there is considerable evidence that Medicaid and Medicare have greatly improved the use of health services by the poor, but these improvements are not so dazzling as to blind us to their limitations. Rates of usage are still not equal across all age groups or for all types of care, and more significantly, they still fall well behind need, which the poor have in greater measure than other groups and which would be the criterion for a truly equitable health care system.

Who Cares for the Poor?

Medicaid and Medicare were intended not only to increase the use of health services by the elderly and nonelderly poor. They were also intended to enable the poor to obtain their care from "mainstream" medicine—that is, the same sources from which upper-working-class and middle-class people get their medical care. How well have they succeeded?

Most people, regardless of income or insurance status, report having a regular source of medical care, an important condition for having access to health services. However, one in four low-income persons does not have a regular physician or other regular source of care, compared with fewer than one in five upper-income persons. Low-income persons *with* a regular source are far more likely than upper-income groups to rely on hospitals and clinics as that source, and to travel longer and wait longer to see a physician.[41] These inequities apply to low-income persons with Medicaid as well as to the poor who have no insurance coverage.[42]

One reason why even people with Medicaid are less likely to have a private physician is that most doctors treat few, if any, Medicaid patients. One-fifth of all physicians see no Medicaid patients at all. Just 6 percent of all physicians care for one-third of all Medicaid patients.[43]

Physicians do not discriminate against Medicare patients in the same way. There are two financial reasons why they do not, both related to reimbursement policies designed to encourage doctors to participate in the Medicare program. First, Medicare pays physicians about the same fees for physician care as does Blue Shield, the medical society plan. A study of fees paid to physicians in 1975 found that for a number of common visits and procedures, Medicare paid only 5 to 8 percent less than the *highest* fees paid by the Blue Shield plans surveyed. Medicaid fees, on the other hand, averaged 20 to 25 percent less than Medicare and Blue Shield fees.[44] Physicians' chief complaint against Medicaid is what they regard as inadequate reimbursement.[45]

Second, the Medicare program permits physicians to bill their Medicare patients their "usual, customary, and reasonable" charge, which is usually somewhat higher than Medicare's fees. Medicaid requires physicians to accept the "assigned" fee because Medicaid patients are considered too poor to pay extra charges. (We will shortly see how this rationale has been increasingly discarded.) In order to meet all of these deductibles, copayments, "unassigned" charges (in excess of those reimbursed by Medicare), and care not covered by Medicare benefits, the elderly have had to buy supplementary private insurance or be eligible for Medicaid supplementary coverage.

The added costs have remained a burden to the elderly whose financial plight Medicare was supposed to relieve. In 1977, Medicare paid for 44 percent of all health care costs for the aged; another

14 percent were met by Medicaid and 7 percent by private insurance. Direct out-of-pocket payments still amounted to 29 percent of the elderly's total health costs.[46] Medicare and Medicaid have not reduced out-of-pocket costs to the elderly as much as they have increased the total amount of money spent on health care per elderly person. Between 1966 and 1977, total health care spending per person sixty-five and over increased nearly four times, while their direct payments increased only two times. Nevertheless, these out-of-pocket costs—including deductibles, copayments, "unassigned" charges, and care not covered by any third-party benefits —continue to be a significant factor in the living expenses of the elderly, more than 16 percent of family incomes for elderly persons with family incomes below $10,000.[47]

Financing: The Leviathan Awakes

It is not simply the fact that fees are absolutely low that discourages provider participation in Medicaid; it is rather that Medicaid fees are low relative to doctors' higher private charges.[48] In other words, in the market for physician services, and consistent with general market dynamics, fees set below the prevailing market price attract few physicians. Ironically, it was the availability of public funds that enabled and encouraged physicians and hospitals to increase their fees.

The injection of public monies into the largely private medical market provided what seemed like unlimited revenues for physicians and private hospitals to order more services and products for their patients, to finance new capital investment, and to raise their prices. Government payments for physicians' services leaped from 7 percent of the total expenditures on physicians in 1965 to 20 percent in 1967 and have remained at 25 percent or higher since 1974. From 1965 to 1967, government payments for hospital care jumped from 39 percent to 55 percent of total hospital costs and have stayed at or near that level since then.[49]

Added to the large and growing private insurance coverage of hospital and physician care, increased public spending encouraged a consequent jump in medical prices. In the five years after the introduction of Medicare and Medicaid, hospitals and physicians raised their charges at more than twice the annual rate of increase in the years before the programs.[50] The "reasonable cost" basis of reimbursing hospitals, which Congress included in the Medicare and Medicaid legislation to appease the hospital industry, created an astoundingly inflationary program.[51] Medicare's "usual, customary, and reasonable" fees, which it paid to physicians, enabled doctors continually to push up prices for their services and to increase their total incomes by ordering more services for their patients. These inflationary spirals reverberated throughout the medical system; price increases contributed substantially more than increases in use did to overall increases in health care expenditures since Medicare and Medicaid began.[52]

The market system in health care works effectively to absorb every additional dollar of public and private funds into increased prices, capital investment, and profits and high incomes. The market system permits each health care unit—whether physician, hospital, nursing home chain, drug company, or other provider—to develop roles based on economic demand and expected profitability rather than on any politically or technically determined assessment of the community's health needs. Market competition among hospitals to attract physicians and their well-insured patients encourages hospital directors to provide the most advanced medical technology and the most modern facilities and services available. Physicians also play a central role in generating demand for hospital care as well as for their own services. Their training, the threat of malpractice suits, and especially the financial incentives in the fee-for-service system encourage physicians to order ever larger quantities of diagnostic and therapeutic procedures. Medical technology companies promote their products to doctors and hospitals regardless of the medical effectiveness or safety of their wares.

Hospitals, for example, used the new programs to their maximum advantage. The cost-plus method of Medicare and Medicaid reimbursement for inpatient care encouraged hospitals to finance modernization and expansion through debt financing, which increased from 40 percent of the total construction costs in 1968 to 68 percent in 1976.[53] With the increased revenues from Medicare and Medicaid, as well as from expanding private insurance, private hospitals' assets per bed increased 124 percent between 1965 and 1975, compared with an increase of only 80 percent in the preceding decade.[54]

Thus, the beneficiaries of Medicare and Medicaid have included more than the elderly and the poor. In 1980, hospitals collected $36 billion, out of their total revenues of $100 billion, from Medicare and Medicaid. Nursing homes collected nearly $11 billion, over half their total revenues, from these programs. Indeed, 41 percent of all state and local contributions to the Medicaid program go directly into the coffers of the largely for-profit nursing home industry. Physicians collected $10 billion from Medicare and Medicaid, more than 21 percent of doctors' total revenues. The drug industry also takes its share, $1.3 billion in 1980. Altogether, Medicare and Medicaid pumped $63 billion into the medical care system in 1980.[55]

Fiscal Pressures on State and Local Governments

These expenditures naturally reflected major commitments of federal and state tax resources. Federal spending for all types of health services grew from $4 billion in 1965 (just before Medicare and Medicaid began) to $15.7 billion in 1970, to $33.8 billion in 1975, and to $65.7 billion in 1980. State and local spending grew less rapidly—from $4.8 billion in 1965 to $31.3 billion in 1980—but represented an even greater burden on the more limited taxable resources at these levels of government.[56]

In California, for example, the state's own expenditures on Medi-Cal totaled $252 million in 1966–67, the program's first year, absorbing 8.4 percent of the state's general tax funds. Ronald Reagan, then in his first year as governor, pounced on the program's liberal benefits, eliminating certain optional services, freezing physicians' fees, and requiring prior authorization for certain kinds of hospital care. Nevertheless, the program's costs to the state continued to rise, in 1971 reaching half a billion dollars in state revenues and consuming 10 percent of the state's general tax funds.[57] By then, Reagan had broader political support from Washington as well as within the state for imposing more stringent cutbacks. His 1971 Medi-Cal Reform Act actually added new groups to the Medi-Cal rolls, but it instituted a stronger prior-authorization requirement for inpatient hospital care, imposed restrictions on reimbursement to providers, and shifted more of the costs of health care for the poor from the state to the counties.

The results were typical of many state efforts to restrain their own Medicaid costs. In the three years preceding this "reform," from 1968 to 1971, the counties' total Medi-Cal share had risen less than 3 percent, despite an increase of 54 percent in the number of Medi-Cal recipients; but in the next three years, to 1974, the counties' share rose 25 percent, compared with an increase of only 4 percent in Medi-Cal beneficiaries.[58] By 1974, Medi-Cal was a major burden on California counties, accounting for four out of every ten dollars they spent on health services. Meanwhile, they had to run an increasingly expensive system of public hospitals and medical care for all the poor who either were not covered by even California's generous Medicaid program or were Medi-Cal eligible persons who could not obtain care in the private sector. Under these burdens, the costs to the counties for public health care programs, including the local contribution to Medi-Cal and unreimbursed costs for county-run public hospitals and other health services, more than doubled between 1967 and 1974.

County health costs took a bigger bite of county property taxes, increasing from 30 percent of the total property tax revenues in 1967 to 36 percent in 1974.[59] A substantial portion of the rising county property taxes is attributable to these increased health costs.

The consequences of these mounting local costs have been significant. Because welfare, Medicaid, and other programs intended to sustain the poor are supported at the local level mainly by regressive property taxes and at the state level by even more regressive sales taxes and somewhat progressive income taxes, they tend to redistribute income from the working class and lower-middle class to the poor.[60] The unpopular tax base of these programs and services, and the fact that they serve mainly the poor and not those who disproportionately pay for them, has made Medicaid, other welfare programs, and public hospitals politically vulnerable. Given the rising local costs of public health care programs and economic and political conditions that impose fiscal constraints, it is not surprising that many California counties have closed their public hospitals. California's once extensive county hospital system has shrunk from sixty-five hospitals operated by forty-nine of the state's fifty-eight counties in 1964, to thirty-three hospitals in twenty-six counties in 1982.[61] It is, of course, the poor—Medi-Cal patients and those who do not qualify for the program—who suffer most from all of these cutbacks.

California is certainly not alone in this situation. Illinois's Medicaid program cost the state 280 percent more in 1973 than it did five years earlier.[62] Gov. Richard Ogilvie in 1971 announced cutbacks, cost-sharing by patients, and restrictions intended to make providers of care "account for the services they deliver to Medicaid recipients," but also forcing recipients themselves "to have more responsibility for their actions in obtaining health services."[63] One of Illinois's tools for cutting the costs of welfare programs, like AFDC and Medicaid, is simply not to increase income eligibility levels to keep up with inflation. From 1975 to 1981, Illinois increased its AFDC and Medicaid income standards by 16 percent,[64] a period when the consumer price index increased 53 percent. Illinois's failure to increase its income eligibility levels has not only kept many of its poor residents off the Medicaid rolls; it has also shifted more of the burden of indigent medical care to the local level. The proportion of Chicago's Cook County Hospital patients who were covered by Medicaid dropped from 65 percent in 1973 to only 27 percent in 1979, adding more patients, and thus more expense, to the county's own tax resources and thereby compounding its fiscal problems.

The Politics of Cost Containment

Throughout the country the litany of state cutbacks and cost-containment devices was familiar. Many of them were encouraged or permitted by the Social Security amendments of 1967, 1971, 1972, and 1981, intended to give the states and the federal government more options and power to control and reduce Medicaid and Medicare costs. The cost-containment strategies included restricting eligibility by reducing maximum income levels or dropping optional groups from Medicaid; eliminating optional medical services; imposing cost-sharing by the patient to discourage the use of services and the purchase of prescription drugs; devising programs to control provider fraud and abuse; introducing restrictive reimbursement practices (to counter the expensive "reasonable costs" reimbursement to hospitals and "reasonable fee" payments to doctors); reviewing utilization in hospitals and nursing homes; and regulating capital investment in health facilities.[65]

The entry of the government into financing health care on such a grand scale assured that it would have to intervene politically to control the system in which it developed a very large stake. However, each of the cost-containment methods tries to compensate for or reduce the irrationalities of the private market, but without challenging essential private control or the market system. Such a challenge is viewed by the economically and politically powerful health industry as being intolerable. Even if individual members of Congress, state legislatures, or governmental agencies were ideologically disposed to eliminate the private control of these public resources now channeled into the health industry, the political costs would be very high and essentially unacceptable.[66]

So, less effective, but politically more acceptable, cost constraints are imposed. In addition to the lower reimbursement rates paid to physicians, Medicare and Medicaid reimburse hospitals at lower levels than do private insurers. In California in 1979, for example, Blue Cross and commercial insurance companies reimbursed hospitals 12 percent more than their "full financial requirements" (which includes the actual costs of providing care, working capital, and capital replacement costs). In the same year, Medicare reimbursed hospitals 4 percent *less* than their full financial requirements, and Medi-Cal paid them *18 percent* less.[67] This differential penalizes public hospitals and private hospitals that serve a large number of poor persons, because of their dependence on Medicare and Medicaid for patient care revenues. Most private hospitals that serve relatively few Medicaid and Medicare patients, however, shift this

unreimbursed portion of their care onto charges for privately insured patients, resulting in an indirect (and regressive) tax paid
through hospital insurance premiums.

Maintaining low reimbursement rates discourages physicians and
hospitals from caring for Medicaid patients. That practice, as well
as restricting the eligibility of low-income persons, tends to shift
the financial burdens onto local governments—in those communities that still have public hospitals and clinics. Both practices, as
well as the curtailment of optional services and the imposition of
cost-sharing by the patient, also shift the burden of containing costs
onto the poor themselves (in the form of out-of-pocket payments
and the foregoing of care), undoubtedly the group least able to bear
the burden but also the least able to oppose such measures. The
earlier California experience with copayments suggests that they
may even result in higher overall costs to the Medicaid program,
because more expensive services (such as hospitalization) requiring
no copayment tend to be substituted for less expensive care (such
as ambulatory services) that had been deferred because of copayment.[68]

Until 1981, major cutbacks were imposed only in Medicaid programs and not against Medicare beneficiaries, because the Medicare
population includes large numbers of voters from all social classes
while Medicaid is limited to the poorer and politically less powerful
groups. In 1981, in order to increase the military budget and reduce
taxes, the Reagan administration and a more conservative Congress
shifted massive amounts of federal funds from public assistance
programs like Medicaid with greater ease than from Social Security
or Medicare. The Omnibus Reconciliation Act of 1981 reduced the
federal match for Medicaid by 3 percent in fiscal year 1982, 4
percent in 1983, and 4.5 percent in 1984, although states may offset
at least some of these reductions by a variety of fiscal and policy
programs or by having an unemployment rate 50 percent greater
than the national average. States were also permitted even greater
latitude in reducing benefits and eligibility. In addition, the administration began an attack on Medicare spending that accelerated
in the next year. In 1981, Congress voted to eliminate or reduce
some Medicare benefits, increase Medicare copayments and deductibles, and reduce reimbursement rates to hospitals. The further
reductions in Medicaid and Medicare adopted in 1982 are likely to
accelerate the shift of costs from the federal government to local
governments, the elderly and poor themselves, and privately insured patients.

The states are unlikely to shoulder the burden that the federal
government is dropping. In 1982, for example, California eliminated its state-funded "medically indigent adult" portion of the

Medi-Cal program, turning over responsibility for its 280,000 recipients to the counties along with less than 70 percent of the $750 million that the state had been spending on the program. The state also formally abandoned its goal of providing "mainstream" medicine for the poor by adopting a policy of contracting with high-volume, low-cost doctors and hospitals to care for all remaining Medi-Cal patients, a major change from the "freedom of choice" principle on which the program had been based since its inception. These actions, which other states are likely to follow, illustrate that government will protect itself from impending fiscal disaster by imposing severe constraints on program expenditures and on the demand side of the medical marketplace.

Both Medicare and Medicaid also attempt to regulate the market by influencing provider behavior. Campaigns against provider fraud and abuse are marginally effective in their financial impact on Medicaid programs, but the high visibility of individual cases of fraud exposed by investigations makes this mode popular with officials and politicians. More significantly, utilization review programs provide for professional peer review of physician decisions to order some kinds of expensive hospital care. Experiences in some states indicate that mandatory review programs tend to retard the growth of Medicaid costs, at least for some kinds of care, although other experiences, particularly with voluntary programs, found no savings.[69] In recent years, state Medicaid programs and Medicare have begun to scrutinize hospital costs and evaluate the reasonableness of costs that were formerly simply reimbursed.[70] In addition, some states have instituted rate-setting mechanisms, some of which reimburse hospitals prospectively rather than on the prevailing fee-for-service basis, forcing hospitals to live within relatively fixed budgets instead of generating as much revenue as possible.[71] All of these methods, together with state-run certification of the need for hospital expansion or the purchase of expensive equipment, have the potential of slowing the rate of increase in hospital costs.[72] Although these methods have gained political popularity among the states because of the danger that Medicaid budgets will drag state treasuries into fiscal collapse, Reagan administration officials opposed such infringements on market prerogatives until their own efforts to control Medicare and Medicaid spending were endangered by the present relatively "free market" state.

LESSONS FOR THE FUTURE

The experience with Medicare and Medicaid improves our understanding of the potential and limits of reform in the health system.

The lessons we learn from this experience will be valuable guides to developing our future strategy.

Value of the Reforms

Without question, Medicaid and Medicare have significantly improved the access of the elderly and the poor to medical services. This conclusion is supported by the increased use of services by the elderly and the poor since the programs began. It is also clear that the poor with Medicaid make greater use of services than the poor who have no insurance coverage.

Nevertheless, these benefits have not been sufficient to remove all inequities. Poor children make fewer visits to physicians than children from nonpoor families. The poor of all ages receive less dental and preventive medical care than the nonpoor. When people's health status is taken into account, the use of health services is still related to income; those better off receive more care than poorer persons in comparable states of health. Similarly, the white population still makes greater use of health services than blacks do, although this difference has also been reduced over the past decade and a half, particularly for the elderly.

Despite these limitations, we should not ignore the very important improvements Medicare and Medicaid have generated. The effects on health status of these increased rates of use is more difficult to determine because most types of medical care have not been proven to lead to better health. Some types of preventive care, such as immunizations and prenatal care, have been shown to reduce the incidence of illness and death. Unfortunately, these are the very kinds of services that remain less accessible to the poor. However, diagnostic and curative types of care are important to all people. They reduce the burden of disease by limiting it, speeding recovery, preventing or limiting disability due to illness or injury, and providing comfort and palliation. These are important benefits of improved access to and utilization of medical services, benefits that the elderly and the poor receive in greater measure now than before Medicare and Medicaid.

Limitations of the Reforms

One of the greatest limitations in the Medicare and Medicaid legislation was the separation of medical care for the poor from the program for the elderly. As a social insurance program, Medicare is paid for by everyone and ultimately benefits all as they reach retirement age. Medicaid, a welfare-linked public assistance program, is paid for by everyone but benefits only those in the bottom classes of society. Thus, Medicare has a broad base of political support while Medicaid's base is narrowed. The importance of this difference in the political base and support was reflected in the ease with which the Reagan administration cut funds from the Medicaid program and the overwhelming opposition it faced when cuts were first proposed for Medicare. Broad-based social insurance programs generate powerful support when threatened, while the dividing line between "deserving" and "undeserving" poor, inherent in welfare programs, shifts almost continuously with changes in economic and political conditions. A single social insurance program for the elderly and the poor would have made health care for the poor less vulnerable.

Medicaid was further limited by its being made a state-run program, whose federal role was limited to contributions and a set of very minimal program guidelines and requirements. State control resulted in wide variations among Medicaid programs, some states providing relatively generously for a substantial portion of their low-income residents and other states creating very stingy programs. A single federal program would have assured at least a uniform base of coverage and benefits. The experience with Medicaid suggests the disaster that awaits health programs under the Reagan administration's block grants to the states, which have replaced many categorical programs funded and monitored by the federal government.

A third limitation in both programs is their regressive financing. Social Security taxes are inherently regressive, since they tax income at a uniform rate at all levels of income up to the income limit, after which additional income is exempt. Even though Medicare's financing is regressive, its benefits are available to everyone, although they are largely deferred until retirement age. The Medicaid program is less regressively financed, but its welfare-related benefits represent a transfer of income from the upper working class and middle class to the poor. If taxes were drawn more progressively, there would be greater equity in the society and less demand for reducing government spending and less vulnerability for either program.

Another fundamental limitation was the integration of both programs into the present market system. Because each unit in the system has the autonomy to stake out its market and seek to maximize revenues and profits, the market system inherently drives up prices and total expenditures. All of these problems are exacerbated, as we have seen, in a fee-for-service context in which providers' incomes are based on the number of services they perform and in which reimbursements are geared to charges and costs for providing each service. In this way, Medicare and Medicaid have turned public funds into subsidies to the privately controlled market. Although the government has in the last decade moved increasingly to regulate the market in order to rationalize it and to reduce the growth of expenditures, it has not attempted to replace private control of each market unit with public ownership or control. Public accountability through public ownership and control would greatly increase the likelihood that Medicare and Medicaid would serve the population's health needs without those needs' having to compete with each unit's desire for profits.

Finally, because they did improve medical care conditions for the elderly and the poor, Medicare and Medicaid have undoubtedly reduced the most pressing needs, and therefore the political demand, for national health insurance. That is, of course, the danger with any reform. Nevertheless, the very existence of Medicare in particular has undermined opposition to national health insurance. After all, Medicare has not made the United States a socialist country, nor has the medical system collapsed—both, dire predictions of the medical profession. Medicare's existence and its obvious benefits have actually legitimized the demand for national health insurance.

Strategy for the Future

The lessons we have learned from the Medicare/Medicaid experience can be translated into several strategic guidelines and principles.

First, to improve equity we should avoid isolating programs for the poor and should broaden the base of support of public health care for all constituencies. Future programs, especially national health insurance, should consist of a single program for all the people—the poor and the nonpoor; the employed, unemployed, self-employed, and retired; primary enrollees and dependents. There must be no distinctions in benefits or coverage, because these will inevitably result in inequities.

Second, to distribute the financial support for health programs more equitably and avoid the backlash experienced by Medicaid and public hospitals, health programs should be progressively financed. In the tradition of social insurance programs, some of the financing may come from payroll taxes. These should be scaled progressively. The majority of support for the entire system, and not only for the subsidies for the poor, should be derived from general tax revenues, and these taxes should be made more progressive than they currently are.

Third, to assure a stronger and uniform base of coverage and benefits throughout the country, decisions on the scope of benefits and coverage should not be left to the states. Local control and administration of national health programs is desirable because it makes the programs more responsive to communities' needs, but local and state administration should be carried out within firm and generous program requirements that apply to every state and locality.

Fourth, a national health service is clearly preferable to national health insurance to eliminate the fiscal, organizational, and programmatic irrationalities in the present market organization of medical care. An insurance program leaves each unit in the system independent of all other units, free to exploit the medical market to its advantage. It thus retains the basic irrationalities in our present medical care system. A national health service would take health care out of the marketplace and make it a genuine public service. There would remain forces that would tend to distort the provision of care from simply meeting the population's health needs: professional groups and bureaucrats would undoubtedly still try to maximize their benefits, even at the expense of the system's intended beneficiaries; and communities would be likely to compete with one another in seeking resources from a necessarily limited resource base. But a national health service permits a degree of public accountability unavailable in any other system, and it greatly increases the likelihood that the health care system will be matched to the population's health needs. The bill introduced into the Congress by Rep. Ronald Dellums would create just such a national health service—a universal and uniform system of benefits and care, progressively financed and locally controlled.

If political conditions do not permit the enactment of such a progressive program, then we can insist on a responsive, accountable, and efficient national health insurance system that controls some of the worst features of the market system. A national health insurance program should be uniform in its coverage and benefits, be progressively financed, have to live within a fixed national budget each year, include a large role for public planning and regulation, and be administered by public bodies at national, state, and local levels.

Finally, to assure the strongest support for needed reforms, we must form broad political coalitions to work for such legislation. The coalitions should include all those groupings that support progressive programs, such as a national health service or comprehensive, universal, progressively financed national health insurance. Such coalitions must reject any attempts to split off fractions with programs geared to a particular grouping's needs. The coalitions working for these long-run reforms should also join and work closely with coalitions fighting cutbacks in Medicaid, Medicare, and other programs that have made a demonstrable difference in the lives of all Americans.

Such a strategy would maximize the opportunity for winning progressive reforms that meet the health needs of the population, building on the successes of Medicare and Medicaid but avoiding many of the most severe limitations of these reforms.

part II

SERVICES FOR SPECIAL GROUPS

4.

occupational
health and safety:

TWO STEPS FORWARD, ONE STEP BACK

Molly Joel Coye
Mark Douglas Smith
Anthony Mazzocchi

I was in Arkansas working for a company that is now part of Monsanto. At that time it was a chemical division of an oil company. They made ammonia, ammonia nitrate and ammonia sulfate at an acid plant, and the fumes from this stack—you know, when the wind was changing—would come down. . . . We went over there to a meeting with the company one day and tried to get them to put an extension on that stack so the wind would catch it and blow it on to somebody else. The company insisted that it wasn't an unhealthy situation, it was just uncomfortable. We suggested to them that it probably was unhealthy too because in that part of the country, as you probably well know, there are trees everywhere, and for about a mile, a mile and a half from this plant, they were all dead. We got the company people to go out to see all these trees, and we said, "Look, if it doesn't hurt you, how come all those trees are dead?" And the company had a very logical answer. They said, "Hell, those trees can't spit it out."[1]

INTRODUCTION

For centuries, workers have known that those engaging in certain occupations or crafts contracted certain diseases: gravestone makers traditionally made their own headstones before they succumbed to silicosis; nitrate workers learned to rub nitrates into their hatbands to fend off headaches on weekends; and pesticide formulators recognized that workers in a certain department were unable to have children. From Paracelsus in his early observations of "phthisis" among miners in the sixteenth century and Bernardo Ramazzini in his treatise entitled *The Diseases of Workmen,* published in 1700, to Sir Percival Pott in his discovery of high rates of scrotal cancer among London's chimneysweeps in the 1770s, scientists have relied upon working people to build their understanding of occupational health. Even the language has been enriched by this accumulated understanding: the expression "mad as a hatter" comes from the recognition that hatmakers did indeed become progressively insane after long-term exposure to mercury in curing felt hats. With this practical knowledge, often gained by tragic experience, workers and scientists have striven for improvements in working conditions.[2]

Yet the state of occupational health in the United States at the beginning of the 1960s reflected widespread public ignorance of the daily carnage wreaked in American workplaces and an almost total lack of effective regulation to protect workers' health. In the decade between 1961 and 1970, some 14,000 workers lost their lives each year in accidents on the job, and the National Safety Council estimated that injury rates had climbed 29 percent over the last decade.[3] More than 2 million workers were disabled by work-related injuries each year. Occupational diseases, frequently more difficult to link to occupational causes because of their gradual development or delayed onset, went largely unreported and uncompensated, although hundreds of thousands of new cases occurred each year.

The 1960s saw the rekindling of many earlier powerful struggles over working conditions. The roots of this modern movement extended back far before the 1960s, but for occupational health, as for many other struggles, the 1960s and 1970s were a time when several factors converged to make significant victories a reality. Spearheaded by the United Mine Workers' massive mobilization for new mine health and safety regulations and just compensation for black-lung victims, labor began to agitate for broader health and safety reforms in the mid-1960s. Joined by a small number of public-interest activists and progressive scientists, this coalition of forces succeeded in passing the Coal Mine Safety and Health Act in 1969 and the Williams-Steiger Occupational Safety and Health Act

(OSH Act) in 1970. The passage of the OSH Act had a tremendous significance, both as a watershed in the struggle over reforms in occupational health and as a demonstration of the vitality of the new forces that had entered this struggle in the 1960s. The OSH Act set forth, for the first time, general as well as specific duties of employers to protect workers; mandated a new standard-setting process; provided for worker participation in standard setting, inspections, and appeals, and for worker education and training; and shielded workers against employer retaliation for health and safety complaints.

This chapter will examine the problems in occupational safety and health targeted by reformers in the late 1960s. They can be divided into four main areas.

The first problem was the lack of governmental regulation of industry, leading to myriad occupational exposures for workers. These took the form of dangerous physical environments resulting in acute injury (unguarded machines, unsafe scaffolding, and the like), of physical agents that led to more long-term injury and disease (radiation, dusts, lead, noise), and, increasingly, of toxic chemicals. The government's role in controlling hazardous occupational conditions had been minimal at best.

The second difficulty was the lack of an adequate compensation scheme for occupationally induced injury and disease. Particularly troublesome was the multiplicity and variation among the compensation systems of different states. Benefit levels and the criteria for determining awards, however, were uniformly punitive and largely ignored occupational disease in favor of a heavy emphasis on injuries.

Third, little attention was given to scientific work in areas critical to occupational health, particularly to the study of occupational disease. There was a lack of basic scientific research in the toxicology and epidemiology of disease among workers, as well as a shortage of properly trained researchers and health care providers in the field.

The last concern was the lack of awareness and knowledge on the part of workers themselves about the hazards of their jobs.

These concerns formed the nucleus around which a coalition of forces fought for basic reforms in occupational safety and health. These can best be described as two different fronts: (1) changes in government structure and regulation intended to modify industry's behavior and (2) changes in the health care system designed to develop the scientific research and core of professionals needed to initiate new forms of health care delivery. We will look at the reforms instituted during the 1970s in both areas and argue that the era must be divided into two main periods.

During the years from 1969 to 1976, pioneer legislation established standards for coal mine safety and health, the Occupational Safety and Health Administration (OSHA), and the National Institute for Occupational Safety and Health (NIOSH). These fledgling reforms were often implemented in forms predominantly influenced by the pro-industry orientation of the Nixon and Ford administrations. Unions, public-interest groups, and committees for occupational safety and health ("COSH" groups) maintained increasing pressure on state and federal agencies on enforcement issues, to issue more standards, and to increase educational programs. The latter half of the decade, the years 1976–81, saw a distinct shift in the character of OSHA and NIOSH, one favorable to the labor movement. As could be expected, this provoked stronger industry reaction and counterattack. In this later period, reform efforts focused on training programs for health professionals and significant developments in state and local occupational health reforms. These efforts deemphasized reliance on direct government enforcement and instead promoted government support of forces considered more likely to effect lasting change.

We examine the results of this decade of reform in occupational safety and health, in measurable improvements in workers' health, in institutional changes, and in the evolution of political and social issues arising from this reform movement, such as the trade-off of productivity and health ("cost-benefit analysis") and the relative importance of job exposures versus individual life-styles in producing disease.

We conclude with the ongoing practical tasks and the theoretical questions that confront workers, unions, and public health leaders and others concerned about occupational illness in America.

BACKGROUND OF THE MOVEMENT

In the context of the social reform movements of the 1960s, two broad forces converged to create a new awareness of job health and safety hazards and of the need for specific reforms to address them: the labor movement and the newly created environmental movement. Economic boom conditions had stimulated a wide range of nonwage demands, and working conditions as a proportion of all strike issues had increased steadily, reaching 30 percent in the years 1968–73. In a 1969 survey of blue- and white-collar workers funded by the Department of Labor, 38 percent of the workers reported health and safety hazards on their jobs, and 71 percent (the highest proportion) considered protection against work-related illness or injury very important among all labor standards problem areas.[4]

The Johnson administration had identified occupational health and safety as part of its labor reform package, intended to maintain the coalition between labor and the Democratic party. In 1967–68, a core of progressive union leadership—from the Oil, Chemical, and Atomic Workers (OCAW), the Steelworkers, the AFL-CIO, and the Industrial Union Department of the AFL-CIO—joined efforts with Ralph Nader's public-interest lobbying group in support of the Johnson proposal. Although the bill was quickly killed by a flood of employer mail, similar legislation was introduced each year until 1970.

The mine workers, who have a long tradition of struggle over health and safety issues, took the lead in the struggle for legislative reform. In 1968, miners from Fayette and Kanawha counties in West Virginia formed the Black Lung Association; in February of 1969, more than 42,000 of West Virginia's 44,000 coal miners staged a wildcat strike demanding enactment of a broad health and safety reform bill, and they stayed out until the state bill was signed into law, three weeks later. When 78 miners were killed in an explosion at Consolidated Coal's huge No. 9 mine in Farmington, later that year, union and public pressure finally forced the passage of the historic Coal Mine Safety and Health Act by Congress.

Industry's reaction to such legislation was predictably hostile. Industry was, first of all, opposed to the *principle* of government regulation (except that which reduces competition or maintains prices). But proposals for occupational health regulations were particularly objectionable to industry because they challenged corporate control over the work process itself. The victory of work force organizing efforts in the basic industries during the 1930s and 1940s forced steel, auto, oil, and other major corporations to bargain with the unions, but most of the concessions wrung from them were economic, that is, dealt with the price of labor in wages or pensions, health plans, and other fringe benefits. Occupational health legislation, however, invaded new ground: it dealt with the substances, the technology and machinery, and the methods of production themselves, as well as rights of access to "trade secrets" about what chemicals they were working with or to medical and environmental monitoring results. This ground was clearly dangerous. In addition, management in nonunionized sectors of the economy feared that health and safety would provide a "back door" entrance for union organizing.

Despite industry opposition, labor continued to press for reform. Labor insisted that all major authority for occupational safety and health be located within the Department of Labor; although the department was Republican dominated under Nixon, after 1968 labor leaders had more hope of influencing it (at least under other

administrations) than the independent board that industry proposed. Labor also fought for certain key workers' rights that had
never existed before: to request inspections of work sites, to see the
results of those inspections, to appeal rulings, to be safe from retaliation, to petition for standards, and to accompany inspectors in the
work site.

By 1970, the passage of some version of a health and safety bill
had become an essential part of even Nixon's blue-collar strategy.
To balance the recessionary measures adopted by the Republicans
in the strong economic boom of the late 1960s, they needed apparent concessions to offer labor. Because of this labor was able to
wrest a far stronger piece of legislation from Congress than industry
had expected. The final OSH Act gave both standard-setting and
enforcement authority to the Department of Labor, leaving only the
review of appealed citations to the review commission favored by
industry.

The second force critical to the development of occupational
health and safety reforms during this period was the environmental
movement. Largely a middle-class phenomenon emerging from student and activist-scientist bases, this movement did not organize
primarily to support legislative reform in health and safety, but was
able to capture media attention and to effect a major change in
broader public awareness of linkages between human disease and
the presence of toxic chemicals in air and water. In the early 1960s,
Rachel Carson's *Silent Spring* was the first book to popularize the
concept that chemicals (or physical agents like radiation) that cannot be seen or smelled in the environment may be slowly creating
disease or a genetic injury that may be passed on to children.

In some industries (such as coal mining or the manufacturing of
asbestos insulation) workers were far ahead of the "experts" in
recognizing the connection between work environment exposures
and later disease. But for workers in industries where exposure
levels are less high, where exposure is not correlated with such a
high incidence of disease, or where the onset of disease occurs years
after exposure, the link between current exposure and future disease is not always so clear. The environmental movement (and an
increasing proportion of young workers who had some scientific
background from high school or college) had a profound impact in
making workers more suspicious of the substances with which thy
worked. Although worker recognition of occupational disease patterns has almost always preceded "discovery" of the associations by
physicians, this increased worker suspicion of exposure on the job
resulted in a wave of "worker epidemiology," with which the occupational health field could not keep pace.

Public health itself was profoundly influenced by the environ-mental movement of the 1960s and early 1970s, but public health leaders did not play a particularly active role in the initial effort to get new health and safety legislation enacted. Although HEW had in 1965 published the first major review of occupational health problems, the Frye report, which called for national expenditures of over $50 million for occupational health and safety programs, there was no significant pressure either from within HEW or from the broader public health community in support of OSHA or sev-eral of the earlier legislative proposals. Nevertheless, statistics generated by HEW, the Department of Labor, the Bureau of Labor Statistics, and the National Safety Council attracted some public attention and contributed to the campaign for the passage of the OSH bill.

REFORMS ENACTED
AND OUTCOMES

The labor movement is not monolithic, and many of the union leaders involved in the struggle to create OSHA had quite distinct reasons for their efforts and for their expectations of the results. Some labor leaders and activists involved in the fight for OSHA felt that a strong enough piece of legislation, and an agency well funded and supported by the administration, could tackle and solve most of the problems responsible for serious disease and in-jury in most workplaces. The process would not be easy, and was expected to be adversary, but much of the importance of electoral politics was precisely to build successful coalitions—primarily around the Democratic party—which would support and imple-ment these reforms.

Others in the labor movement had little expectation that OSHA itself could or would actually protect most workers from job haz-ards. The importance of OSHA lay, as they saw it, in creating a stage upon which issues previously hidden within the workplace could be publicly discussed and examined. Workers, their families, and the public would learn about job hazards and about their rights to information and to protection. Defenses and positions taken by industry would also be made public and discussed. The struggle for right-to-know legislation (the labeling standard proposed by the federal OSHA, and similar legislation passed by a number of state and city governments), for example, caused more workers to won-der what they are exposed to, to demand information, and to use both collective bargaining and OSHA mechanisms in the struggle to get that information; it also created public discussion of such concepts as "trade secrets" and "cost benefit."

Regulatory Issues:
Standards and Enforcement

In the area of standards and enforcement, OSHA's initial performance was a severe disappointment. Only four new standards had
been promulgated by 1976, each of them issued only after court
suits *by* unions (frequently in cooperation with the Health Research
Group) *against* OSHA. The 450 preexisting consensus standards
adopted with the OSH Act were grossly unscientific and offered
little protection. The number of OSHA inspectors was clearly
inadequate to reach most workplaces; and the average fine for non-
serious violations was less than $50, that for serious violations
approximately $625. Industry had a field day ridiculing OSHA with
cartoons of the "Cowboy after OSHA" (replete with portable toilet,
guardrails, hard hat, and safety goggles) and pointing out the "nit-
picking" safety regulations (most of them inherited from the old
Bureau of Labor Standards). Nixon and Ford had appointed OSHA
administrators who were obviously antagonistic to labor, and the
political nature and uses of OSHA were made particularly clear
with revelations such as the "Guenther memo," in which then
OSHA chief, George C. Guenther, reassured his superiors in the
Department of Labor that "no highly controversial standard [i.e.,
cotton dust, etc.] will be proposed by OSHA or by NIOSH," that
the political registration of all field Regional Administrators was
being checked, and that he would submit OSHA's hiring plan to the
Republican National Committee and to the Committee to Re-Elect
the President.[5]

Despite these marked problems with OSHA's enactment, a tremendous public debate had been stimulated about job health and
safety hazards, about the best means of combating them, and about
worker roles and rights in the struggle for health and safety.

OSHA was a significant campaign issue in 1976, and Carter promised an administration that would support OSHA and push for the
enactment of more standards and for more rigorous enforcement of
existing ones. The significance of his campaign pledges and, perhaps
more important, of the general attitude of workers to the Democratic victory in 1976 was attested to by a dramatic upsurge in
worker complaints—requests for inspections—to OSHA in the period 1977–80. This surge coincided with his appointment of a tox-
icologist from the University of Cincinnati, Dr. Eula Bingham, as
assistant secretary of labor for OSHA. Dr. Bingham's appointment
was widely regarded as evidence of a new swing away from the
agency's previous strong pro-industry stance.

Supporters of health and safety had not been dormant though the

Nixon and Ford years. Labor unions, public-interest groups, and others had continued to push OSHA and NIOSH for changes in policy and practice. In addition, they had learned how to find their way through state and federal bureaucracies and procedures. Hundreds of local union health and safety committees had been formed. A corps of health, technical, and legal professionals had been developing, often volunteering time to assist unions in health and safety and compensation through COSH groups and other such forms. Thus when the Carter administration took office, in 1976, the occupational health movement had built a base capable of utilizing the opportunities presented by more progressive federal officials.

Policies developed during this period by Bingham at OSHA and by Anthony Robbins at NIOSH demonstrated a growing awareness of the importance of direct worker involvement in the struggle for health and safety reform. Although it was clear that OSHA would never be able to field enough inspectors to effectively police workplace conditions, a work force well informed about its rights under OSHA could successfully use the *threat* of OSHA intervention to win protection for themselves. Similarly, the new standards promulgated by OSHA were important and effective, not because OSHA itself had the capacity to oversee their implementation in all or even most workplaces, but because organized workers could refer to these standards in negotiating contracts or in short-term struggles over health and safety working conditions in the shop floor. The key to greater effectiveness for OSHA, from labor's point of view, lay in the passage of more standards with more focus, in the enforcement of policies, and in the provision of resources for the education of their own memberships about health and safety issues and legal rights.

By December 1980, the total number of standards enacted by OSHA had reached only eleven; OSHA safety regulations were still amended fewer than ten times a year, on the average, each standard promulgated was promptly appealed by trade associations in court, and the benzene standard had been overturned by the Supreme Court in 1980 on grounds of insufficient documentation of risk at the low exposure levels that the standard prohibited.

Yet OSHA policy on the development and promulgation of standards had changed fundamentally under Eula Bingham's leadership, and OSHA had been far more vigorous in creating and supporting new types of standards. Recognizing the escalating rate at which new chemicals were being introduced into the workplace, as well as the enormous number of chemicals already in use for which no standards existed, Bingham promoted the concept of "generic standards," which could address whole categories of chemicals. The Cancer Policy Standard was the first generic standard to be proposed, and it was even more controversial because it was also the first standard to rely primarily on nonhuman data (combinations of bacterial mutagenesis assays and mammalian tests for carcinogens) in classifying chemicals as toxic to humans.

The lead standard also incorporated two new concepts. "Rate retention" required that all workers removed from their job because of high blood lead levels had to be retained at their previous rate of pay and seniority level, whether working in a lower job category or not working at all, until the levels returned to normal or for up to eighteen months. Second, previous standards had contained no provision for early removal from exposure. "Medical removal protection," also incorporated into the OSHA lead standard, allowed physicians to remove certain workers with blood levels greater than 30 ug/dl from lead exposure for up to eighteen months (with rate retention protection) in order to prevent potentially irreversible health effects; for example, workers attempting to conceive a child and those suffering from renal disease, hypertension, or other diseases that lead exposure might be expected to exacerbate.

Finally, Bingham pioneered an entirely new type of standard with the labeling and medical-records-access standards—standards that stipulate the right of workers to certain kinds of information. The labeling standard (proposed by OSHA in 1981 but never actually promulgated because of Carter's last-minute campaign maneuvers) would have directed employers to provide information on the generic-chemical content of and potential toxic effects of chemicals used in their workplace. Broadly referred to as right-to-know legislation, similar standards have been enacted in New York, California, Maine, Michigan, and Philadelphia. The movement for right-to-know legislation on all levels—local, state, and federal— has been one of the most successful organizing issues in health and safety for unions and for labor support groups.

The second standard giving workers new rights to health and safety information was the medical records access standard promulgated by OSHA in 1980. This gave workers the right to see and obtain copies of employer records of workplace monitoring, of biological monitoring, of the chemical name and potential effects of a toxic substance or harmful physical agent, and of medical records. OSHA suffered some setbacks in court rulings on enforcement procedures, the most serious being the *Barlow* decision by the Supreme Court, in 1978, which denied OSHA inspectors the right of entry to inspect workplaces without a warrant. The decision did give OSHA the right to obtain ex parte warrants (without demonstrating probable cause), but as lower courts rule on the basis of *Barlow* its inhibiting effect has become apparent. At the Pool Offshore Oil Drilling Company in Louisiana, for example, OSHA was denied access for an inspection even after a total of five deaths had occurred in the preceding nine months.[6]

The issue of employer retribution against workers requesting health and safety inspections had been addressed in the original OSHA legislation under Section 11c, which gave workers the right to appeal to OSHA if their employer discriminated against them by reducing their pay or by firing them. As the number of 11c complaints escalated, so did OSHA's backlog of cases. Practically, workers soon realized that risking a three-year wait for an OSHA investigation and an eventual court decision made Section 11c a less-than-effective guarantee; only where they had a union prepared to fight retaliation through grievance procedures and other nonregulatory approaches could they afford to press for health and safety on the job.

Where union locals were strong, however, the workers were able to use OSHA's existence to win significant improvements in health and safety, frequently without directly asking the agency to intervene. When the posting of arsenic warning labels at a geothermal energy production unit raised concern among the members of the International Brotherhood of Electrical Workers in northern California, the union filed a grievance referencing the new OSHA arsenic standard rather than asking for (and waiting for) an OSHA inspection. Local 1245 health and safety staff monitored the arsenic levels at the unit and found them to be above the OSHA standard, and publicized the results widely among their members. Within a month, the company had agreed to produce a new slide show for employee training, to institute new work practices which in some cases went beyond those required by OSHA, and to provide data on future monitoring. As local officials said, they could always go to OSHA if the company reneged on its agreements; they did not believe they could have won this victory without the existence of a strong OSHA standard and the backup threat of OSHA intervention.

The "New Directions" program created by OSHA in 1978 became both a symbol of OSHA's new emphasis on worker involvement and a major funding program in its own right. Established to fund worker education programs in health and safety, initial grants distributed $6.4 million to unions, universities, trade associations, and nonprofit groups. By 1980 the program budget had risen to $15.1 million; an estimated 75,000 workers attended training programs in health and safety as a result of New Directions–funded efforts, and 5 million were reached indirectly on a regular basis— for example, by union health and safety newsletters.[7]

While workers were becoming more educated and more sophisticated about occupational health and safety issues, environmental health issues were receiving more attention in the public media. Love Canal and other toxic-waste dump sites were the focus of most of this attention, together with "acid rain," urban smog, and other industrially generated pollutants. In each case of environmental pollution, workers employed in the relevant industries were goaded to form deeper suspicions about the effect of these pollutants on their own health, and frequently to resent the public attention given to more diffuse environmental exposures at the expense of their own more concentrated risk. The cavalier response that often emerges at first ("I've been working around it for years, hasn't done anything to me") slowly yields to concern, as patterns of chronic disease are discovered or as the media take the effects associated with exposure more seriously (such as those in the case of Agent Orange).

Increased public concern about the toxic effects of environmental pollution also resulted in the creation of a number of other regulatory agencies, such as the EPA and the Council on Environmental Quality. Unfortunately, many of these agencies with overlapping jurisdictions did not develop functional ways of coordinating their efforts, and rarely demonstrated the awareness of or concern for worker exposure that OSHA showed. In the area of agricultural workers and pesticide usage, for example, OSHA and the EPA became embroiled in a bitter contest for authority to set standards and enforce them. OSHA lost most jurisdictional rights to protect fieldworkers to the EPA, although the EPA was notorious for its lack of enforcement of even the minimal standards governing pesticide usage.

Workers' Compensation

The original workers' compensation compromise between labor and industry made it illegal for workers to sue their employers, in return for a promise of compensation for medical expenses and part of the lost wages. The system has remained fragmented among the states, and estimates of current compensation for all costs (medical, lost wages, other family expenses) associated with occupational injuries and illnesses put it at approximately 20 percent.[8] This had been the second major target of labor reform efforts, and in 1972 the National Commission on State Workmen's Compensation Laws made its report.

The commission concluded that the state systems were inadequate and inequitable; it recommended nineteen minimum essential improvements designed to extend coverage to more workers and to provide higher benefits. One recommendation was that maximum temporary- and permanent-disability benefits be at least equal to the average weekly wage for that state; only Arizona met this in 1972, but maximum-benefit levels in all states rose by an average of 84 percent between 1973 and 1977.[9] The black-lung benefit program was implemented, and in a number of local regions unions and retired workers had formed groups to press for increased benefits and more liberal definitions of compensable disease.

Despite the bleak picture of state workers' compensation programs represented by the review commission report in 1972, there was no major effort to federalize workers' compensation during the 1970s. Coverage of such elements of the work force as agricultural workers, domestic workers, and employees of small firms had not increased significantly, and by 1980 state programs were in compliance with an average of only twelve of the review commission's nineteen principal recommendations.[10]

In 1980, the Department of Labor published the *Interim Report to Congress on Occupational Diseases,* a survey of disabled individuals between the ages of twenty and sixty-five (excluding most retired persons). Two million workers reported severely or partially disabling conditions resulting from occupation-related diseases—not injuries—and 700,000 of them suffered long-term total disability. The 1978 income lost because of disabling occupational diseases was estimated to be $16.4 billion; only 40 percent of this lost income was replaced by income support programs of all types, although 60 percent of the wages lost because of occupational injuries was replaced. Furthermore, only 5 percent of the victims of occupational disease received any income support from workmen's compensation, and one out of four got no income support payments at all.[11]

The major blockages to compensation for occupational disease were found to be due to the delayed onset of the diseases, the multiple causation of diseases, and the requirement that diseases be associated with employment at one or more specific firms in the past. The average worker suffering from an occupational disease waits a year or more before receiving the first compensation payment (compared with two months for injury victims); 60 percent of the claims are initially denied by employers (compared with 10 percent for injury victims); more than half of the claims are settled by "compromise and release," which absolves the employer of further liability even if the condition worsens (compared with 16 percent of the injury claims); and a totally disabled worker receives an average of $9,700 in total compensation benefits against expected future earnings averaging $77,000.[12]

Although inflation has largely eaten up the apparent gains in benefit levels for workers' compensation since the early 1970s, waiting periods until compensation benefits payments begin have been reduced in many states, and the battles to establish certain diseases as compensable have raised union and public consciousness of the need for further reforms in this area. Because the time lag between exposure and development of disabling disease is often a matter of decades in some chronic and delayed-onset diseases, such as asbestosis or cancer, industry is rarely forced to internalize the costs of these diseases—workers have retired or moved on to other jobs long before the diseases develop. Workers' compensation insurance premiums therefore do not reflect the actual damage that companies inflict upon the health of their employees. Furthermore, under workers' compensation legislation, workers cannot sue their employers directly for job-related injury or illness. In the late 1970s, there was a sudden upsurge of "third party" suits, in which workers sue the original manufacturers (the third party) supplying a toxic substance to their actual employer; although some of these cases win substantial awards and attract widespread attention, they are too limited to effectively alter the economic incentives for industry to ignore many health hazards.

Development of Research and Professional Training

In the early 1970s, from the fight for passage of the OSH Act until the end of the Ford administration, public health and medical leaders did not as a whole play an active role in occupational health reforms. Schools of public health and medicine saw little need for increased emphasis on occupational health and medicine. For example, the dean of the Johns Hopkins School of Hygiene and Public Health, Dr. John Hume, commented in 1972 on the need for more occupational medicine specialists: "What we need are more people in the other specialties. . . . Workers really have no problem, because if they have health problems they can always go to their company doctor."[13] Research was predominantly financed by industry and rarely obtained informed consent from the workers; workers were frequently not even informed that they were participating in a study, were not given the results of their own tests, and were still less often informed of the results of the study as a whole.

NIOSH had been charged under the OSH Act with responsibility for developing the scientific basis, known as criteria documents, for new health and safety standards, for training occupational health professionals, and for conducting both basic science and field research in occupational health. But in the first five years of the program, more than half of the total NIOSH budget went to the development of criteria documents, despite clear signals that few new standards would be promulgated by OSHA, and relatively little funding or programmatic effort went into encouraging research or training.

The need for a major increase in training programs was acute. Fewer than 6 of 10,000 medical students graduating each year in the early 1970s entered occupational medicine, and three-fourths of the residency positions went unfilled each year. Only 12 of the 100 medical schools in the country even included occupational medicine formally in their curriculum, and only 5 of the 19 schools of public health had programs in occupational health, with a total enrollment of 53 students per year. An estimated 6,000 physicians practiced occupational medicine, with only 450 board-certified specialists in occupational medicine.[14]

In fact, the greatest activity in occupational public health and medicine occurred outside of these formal research and training programs, beginning in the 1960s with the Medical Committee for Human Rights' Occupational Health Project, the Health Policy Advisory Center *Bulletin* articles, and with early cooperation between occupational health professionals and unions, as in the 1973 OCAW strike and boycott against Shell Oil over health and safety issues. The Shell strike—the first major political event to bring environmentalists (primarily students and scientists) and workers together—belied the "workers don't care about their health" myth that many health professionals believed, and opened up a new era of outspoken prolabor advocacy for many public health workers.

These early links between unions and individual medical and occupational health workers became a crucial part of the overall development of the field during the 1970s. Work by Dr. Irving Selikoff at the Mount Sinai medical school in New York had broken the industrial hegemony over medical and personnel information on asbestos disease by using welfare and retirement records from the asbestos insulators' union as the basis for his epidemiological studies, and he stimulated a generation of researchers in pulmonary medicine. Dr. Lorin Kerr of the United Mine Workers had inspired medical and public health activists for years, and agitated within the American Public Health Association (APHA) for greater attention to occupational health issues. In 1974 Dr. Kerr was elected president of the APHA; in 1975 the theme of the APHA's annual meeting was "Work and Health," and for the first time other fields in public health began to search for linkages with occupational health. Dr. Sid Wolfe at the Health Research Group took student interns and made them passionate, effective advocates for job health and safety. While on the OCAW health and safety staff, Drs. Jeanne Stellman and Susan Daum wrote *Work Is Dangerous to Your Health* to educate workers about job hazards—and wound up educating medical and public health students about how to work with workers.

These efforts and others led to the creation of a new generation of health care providers, lawyers, public health workers, and community activists interested in occupational health. They provided the backbone for the Committees on Occupational Safety and Health (COSH groups) that sprang up around the country. Following the example of the Chicago Committee on Occupational Safety and Health (CaCOSH), these groups have been an important bridge between the academic/technical community and the labor movement, and have been the training ground for many people now working professionally in the field. In addition, they have provided much needed technical expertise for occupational health activists and for groups of "victims" of occupational diseases, such as the Brown Lung Association and organizations of asbestos victims.

The developments of the early 1970s also had an impact on the "establishment" within occupational medicine—the American Occupational Medicine Association, composed almost entirely of corporate physicians or physicians contracted to industry, with a sprinkling of academics. A spate of articles appeared in the mid-1970s in the *Journal of Occupational Medicine* (published by the AOMA) on such topics as "Whose 'Agent' Is the Occupational Physician?" and "Elements of Credibility—Changing Perceptions." In 1977, one author complained that "our specialty currently has no mechanism for the individual physician who wishes to report occupational hazard information but encounters constraints by management," and called for the development of a review and mediation procedure for the relief of industrially employed physicians.[15] The AOMA convened a special committee to develop a new Code of Ethical Conduct for Physicians Providing Occupational Medical Services, which was adopted in July 1976.[16]

NIOSH's almost exclusive emphasis on the production of criteria documents during the first five years of the OSH Act was severely attacked by labor and by public health workers. They pressed continually for programs to meet the enormous need for health professionals and for research in occupational health, and the passage of the Health Professions Education Assistance Act in 1976—establishing ten regional occupational health and safety training and education centers—marked a significant budgetary and policy change for NIOSH. Resources were ultimately shifted not only to the training of health professionals but also to field research in response to worker and industry requests (Health Hazard Evaluations) and to funding for basic and applied research in such key areas as new energy technologies and reproductive effects.

The regional training centers, which became known as educational resource centers (ERCs), received their initial grants in 1978.

By 1980 a total of thirteen ERCs had been funded, and two large occupational health centers had been established by the state legislature in California. Because the five targeted fields (occupational medicine, nursing, toxicology, epidemiology, and industrial hygiene) had had so few resources prior to the ERCs, NIOSH funding attracted scientists originally trained in related fields of medicine, nursing, toxicology, and epidemiology to occupational health. In some cases, of course, scientists simply relabeled their ongoing work as "occupational" medicine, toxicology, and so on, in the academic tradition of making chameleonlike adjustments to changes in funding programs.

A second major target for reform was the lack of integration of occupational medicine into the mainstream of medical training and practice. Although very little research had been done on the prevalence of occupational disease among general-medicine patients, an early study commissioned by NIOSH found that 31 percent of all medical conditions among a heterogeneous group of workers were of probable occupational origin.[17]

In 1978, the American Medical Student Association established a task force on occupational health that held regional meetings, developed resource guides for curriculum development and electives in occupational medicine, and published a newsletter to exchange program ideas, including internship programs linking medical schools with various unions. In 1979, HEW created a new grant program to fund curriculum development projects in occupational medicine for undergraduate medical education; these grants reached many medical schools that did not have ERCs or other sources of expertise, and it encouraged innovative programmatic approaches by medical students participating in many of these projects.

As scientists sympathetic to the labor movement and trained in the fields of medicine, toxicology, and epidemiology entered occupational health, they were frequently openly critical of the old school of practitioners represented in the American Occupational Medical Association. Drs. Samuel Epstein and Irving Selikoff founded the Society for Occupational and Environmental Health in the mid-1970s, and in 1980 Dr. Selikoff began publication of a new scientific journal, the *American Journal of Industrial Medicine.* The occupational health section of the American Public Health Association took on new vigor in response to the persistent efforts of Dr. Kerr, many with the participation of younger activists who had worked for or with the labor movement. An increasing number of occupational health professionals, in fact, began to move between academia and public interest and union health and safety jobs.

Worker Consciousness and Organizing on Health and Safety

Throughout the first half of the 1970s, worker interest in health and safety issues continued to grow. Although the National Labor Relations Board had not established health and safety issues as mandatory subjects for collective bargaining until 1966, many union locals and some internationals had attempted to negotiate on job health and safety earlier. IBEW Local 1245 in Walnut Creek, California, had first raised its demand for a joint union-management health and safety committee in the 1953 bargaining sessions; not until 1974 did it finally succeed in winning this language. By 1973, federal mediation officials noted that for the first time in the history of major industrial bargaining, health and safety demands were a leading issue in contract stalemates.[18]

At Kawecki-Berylco Industries, the Oil, Chemical, and Atomic Workers were able to win a major contract victory without resorting to a strike. In 1971, the union learned that the levels of beryllium metal dust at the DOD-contract Kawecki-Berylco plant exceeded existing federal limits by more than 1,000 times and that 10 percent of the work force there had berylliosis, a chronic lung disease. Over the next two years, the union health and safety department carried out an intensive educational program with the membership in this unit, and in 1973 the local was able to negotiate a three-part health and safety program into their contract: a union industrial hygienist would be allowed to take independent measurements of dust levels in the plant and to recommend improvements; two local members would be trained in dust sampling and be given their own equipment and paid time to conduct periodic monitoring; and union-designated physicians would be paid by the company to implement a program of medical surveillance. More frequently, however, the OCAW and other unions interested in health and safety improvement found themselves up against intransigent negotiators for industry.

By 1974, according to the Bureau of Labor Statistics, 93 percent of all contracts involving 1,000 or more workers contained health and safety provisions. The UAW 1973 contracts, for example, had instituted a sweeping health and safety program guaranteeing the union's right to strike over health and safety issues, establishing a system of company-paid but union-designated full-time health and safety representatives in large plants, and giving the union access to all plants for monitoring and medical surveillance. Unions were increasingly aware that they needed their own medical, industrial hygiene, and epidemiological expertise in order to evaluate the workplace environment and the medical and hygiene data being provided under these new contract terms.

The growing worker interest in and sophisticated knowledge about chronic-disease patterns led to a rapid upsurge in what has come to be known as "worker epidemiology": the detection by workers of associations between job exposures and disease, often with relatively complex and accurate analytic approaches. Michael Bennett, the president of UAW Local 326 in Flint, Michigan, investigated his members' suspicions of an elevated rate of cancer deaths in their machine shop and presented the international union health and safety staff with a full study of the proportional mortality rate with appropriate controls.[19]

The 1980 Schweiker amendment proposing sweeping changes to limit OSHA's scope and enforcement powers tested the new commitment of many labor leaders to health and safety reforms and gave reformers within OSHA a chance to gauge the depth of rank-and-file worker support. In effect it would have exempted more than 90 percent of the small businesses from most OSHA oversight, although 41 percent of deaths on the job occur in these workplaces. The labor unions that had been most active on health and safety mobilized a remarkable protest against the Schweiker bill and with the active support of the AFL-CIO and COSH groups, managed to defeat the Schweiker amendment.

Industrial Reaction to the Reforms of the 1970s

Schweiker's proposed legislation was an attempt by industry to capitalize on what was perceived as a growing rightward trend in the country, and to roll back the reforms of the past decade. It was, however, only part of an ongoing attack on several fronts, including legal challenges and the ideological recasting of health and safety issues.

In legal challenges, trade associations such as the American Petroleum Institute, the Society of the Plastics Industry, the American Industrial Health Council, the Chamber of Commerce, and the National Asscociation of Manufacturers have encouraged individual employers to appeal OSHA citations and have frequently joined them in their appeals. The average appeal takes three years to settle, unless it goes to the Supreme Court, in which case it may take five years or more. Meanwhile, abatement of the hazardous condition is delayed until settlement, and the costs of litigation are tax deductible for the industry in question. Between 1973 and 1979, the number of contested enforcement cases increased by more than 400 percent. In 68 percent of those contested cases that reach the Occupational Safety and Health Review Commission for a hearing, full or partial relief is granted and penalties are reduced or eliminated altogether. OSHA standards themselves are regularly challenged by industry upon promulgation and have been defended with varying success.

The struggle to shape public conceptions of OSHA in particular, and of occupational health and safety reforms in general, has engaged a large part of industry's attention. Three major themes are emphasized by industry in this effort: (1) that OSHA is overly bureaucratic, to the point of nit-picking; (2) that OSHA has unreasonably played a "policeman's role" in regulation rather than fostering cooperation between employers and the agency; and (3) that the benefits of protecting worker health and safety, when weighed against their costs in terms of plant closings, the transfer of investment capital abroad, and their overall impact on economic growth, are often overvalued by OSHA and that this results in decisions against the interest of the nation as a whole.

Criticism of OSHA for acting as a "policeman" rather than in cooperation with industry escalated during Bingham's administration. This "adversary" stance on the part of OSHA—adversary to industry rather than to labor, as during the Nixon and Ford administrations—was particularly assailed during the Schweiker amendment hearings. In 1980, the Heritage Foundation—a right-wing policy center—issued its report, which was considered a major statement of Reagan's position on regulation. The report reiterated criticism of OSHA for its "policeman's" orientation and recommended that OSHA send complaints about worker health and safety directly to management, write performance-based standards to permit employers "flexibility" in compliance, and place major emphasis on cooperative labor-management programs. In 1981, six months after he had been appointed head of OSHA by Reagan, Thorne Auchter proposed that OSHA exempt employers with better-than-average safety records from inspections, send employee complaints to employers instead of conducting an inspection unless an imminent danger was suspected, and exempt employers with health and safety committees from most inspections.

In effect, Reagan is accomplishing by fiat what Congress refused in the Schweiker amendment. OSHA was not initially targeted for major budgetary cutbacks; instead, a significant number of regional enforcement offices were closed and enforcement efforts were sharply curtailed. Although later budget cuts were more pronounced, such cuts have been proportionately more severe in the NIOSH budget. In addition, Anthony Robbins—a leader of liberal reform efforts in public health before he became director of NIOSH, and a strong advocate of sound scientific and professional programs in defense of worker health while at NIOSH—was summarily fired in a startling move shortly after Schweiker took office. The firing came one day after publication of a scurrilous attack on Robbins in *Washington Watch,* the U.S. Chamber of Commerce newsletter on regulatory actions.[20]

The final and perhaps most important theme that industry stressed in its attack on OSHA, and on health and safety reforms in general, is the contradiction between productivity and health. Cloaked in the pseudoeconomic jargon of "cost-benefit analysis," this issue has been repeatedly and effectively used to forestall the establishment and the enforcement of standards. The strong impact of this argument is understandable; protecting worker health does cost money, and in an era of rapid inflation and growing unemployment, conservatives have built much of their antiregulatory drive on the economic difficulties and fears of working people.

The argument that the protection of worker health is actually in the long-run, if not the short-run, in the interests of employers because they benefit from a healthy work force was made in the 1960s but is rarely heard now. Workers and the general public are more sophisticated and understand how little of the individual or social costs of job-related disease are borne by the industries that create them. Instead, industry asserts frankly that we cannot afford health.

To counter this position, occupational health and safety activists have developed several positions. They argue, first, that OSHA regulation has not meant a significant economic hardship for employers. In a McGraw-Hill survey of 2,000 employers reported in 1980, 83 percent said that OSHA had not caused economic hardship for them. (They also stated that they expected expenditures for compliance to drop by 9 percent in 1982.)[21] In specific terms, the effect of the vinyl chloride standards promulgated in 1974 is frequently cited; industry had originally stated that the standards would eliminate vinyl chloride production in the U.S. and cost millions of jobs, but production has in fact risen by 17.5 percent and four new firms have entered the vinyl chloride industry since the standards took effect, in 1975.[22]

A second argument holds that environmental and occupational regulations actually force technological innovation, the modernization of faltering industries, and the growth of new pollution-control industries providing many new jobs. Industries that manufacture ventilation-exhaust systems, asbestos substitutes, equipment to enclose the processing of toxic chemicals, and other products necessitated by regulation have expanded enormously since 1970. Whereas the Council on Environmental Quality estimated in 1980 that environmental regulations have added only 0.1 to the consumer price index, have decreased employment by 0.4%, and have increased the gross national product by $9.3 billion,[23] sales in the pollution-control industries grew by 16 to 22 percent annually (compared with an average of 9 percent for general manufacturing) during the first half of the decade, and profits in these industries are expected to continue to exceed those on other product lines.[24]

The third position of occupational health activists is that cost-benefit analysis in fact measures only the costs to industry of potential regulation. As Dr. Samuel Epstein recently pointed out, "cost-benefit analysis is superficially an attractive basis for public policy, because it appears to strike a 'neutral' balance between the costs of proposed regulations and their anticipated benefits. But while the costs of regulation are immediate and can easily be given a dollar figure, the benefits—such as the prevention of future disease—are delayed often by several decades and can only be assigned a dollar cost with difficulty, if at all."[25] Furthermore, the benefit accruing to society as a result of economic growth stimulated by deregulation or nonregulation is general, while the costs of inadequate regulation—both economic and personal—are borne by a relatively small group of workers in each case who are specifically, not randomly, at risk.

LESSONS LEARNED AND STRATEGIES FOR THE FUTURE

Lessons from the 1960s and 1970s

Health professionals, workers, and others interested in occupational safety and health can learn from both the successes and the failures of attempted reforms in the past thirteen years. From among the many lessons of the 1970s, the following five stand out.

(1) *There is no necessary link between the scientific knowledge of hazardous conditions and the protection of workers.* The struggle over health and safety in the workplace only secondarily concerns gaining more knowledge about the danger; it is principally a political one. Advocates of reform who thought that "more research" and "harder data" would provide the key to change found that a great many workplace hazards already well known and well documented have persisted because of the economic costs of removing them.

(2) *Worker initiative and control is crucial in creating and maintaining a healthy workplace.* From the beginnings of OSHA, it was clear that government inspection could not be relied

upon to enforce standards, because the number of inspectors could never be great enough. A more fundamental limitation is that the U.S. government, despite concessions won by working people, remains predominantly subject to the pressures and interests of the corporate class. As examples cited earlier document, the existence of standards and the threat of enforcement are most effective as tools of an organized and active workers' struggle for health and safety.

(3) *The current crisis in the American economy has profound implications for occupational health.* The economic crisis has brought with it a general offensive against organized labor, with a new wave of union busting and an ideological onslaught under the rubric of "cost-benefit analysis." Citing the deterioration of America's competitive position and the need for greater "productivity" to restore U.S. industry, champions of deregulation argue that anything that threatens productivity must be sacrificed. The crisis also directly increases health hazards in production, as industry cuts back on expenditures for maintenance and upkeep.

(4) *Workers cannot be protected from hazardous substances on a one-by-one basis.* The number of new chemicals introduced annually into the workplace over the last decade far outstrips our current ability to test for possible dangers, and even attempts to regulate substances with *known* effects are stubbornly resisted by industry. Generic standards based on animal and other assay systems, and recognizing the related effects of structurally similar chemicals, must be used to confront this problem. We cannot continue to make workers' deaths the standard of proof necessary for regulation—the "body-in-the-morgue" method of epidemiology is too costly.

(5) *The detection, prevention, and treatment of occupational disease must be integrated into the overall health care system.* Despite a significant increase in the number and training of occupational health specialists, most people have and will continue to rely on private physicians, clinics, HMOs, and other general medical providers for their health care. There are many examples of occupational diseases discovered or confirmed by observant internists and family practitioners. As more becomes known about the effects of occupational exposures, health care providers will need and want greater knowledge of occupational medicine in order to adequately care for their

patients. For all these reasons, the training and practice of health care providers must increasingly incorporate aspects of occupational medicine. The broader health care system is, of course, not meeting the needs of the population effectively now and no significant improvement in the health of working people will be achieved without concomitant improvements in the prevention of diseases with occupational and nonoccupational causes.

Practical Tasks Ahead

The gains won in occupational safety and health in the 1960s and 1970s are now under increasing attack, as are advances in many other areas. The current political climate and the unmet needs present a number of new tasks that must be taken up by activists in the field.

(1) *Supporting and expending unions' commitment to health and safety.* Many unions have made great progress in the past ten years in building up health and safety staffs, developing rank-and-file committees, and pushing for health and safety contract language. The issue is, however, still seen as peripheral in some quarters—an "extra" service —rather than as a fundamental and ongoing concern. The withdrawal of New Directions grants and other federal funds that were used to initiate many of these efforts severely test labor's commitment to health and safety, especially when many unions are on the defensive and struggling for their very existence. Cooperation between unions and health professionals on health issues should be strengthened; company attempts at blackmail with threats of plant closings if health standards are enforced must be exposed and combated.

(2) *Building coalitions and educating the public to oppose the roll-back of standards and enforcement.* The Reagan administration has implemented its commitment to "deregulation" and the "voluntary compliance" approach of the Nixon-era OSHA. Advocates of health must find creative ways to publicize these issues—to dramatize them in human rather than in simply financial terms. The successful effort to block the Schweiker amendments was an excellent model of national coordination and cooperation between health, labor, academic, and public-interest groups. In addition, the broad base of public

concern about environmental issues should be tapped for related occupational health issues. Public concern about the spraying of malathion to control the Mediterranean fruit fly in California, for example, ignored the far more dangerous pesticides routinely sprayed on crops, with far more significant farm worker exposure.

(3) *Developing more technical competence.* Mere advocacy and sympathy will not do. The field of occupational health has developed tremendously in the last ten years. The battle between reform advocates and industry is increasingly a battle waged with studies, data, and interpretations. While the essential political nature of this battle should not be forgotten, it must be recognized that good politics alone will not defeat the increasingly sophisticated and competent army of industry experts. Fifteen years ago, for instance, textile manufacturers denied that the disease of byssinosis even existed. Since this is no longer a viable strategy, they call on hired staff physicians and epidemiologists, consultants, and purportedly "independent" academics for more sophisticated evasions of responsibility. Advocates of workers' health must be able to draw upon technical expertise to expose the fallacies of these arguments.

(4) *Developing new forms and institutions for research, medical surveillance, and treatment of occupational diseases.* Several observers have correctly pointed out that business should pay its share for the investigation of occupational illness, without prejudicing the outcome of that work. In addition, it is a fact of life that most of the increasing number of occupational safety and health professionals—nurses, industrial hygienists, doctors—well trained and conscientious for the most part—will have to work for industry. It is therefore vitally important that efforts be made to establish new ways of carrying out this work: research teams and clinics funded jointly by doctors and management, autonomous consulting groups or institutes with proper controls to practice their independence, and so on.

Theoretical Problems

The movement for occupational health reform has, like any movement, brought about changes that bring new theoretical issues to the fore—"theoretical" but not irrelevant, because their discussion and resolution is important for guiding the day-to-day work of

practitioners in the field. We conclude this essay with a brief enu-
meration of these issues.

(1) *Technological development and its implications.* The advance of
modern technology contains a paradox for occupational
health: the same explosion of knowledge that makes
possible sophisticated engineering controls and the
elimination of hazards also creates *new* untested substances, processes, and environments at a dizzying pace.
One of the pressing tasks in occupational health is to
anticipate problems before they arise, thus avoiding the
necessity of costly and difficult "retrofitting" or product
abandonment after the hazards have taken their toll.
One current example is the rapidly growing investigation of problems faced by office workers—a group
previously thought to be relatively free of risk. The
development of energy-efficient, "tight" buildings
stimulated by the energy shortage of the 1970s has
produced a host of difficulties with indoor environmental pollution. Thus, while we still battle the hazardous
legacies of steel mills built in the 1930s, we must
reckon with the changing character of work and of the
work force in the 1980s and 1990s. What will be the
occupational health issues of the next decades?

(2) *Occupational health as an organizing issue for labor.* Closely
connected with the changes in the character of the work
force is the necessity of revitalizing the labor movement. Only 20 percent of all American workers belong
to unions—a percentage that continues to drop as older,
organized industries and areas decline. Many unions
are faced with mergers to consolidate their resources.
Union leaders understandably question whether major
commitments to health and safety will aid their most
pressing task—organizing the huge unorganized population. And while it has long been conventional wisdom
among occupational health activists that the issue is
tailor-made to assist organizing, many veterans of the
labor movement, including some who have been very
active in health and safety work within their unions,
disagree. They argue that health and safety activity is
vital for *already organized* unions, but that it does not lend
itself to organizing. It is, in fact, difficult to point to
many instances of the successful use of health as a key
issue in recent organizing drives. Is this simply a lack of
appreciation of its potential by organizers, or are there

inherent limitations in using health as an organizing tool? How can these limitations be overcome?

(3) *Individual life-style versus collective risks.* Industry spokespeople attempting to minimize the apparent risks of job-related exposure have increasingly pointed to "life-style"—smoking, drinking, diet, overeating, and so forth—to explain patterns of chronic disease. Their solution to such socially produced habits as smoking or overeating is to prescribe individual action: "don't smoke," "jog," and "don't overeat." Similarly, within the realm of admittedly occupational disease and injury, they have attempted to shift the blame to individual workers for not wearing personal protective equipment such as respirators or earplugs.

Occupational health advocates have correctly opposed this victim-blaming approach, pointing to irrefutable evidence of workplace-induced disease and arguing for reliance on engineering controls rather than on personal protective equipment. Furthermore, they have pointed out that job-site exposures are not voluntary but imposed—particularly in an economy with steadily rising unemployment rates—while smoking is at least not a condition of earning one's living. But the inescapable fact is that asbestos workers who smoke *do* get cancer far more often than those who do not (both groups, of course, far more than their non-asbestos-exposed counterparts). There is, then, the nagging question of how the movement should handle individual responsibility for one's health without either capitulating to industry's position or ignoring the question altogether. After all, people can and do stop smoking, wear earplugs, or lose weight. How can and should this question be addressed in research, educational, and bargaining efforts?

(4) *The contradiction between productivity and health.* The current offensive against strong on-the-job health protection uses cost-benefit analysis to argue the allegedly beneficial effects of deregulation. The intention is clearly that more lenient regulations should "cost" the worker his or her health and "benefit" industry. How should this attack be fought in the political and ideological spheres?

One question is whether the contradiction between productivity and health necessarily exists. Some have held that this antagonism exists solely under capitalism

—that is, the private ownership of the means of production. But the experience of the 1960s and 1970s has shown that the socialist countries, though they have often taken great strides forward in occupational health and safety, have by no means eliminated the contradiction; in fact, because of the relative poverty of countries like China and Cuba, which are still emerging from semicolonial status, the contradiction may be even greater. What has been the experience of the more developed socialist countries in Eastern Europe and of the Soviet Union? And if the contradiction is a necessary one, how do we handle it in the deteriorating U.S. economy? Can we take a "money is no object" stance toward workers' protection and expect to win the battle for public opinion?

A case in point is the contention by industry that stringent health regulations are forcing them to close U.S. plants, lay off U.S. workers, and move their operations overseas to less regulated climates. This threat, unless countered, obviously has the potential to split the labor movement along "health versus jobs" lines, similar to its current split over nuclear power.

We do not believe that occupational health regulation has been in fact a major cause of runaway shops and other disinvestment patterns in the past between geographical regions of the United States or abroad. But little research has been done on this issue, and the threat will continue to be widely used by industry. For this reason we must refine our theoretical and practical understanding.

The authors wish to acknowledge the generous help received from Jane Halpern, Ellen Widess, Richard Walker, and Peter Orris.

5.

the women's
health movement:

WOMEN TAKE POWER

Helen Rodriguez-Trias

Out of scattered small groups meeting in each other's homes, women forged a women's health movement of national dimensions in less than two decades. Though its effect on specific health issues was profound, the movement's main contribution was a new feminist consciousness. Feminist vision expanded beyond the concerns of women in relation to doctors to concerns of *people* in relation to the socioeconomic realities of the health care *system.* Its proponents were and still are primarily white, well-educated middle-class young women who had to confront their ideas on race, class, and sex privilege as they built coalitions for what became known in the 1980s as reproductive rights. In their effort to organize, they came into conflict with working-class and Third World women organizing for welfare and health rights in the community. From these clashes among women of different class and ethnic origin, with different concerns and priorities, came a unified view that brought major advances. Nowhere was this more apparent than in the movements for abortion rights and against sterilization abuse.

BEGINNINGS

In the consciousness-raising groups of the sixties, women became more aware of their concerns and dissatisfactions with much of their health care. More and more tales of discomfort, humiliation, and abuse at the hands of professionals emerged. A distrust of medical technology grew, along with a suspicion that much of it answered the needs of profit rather than of patients. Reports of unnecessary surgery, particularly on women, led to more questions, as did the medicalization of childbirth, menstruation, and menopause. As patriarchy in the family was questioned, so was patriarchy in the doctor-patient relationship.[1]

Women began to realize that they were by far the most frequent users of health services for themselves, their children, or other dependent family members. A women's consumer movement emerged. Its evolution was typified by a group of women in Boston who met in 1969 to discuss their concerns about their bodies, their sexuality, and their health. Soon their activities expanded into educational seminars for women in their homes, day care centers, nurseries, schools, and churches. From these discussions came the first mimeographed edition of *Our Bodies, Ourselves*, which in less than ten years was to reach around the world.[2]

Women continued to discuss, expose, publicize, organize. They wrote newsletters, magazine articles, and pamphlets. They read and studied important critiques such as Ehrenreich and English's *Witches, Midwives, and Nurses* and *Complaints and Disorders*, which stated that health care had once been primarily in the hands of women.[3] In less than a century it was usurped by men who organized medicine to exclude not only white women but also black people and people from the working class.

The feminist viewpoint was that women's reproductive functions, which are normal life events, were turned into "medical conditions" and were commercialized by men. Some feminists, going further, placed blame on a corporate establishment that put profits first and exploited illness, both real and that created by the medical world itself.

Although many who joined the women's health movement participated in broader health care reforms for community centers, worker organization, free clinics, and such, they focused on specific women's health issues. For example, some created the self-help movement on the premise that women could learn about their bodies and provide routine gynecological care for themselves and others. Many who had organized storefront clinics later organized self-help clinics along similar egalitarian patterns.

A narrower focus permitted the concentration in several key areas: contraceptives and experimentation on women, gynecological and obstetrical care, the use of dangerous drugs, particularly of diethylstilbestrol (DES), women in the health professions, and reproductive freedom.

While predominately white middle-class women organized a health movement around their concerns, putting emphasis on changing their relationship to doctors and controlling their own bodies, working-class and Third World women were clamoring for day care, welfare rights, entry-level jobs in the health care system, and the establishment of community health centers. White women concentrated on *health care,* women of color and of the working class on *health status* with a gut understanding of its socioeconomic determinants. The two points of departure initially made for parallel movements, which nevertheless converged with great effect in the arena of reproductive rights. Before this convergence and the lessons it produced are described, a brief sketch of the problems and progress in the other key areas of work will serve to provide an overview of the women's health movement today.

CONTRACEPTIVES AND EXPERIMENTATION ON WOMEN

Barbara Seaman's widely read book *The Doctors' Case against the Pill,* published in 1969, and later exposés revealed that women were experimented on with oral contraceptives.[4] Furthermore, there was evidence that manufacturers concealed hazards and that the Food and Drug Administration did not conduct or require adequate tests. The original study of the pill—in Puerto Rico, in the 1950s—included only 132 women and left uninvestigated two or three suspicious deaths as well as using doses of estrogen considered prohibitive by U.S. standards.[5]

Third World women in the United States were frequent subjects of unethical experiments, such as one pill test in 1970 in which 76 Mexican-American women were given placebos without their consent. Ten became pregnant! Doctors did not even censure the investigators; on the contrary, the paper presenting the results of the experiment was well received. When questioned on methodology, the investigator replied, "If you think you can explain a placebo test to women like these, you have never met Mrs. Gomez from the West Side."[6]

Depo-Provera, an injectable, long-acting contraceptive, carcinogenic in animal testing, became another source of bitter controversy. The drug companies have continued an effort to obtain FDA approval while members of the consumer movement have continued to the present to oppose it as unsafe.

Intrauterine devices had proliferated greatly without demonstrations of safety. By 1974, some 2 million women had the Dalkon shield in their uteri and another million had other devices—all virtually untested for their long-term safety.

As the reports of deadly complications of pills and IUDs grew, so did women's anger at being used. Women exchanged information through newsletters and other publications, organized, participated in hearings, and initiated lawsuits. The National Women's Health Network, founded in 1975 by Barbara Seaman, Phyllis Chester, Belita Cowan, Mary Howell, and Alice Wolfson, quickly became involved in pressuring the FDA for safety standards.[7]

After a lengthy court battle on pill information, a victory was won in 1978. Manufacturers are now required to include information on hazards in packages of estrogen-containing pills. Another victory was a court mandate that the FDA "regulate medical devices, including IUDs and clips, rings, and bands for sterilization—products over which the agency previously had no clear statutory jurisdiction. Devices already on the market are now required to apply for approval and submit evidence of safety and effectiveness."[8]

The battle over Depo-Provera rages on as manufacturers in the United States continue to press for FDA approval for wide-scale use. Through several conduits, including the federal Agency for International Development (AID) and the International Planned Parenthood Federation (IPPF), large amounts of Depo have been exported and injected into 5 million women in countries as disparate and far removed as Thailand, the Philippines, Egypt, and Chile—in fact, in a total of seventy countries![9] Today many people in the health movement condemn these practices, thus taking the side of others who expose and deplore them.[10]

GYNECOLOGICAL AND OBSTETRICAL CARE

Women's contentions that gynecological care was perfunctory, impersonal, and generally demeaning in the hands of most gynecologists seemed well substantiated by their experience. Moreover, the frequency of gynecological surgery in the United States far surpassed that in other countries. In the seventies, hysterectomy became one of the most frequently performed major operations—over 400,000 per year. Audits suggested that perhaps one-third were unnecessary.

The self-help movement, revolutionary in its concept that women could provide gynecological care for themselves and each other, challenged the control of gynecologists. Begun by Carol Downer and other West Coast women in 1971, the movement grew rapidly as thousands of women trained themselves in the use of the speculum, in menstrual extraction, and in simple remedies for common vaginal infections. When Carol Downer and Coleen Wilson were arrested in 1972 and charged with practicing medicine without a license, women across the country rose in support. Margaret Mead, who was among the supporters, observed that "men began taking over obstetrics and they invented a tool that allowed them to look inside women. You could call this progress, except that when women tried to look inside themselves, this was called practicing medicine without a license."[11]

After her acquittal, Carol Downer continued as the recognized leader of self-help, aiding in the creation of thousands of clinics. Although the movement challenged doctors and hospital hierarchy, it remained small and peripheral enough to be ultimately nonthreatening to the establishment as a whole.

Women's experiences with childbirth practices were no happier than with gynecological care. Any delivery of an infant in a hospital was an elaborate, frequently traumatic procedure, fraught with the discomfort of monitors, extensive laboratory tests, intravenous medications, analgesia, anesthesia, episiotomies, and other questionable, if not downright dangerous, routines. The risk of a Caesarean section was increasing, with rates from 20 to 30 percent becoming common.[12]

Nurse-midwifery programs were virtually nonexistent. It was practically impossible to obtain any but the most interventionist forms of childbirth services. Only a few elite clinics even practiced natural childbirth.

The International Childbirth Association, whose outspoken president, Doris Haire, is one of the foremost exponents of spontaneous birth in homelike environments, and many others had campaigned for decades.[13] Hospitals that catered to a middle-class, educated clientele finally put their anesthesia machines, monitors, oxygen tanks, and the like out of sight, decked birthing rooms with curtains and other amenities, allowed fathers to participate, and permitted babies to remain with their mothers from birth. Some even brought midwives to deliver infants in their traditional, supportive, noninterventionist ways.

Still, today, the vast majority of women and infants are subjected to the trauma of unprepared childbirth among strangers. Hospitals have numerous routines that interfere with mother-child bonding, family participation, and breast feeding. The alarming rise in the rate of Caesarean sections continues.[14] Doctors offer innumerable justifications for their increasing use of surgery, the most frequent being their fear of malpractice suits if a baby is "less than perfect" after vaginal birth.

Women exert little or no control over institutional practices that entrap them once they are in the hospital. In her article entitled "The Caesarean Epidemic," Gena Corea uses the story of Laurie

Olsen.[15] Laurie is the daughter of Tillie, the feminist writer, and Jack, a teacher of labor history; she is also the sister of three feminists, and herself a policy researcher and writer. Laurie's labor in an Oakland, California, hospital went from one procedure to another in a choreographed sequence from the rupture of membranes, which occurred before her arrival, to the electronic fetal monitor, to the induction by Pitocin and the Caesarean section, when the Pitocin did not seem to work. Laurie herself later commented that natural childbirth and other reforms had remained marginal to institutional practices.[16]

D E S

Diethylstilbestrol (DES), a synthetic estrogen, was in the news in early 1971. At Harvard, Dr. Arthur Herbst discovered that a rare and frequently fatal form of vaginal cancer attacking girls in their teens could be traced to DES given to their mothers while the girls were in utero.[17]

DES was given to an estimated 6 million pregnant women between 1943 and 1959, thus exposing at least 3 million children to its toxicity.[18] The drug was originally popularized in the forties for the prevention of miscarriage and later used widely to stimulate "better placental function and hence bigger and healthier babies."[19] Even after Dr. Herbst's discovery had become widely publicized and despite pressure from the Cancer Control Bureau of the New York State Department of Health and numerous investigators that the FDA ban the use of synthetic estrogen in pregnancy, no action was taken for nearly a year. It was only under pressure from DES mothers urging Congress that the FDA finally acted. Its delay exposed an estimated additional 60,000 children to DES, now known to also cause genital abnormalities in boys.[20]

As women learned about the resistance of the public health agencies and doctors to the gathering and sharing of information that would lead to earlier detection, they became incensed. DES lawsuits were initiated in almost every state. In Michigan and Massachusetts, women organized to bring class action suits that would make Eli Lilly and the other manufacturers pay damages for the treatment of DES daughters and sons. Others followed. After several years of agitation spearheaded by DES mothers in New York, California, and other states, a national action group on DES was formed in 1976.

Their campaign to educate the public, physicians, and health officials resulted in screening programs in most states and in an increasingly vocal, educated public. Nonetheless, DES is still widely used today as the "morning after" pill to avoid conception, for the prevention of breast engorgement in women who do not breast-feed their newborn infants, as replacement therapy for women in menopause, and most of all in cattle feed to stimulate greater weight gain. Women are therefore continuing to wage the struggle against this widespread prescription of a proven carcinogen.

WOMEN IN HEALTH PROFESSIONS

Women, who compose over 70 percent of the health work force, are notoriously absent from the higher professional echelons of doctors and administrators. In 1970 the situation was even worse: only 8 percent of all doctors were women, and women made up only 3 percent of all obstetrician-gynecologists.

Partly owing to the distrust of professionals and partly to its community bases, which were outside of institutions, women's health organizations were not particularly concerned with the increased entry of women into medical school or into obstetrics and gynecology. Their thrust was more toward educating women to choose doctors wisely, self-help, and development of referral services. Nevertheless, the women's movement did generate sufficient pressure that, from 1970 to 1980, admissions of women into medical school rose from less than 10 percent to nearly 30 percent. A perhaps more important effect of the women's movement is on the women applicants themselves. Few are untouched by its activism and affirmation of women's rights. Before they attended medical school, many had already been advocates on health or women's issues. They bring organizational experience, which they put to good use in providing supportive networks for each other.

In some medical schools women students have successfully petitioned for the removal of lecturers whose remarks were particularly offensive and for the inclusion of research studies by women on women's health issues in the curriculum. Because of the efforts of sensitive educators, teaching by trained patients who became teaching assistants has become established in several medical schools. The teaching assistants are articulate in their guidance of students as these learn to perform pelvic and breast examinations on them. Students report that their sensitivity to patients' reactions increased on a par with their interviewing and physical-examination skills.

Despite increased admissions of women, several areas of concern remain. Minority admissions are now hitting a new low,[21] and it seems that the gains by women are coming at the expense of setbacks for black, Hispanic, and native American men. The stage is set for destructive competition. In addition the admission of women has not resulted in any increase in status for women faculty in medical schools.

REPRODUCTIVE FREEDOM:
CASE STUDIES IN ABORTION
RIGHTS, STERILIZATION ABUSE,
AND POPULATION CONTROL

Beginning in the 1800s, legislation restricting abortion services to all but the few sanctioned by teams of doctors in medical centers existed in all states, despite the grim reality of women sick and dying from illegal abortions.[22] Sometimes the very same doctors from the medical centers performed highly illegal but profitable abortions at other sites.

The abortion rights movement, which began taking shape in the 1960s with advocates among the professionals—the American Law Institute (1959) and the Association for the Study of Abortion (1964)—soon received a major impetus from feminist groups. Although not in complete agreement, women were increasingly advocating repeal rather than reform of the laws governing abortions. The second National Organization for Women convention, in 1967, demanded access to contraceptive information and repeal of restrictive abortion legislation.

By 1970, laws in Hawaii, Alaska, and New York had been repealed, albeit with some qualifications regarding residency status, dates beyond which an abortion could not be performed, requirement of spouse or parental consent, and performance in a hospital.

Feminists had organized the NOW Task Force on Reproduction and Its Control, New Yorkers for Abortion Law Repeal, and the Women's National Abortion Action Coalition (WONAAC). These were joined by other general abortion rights groups, such as the Association to Repeal Abortion Laws (ARAL) and the National Association for Repeal of Abortion Laws (NARAL).[23]

Dramatic demonstrations and hearings were held in major cities. Women, dressed in mourning, disrupted hearings, invaded rallies against abortion reform, and demonstrated at the AMA convention in Chicago in 1970. Feminists organized and joined others in the underground abortion referral network, which consisted mainly of out-of-state physicians and unfortunately usually entailed an expensive package inaccessible to poor women. Some groups broadened their direct services, and in Chicago the Women's Liberation Union organized a service group that performed 11,000 abortions in four years at the low cost of $50. No one was denied an abortion for lack of funds, and no one died.

In 1973, the millions of signators, thousands of marchers, hundreds of organizers, and dozens who had laid their personal freedom on the line risking prosecution were elated—the U.S. Supreme

Court decided in *Roe* v. *Wade* and *Doe* v. *Bolton* that during the first three months of pregnancy, abortion was to be a free choice to be negotiated between a woman and her physician.[24]

Women were unprepared for the mushrooming of abortion programs that followed. Some, more experienced than others, were able to organize their own clinics; others acted as referral sources or as workers in the clinics. Their vast experience as patients (often humiliating), as advocates, and as counselors (revealing) brought a new consciousness of the economics and politics of the health care system to the most advanced groups. The focus became quality care, although even nominally safe abortion services were still far from available for millions of women who lacked money and were in communities that failed to provide them.

Through the years 1973–77, as safe abortion services became more accessible to white, middle-class, urban women, who made up the backbone of the abortion rights movement, a certain complacency took hold. The movement generally failed to address charges by Third World women that they were sometimes pressured into having abortions at welfare centers or by low-income women that they were being forced to accept "package deals" of abortion and sterilization at the medical centers that had abortion programs.[25] Planned Parenthood Federation and others in the forefront of the abortion rights struggles also supported government programs for birth control, which were considered suspect by blacks and members of other minority groups.[26]

As this complacency was growing, the forces of reaction were gathering strength under the slogan "Right to Life." Rushed by those forces, the Hyde amendment passed in 1977 and each year after that effectively cut off Medicaid funding for abortion in all cases except those in which pregnancy would endanger the life of the mother or in which it had been caused by rape or incest. In June of 1980 the Supreme Court ruled it constitutional.

The abortion rights movement, now known as Pro-Choice, still reeling from the blows dealt by an increasingly strident, violent, and well-funded "Right-to-Life" movement, was forced to begin to reevaluate its partial neglect of the concerns of low-income women.

Rosie Jimenez, a Mexican-American Texan, was the first documented victim of the Hyde amendment.[27] She died following an illegal abortion performed in Mexico, her Medicaid card in her purse. Increasingly, black and Hispanic women spoke more loudly at rallies. Welfare rights, the Black United Front, the Third World Women's Alliance (now known as the Alliance against Women's Oppression), and other organizations representing poor and Third World women became more involved in the struggle to maintain women's right to choose. The seeds of unity were sown. Soon even the most elitist Pro-Choice organizations were modifying their messages on the "need to reduce welfare rolls." Today, as Congress debates a constitutional amendment granting full civil rights to the fertilized ovum, which might well make abortion a capital offense, women once more march, petition, demonstrate, and get arrested. As the threat to reproductive freedom grows, the coalitions grow broader.

If the weaknesses of the abortion rights movement could largely be attributed to its failure to address the concerns of black, Hispanic, native American, and other working-class women from its beginning, the strength of the movement against sterilization abuse certainly came precisely from its roots among these same disenfranchised groups. It quickly developed a constituency among these very same groups, whose members were able to confront members of the women's health movement about their racism and attitudes of class superiority.[28]

THE MOVEMENT TO END STERILIZATION ABUSE

By the early seventies, numerous community organizations, particularly National Welfare Rights, had become alarmed at reports of the forced sterilization of women on welfare and of those receiving care in city, county, and other government hospitals. *Relf* v. *Weinberger,* (1973), brought on behalf of two black, allegedly retarded girls, aged twelve and fourteen, who had been sterilized without their knowledge or consent in a federally funded program in Alabama, rocked the conscience of many sectors.[29] Civil libertarians, newspaper editors, jurists, politicians, journalists, and civil rights activists gave wide publicity to the case. The resultant pressure prompted the Department of Health, Education, and Welfare to promulgate, in April 1974, guidelines to curb sterilization abuse. The regulations, which included a moratorium on the sterilization of incompetent people and those under twenty-one, were largely ineffective and unknown or ignored by providers of sterilization services, even a year or two later.[30]

Simultaneously the number of sterilizations was rising at a rapid rate, particularly after 1973.[31] From the Los Angeles County Hospital staff came information that Mexican women were being sterilized in large numbers, in many cases without properly obtained informed consent. Interviews showed that abuses were widespread. They consisted of waving consent forms before a laboring woman's eyes, requesting the signature of forms in English from patients who spoke only Spanish, and operating without consent.[32] In New York sterilization rates in city hospitals serving Hispanic and black communities had risen alarmingly.[33]

Several women's organizations united around the issues raised by forced sterilization. The Committee against Forced Sterilization, on the West Coast, and the Committee to End Sterilization Abuse (CESA), in New York City, were representative of groups that carried out community education, publicizing and campaigning against the excesses of doctors and hospitals.

In several cities that contained major academic medical centers the presence of Programs for International Education in Gynecology and Obstetrics was exposed. These programs train gynecologists from Third World countries to sterilize women using the laparoscope and send them back to work in AID-supported programs in their nations. Women's health organizations in California and New York developed coalitions promulgating guidelines to promote informed consent and thus protect women from abuses. In California the focus was on guidelines to be approved and implemented by the state department of health. In New York, the Health and Hospitals Corporation (HHC), which has the administrative responsibility for the city hospitals, was targeted for pressure.

The Committee to End Sterilization Abuse (CESA) was organized at a showing of "Blood of the Condor," a film exposing AID sterilization of Bolivian Quechua Indians. In the ensuing discussion several people in the audience revealed personal experiences or friends' experiences with forced sterilization and agreed to organize. Although its original focus was the exposure of population control programs as a means of continuing the exploitation of people, the committee became more and more involved in sterilization abuse as an infringement of individual rights.

In its activities in the community, members approached Puerto Rican and black organizations—at community centers, churches, political headquarters, and schools, for the opportunity to speak. They quickly gathered story after story of abuses similar to those in the rest of the country. The Advisory Committee on Sterilization Guidelines for New York City Hospitals undertook the task of developing more effective regulations for hospitals. A broad representation of hospital community boards, health advocacy groups, health care professionals, consumers, civil rights, legal rights, and Third World community groups brought their viewpoints to the discussions. The representation of such diverse groups as the National Black Feminist Organization, the Lower East Side Neighborhood Health Center, Healthright, Health-PAC, CESA, the Center for Constitutional Rights, the Family Planning Division of the Human Resources Administration, the Puerto Rican Socialist Party,

Ms. magazine, and the National Organization for Women ensured the sharing of many experiences, opinions, and positions. It quickly became evident that the issue of sterilization abuse could mobilize much broader segments than could that of abortion rights.

This coalition drafted the following guidelines for performing sterilizations: a thirty-day waiting period; an interdiction of consent at times of delivery, abortion, or hospitalization for any major illness or procedure; the requirement that full counseling on birth control be available so that alternatives are offered; the stipulation that the idea of sterilization not originate with the doctor; and the provision that informational materials be in the language best understood by the woman.

The guidelines also stated that if she wished, the woman could bring a patient advocate of her choosing to participate at any stage of the process. She could also have a witness of her choice sign the consent form. Perhaps the most important point was that a woman should express in her own words, in writing on the consent form, her understanding of what the sterilization entailed, particularly its permanence.[34]

Although the main thrust of the effort was to pass and implement the guidelines, discussions of basic issues also took place during the many months of work. Several of these issues continue to be crucial to the women's health movement.

Regulations as a Focus

The question was whether regulations really addressed abuses and whether they would decrease the likelihood of their occurrence. We were all too painfully familiar with institutions and their blatant disregard for regulations that interfered with expedient, profitable, or simply established practices. Was all the effort for naught?

It was agreed that the process of proposing, obtaining, retaining, and enforcing regulations educated and organized people and was worthwhile, if for no other purpose than to strengthen organization per se. It was also evident that the very fact of such a diverse group's working together on a set of tasks had produced an exchange that would otherwise not have happened and that was absolutely necessary for coalition building.

Work within Institutions and Outside Them

Some members of the committee agreed that enactment of guidelines could be gained by knowing how the HHC worked, reaching key people in decision-making positions, and proceeding to develop an internal strategy for approval. Others emphasized that the organization of communities, and the pressure that it could bring to bear, was essential in order to move the corporate structure.

Out of the many discussions a pattern of activity evolved. There were people working in the city hospitals who gave information and reached health workers such as social workers, counselors, nurses, and members of the community advisory boards. These last, although indeed "advisory," exerted much pressure on the governing board of HHC and helped to shape its policy.

Members of the Advisory Committee on Sterilization Guidelines met with the groups. The insiders discussed documented incidents and supported efforts toward implementing the guidelines. Others who belonged to community organizations or groups developed petitioning and letter-writing campaigns. Efforts at the local level, however, made it clear that no amount of lobbying for the guidelines could have overcome the organized opposition of professionals without tremendous community support and a mechanism for voicing that support within the structure of the hospitals.

Single Issue or Programmatic Approach

Most organizations that took up the struggle on sterilization abuse had broader programmatic goals in the general area of rights. The sterilization issue was seen in a larger context of social gains for oppressed groups. The Center for Constitutional Rights, Healthright, Health-PAC, and others that represented the most progressive part of the abortion rights movement saw sterilization rights as one aspect of reproductive freedom and of women's right to control their own bodies. Others, such as the Puerto Rican Socialist party, were political entities with revolutionary programs, which in the case of the PSP include the total liberation of Puerto Rico from U.S. domination. These groups saw sterilization of minority women as one more form of oppression of minority people and held that it had to be combated as such.

Although there was no resolution of how to determine the emphasis given to a single issue at any one time, a style of work that showed an understanding of the different priorities of different organizations again emerged. In order to successfully carry out campaigns, demonstrations, and mass meetings, the support of the organizations with programs and platforms was essential. The day-to-day sticking with the issue, the meeting to develop guidelines, and the shepherding through the bureaucratic maze were possible only through the work of the few individuals in CESA and HHC who were dedicated to the "single issue."

''Providers'' versus ''Consumers''

As the women organizing abortion clinics had learned before, the committee members had to grapple with the question of including doctors in the process of guideline development. No one had illusions as to the depth of conflicts over the empowerment of patients. Doctors, once included in the discussions, fought the guidelines with arguments ranging from contemptuous dismissal of women as "habitual aborters" who needed sterilization on the spot to concern for their own right to counsel women as they saw fit. Painful as it often was, the exchange was nevertheless an essential process.

The "consumers" in the committee came to realize that no matter who regulates, the "providers" still do the actual procedures and need to be consulted and, on some level, convinced so that they may change their practices.

The Role of Influential Organizations in Disagreement with Guidelines

Again the controversy surfaced in all its complexity. The opposition to guidelines ranged from that of the Association for Voluntary Sterilization (AVS), well known for its aggressive positions and programs to combat "overpopulation" (funded through AID, it sterilizes myriads of Southeast Asians, Filipinos, and others) to that of the milder Planned Parenthood Federation (part of the Pro-Choice movement, considered by many feminists a friend, it has some of the best-run reproductive-services clinics in the country).

Agreement was never reached on how much effort and time were worth spending to gain support from the latter type. AVS was surely not a potential or even a desirable ally. The attitude toward Planned Parenthood was not as clear. Most organizations decided to share platforms with it to defend abortion rights, but only after having been assured that there would be no attack on the guidelines on sterilization.

The Identification of Areas of Irreconcilable Conflict

The HHC Advisory Committee was unprepared for the furor that greeted its initial position paper. The ferocity of the opposition was vented in letters, articles, meetings, and ultimately, in September 1975, a suit against the guidelines.

Typical of the power conflict over who makes the rules or who regulates whom was the suit by the six professors of obstetrics and gynecology, alleging that the guidelines infringed their right to free speech, since doctors were mandated to discuss sterilization only in the context of other methods of birth control.[35] Their suit, eventually dropped, was against *all* guidelines, including those of HEW, the state, and of course HHC. It made patent their unwillingness to abide by any regulations except their own. Some physicians had already expressed the fear that one set of regulations would lead to another and that they would soon be told when and how to perform surgery.

A related conflict emerged over the right of a consumer group, albeit one functioning within a corporate structure accountable to the public, to develop regulations by which the hospitals must abide. This incursion into the institutions called for advocacy, counseling, interpreters, and educational and other services as requisite for the process of obtaining informed consent. The structure of institutions was being altered.

As the groups opposing sterilization abuse continued their work, more and more conflicts with and within the women's health movement surfaced. Typical responses occurred at the 1975 Women's Health Conference held in Boston, where members of the nearly all-white audience challenged the four panelists who spoke on population control. After the speakers presented critiques of U.S. government sponsorship of population control programs in Latin American and other countries, some members of the audience objected to the views presented. A few defended the need for population control programs as a means of maintaining the environment or promoting peace or furthering economic development. Others defended the compulsory sterilization of mentally retarded individuals on the grounds that they are unfit for parenthood. Most women who took exception to the guidelines or legislation did so on the basis of personal experience. In the past they had been denied their request for sterilization because of their status (unmarried) or the number of their children (usually the doctor thought they had too few). They therefore opposed a waiting period or any other regulation that they interpreted as limiting access.

It became clear once more that personal experiences made for divergent viewpoints. While young white middle-class women were denied their requests for sterilization, low-income women or women of certain ethnicity were misled or coerced into them. The ensuing debate, like many others that followed over the years, had a healthful effect. Several organizations, including the Boston Women's Health Book Collective, made the issue of sterilization abuse their own, initiating campaigns to combat it.

In New York City the organizations took to the streets as the

successful movement for HHC guidelines grew to one for city council legislation. The elevation to the public level created conditions
favorable for new coalitions, including the prestigious National
Council of Churches, which through its project called Interreligious
Foundations for Community Organization (IFCO) sponsored the
National Conference on Sterilization Abuse in Washington, D.C.,
in September 1979. Over eighty people, half of whom were from
ethnic minorities and one-tenth of whom were men, met to present
testimony. Representatives from civil rights groups, women's
groups, and church organizations denounced U.S. government policies promoting the sterilization of minority women. Mary Ann Bear
—from Lame Deer, Montana—moved the conference when she
presented testimony on the massive sterilization of Indian women.
Such action "threatens our survival, tampers with basic religious
values and human rights to reproduce," she said, adding, "As a
minority we native Americans do not have to limit our numbers."
    The growth of these new coalitions not only ensured the success
of the legislation in New York City but also generated sufficient
pressure on a national level on HEW that in 1978 it promulgated
new, stronger guidelines patterned after the New York City law
(Public Law 37). In HEW's ten regions, its officials heard hundreds
of people testify in favor of more stringent guidelines and stronger
enforcement than those of 1973 provided.[36]
    Sterilization abuse, formerly recognized only by those who had
been its direct targets, became a generally acknowledged problem
that could no longer be denied. Third World women and their allies
had made their point; they had succeeded in escalating the struggle
for guidelines to legislation, from local to national arenas. The existence of the HEW guidelines gives substance to the current work
in monitoring that the National Women's Health Network now
spearheads.[37]

POPULATION CONTROL

The work on sterilization abuse catalyzed a change in yet another
realm from national to international perspectives. Puerto Rican
women described the events in Puerto Rico, where over a period of
thirty-five years privately funded foundations based in the United
States and the Puerto Rican government, with U.S. government
funds, had by 1968 sterilized over one-third of the women of child-
bearing age.[38] In the forties, just when women were joining the
work force in large numbers as industrialization opened up job
opportunities, sterilizations were provided at minimal or no cost.
Women suffered from lack of safe, legal abortion services, alternative methods of contraception, day care services, and general health

services, yet they were offered sterilizations. Large numbers of those sterilized believed that it was temporary.

Through this example from Puerto Rico, many women in the women's health movement came to understand that the nature of the colonial relations between Puerto Rico and the United States made coercion possible through a population control program.

Black women spoke of the increased sterilization in the South, the use of hysterectomy as a way of sterilizing young black women, and the move in at least ten states to pass laws permitting the compulsory sterilization of welfare recipients.[39] At the same time, they noted the presence of AID population control programs in Africa, Latin America, and Asia.

Native American women and men exposed the unprecedented number of sterilizations on reservations without evidence of informed consent,[40] while they showed the efforts of several corporations to deprive them of their land, particularly that which contained uranium.[41] Mexican women told of increasing sterilization programs just across the U.S. border, in Juarez and other border cities where U.S. industries have established plants employing thousands of women.

As the picture emerged, the militancy against the U.S. corporations and the government-supported agencies involved in population control programs overseas increased.

A new development among women workers in U.S. industry in 1979 raised additional concerns for health and safety on the job. In that year, some women employed by the American Cyanamid Company in West Virginia charged that the company had threatened to fire them from the lead pigments division of the plant unless they underwent sterilizations. Lead exposure is harmful to all workers, but this is especially so for unborn children. The company feared the possibility of pregnancies.

In public forums, women debated representatives of the Association for Voluntary Sterilization, Zero Population Growth, International Planned Parenthood Federation, and other organizations involved in population control. The activities of U.S. government agencies were exposed in a vast network of newsletters, journals, and magazines, as well as in a prolific output of scholarly books. Information on sterilization abuse and its complex connections to U.S. corporate interests was widely disseminated.[42]

THE PAST AND THE PROMISE

The women's health movement, to its credit, challenged one of the largest industries in the country. Its greatest challenge was to professional authority in its demand for control of women's bodies.

The struggle for control took many forms: legislation pertaining to women, the participation of women in their own health care, the marketing of products. To a lesser degree, women's demands altered the childbirth and abortion practices in hospitals, the admission of women to medical schools and their curricula, and the organization of services such as self-help clinics. But there has been almost no impact on surgery on women, particularly Caesarean sections and hysterectomies, on the prescription and exporting of dangerous drugs and contraceptive techniques, or on the relationship of patients to health care institutions. Moreover, the movement affected only a relatively small number of women and not the many who because of education, age, or geographic or other circumstances were beyond the reach of organizing efforts.

The most serious weaknesses of the movement remain its failure to cement alliances with working-class women and women from ethnic minorities. When women in the movement posed utopian solutions such as filling health needs through self-help, they alienated women who struggled to bring medical care into their communities. The frequently expressed, narrow feminist view that men were the enemy further alienated potential allies among men and some progressive organizations.

In addition, the women's health movement did not seek to understand or expose the poor working conditions in the health industry itself or to link the concerns of women health workers with those of consumers. Often the thrust was individualistic and at best reformist, as if being in the "know" and shopping for better care were the goals. Ultimately, its greatest weakness was its overall failure to address the need for power within the institutions where most of the abuses were taking place.

However, the tremendous importance and potential of the movement lies in its ability to catalyze revolutionary changes in its participants. The structure and models it created also have lasting value. The Boston Women's Health Book Collective spoke of this process of transformation of women's consciousness: "We are white, midde class women, and as such can describe only what life has been for us. But we do realize that poor women and nonwhite women have suffered far more from the kinds of misinformation and mistreatment that we are describing in this book. In some ways learning about our womanhood from the inside out has allowed us to cross over the socially created barriers of race, color, income, and class, and to feel a sense of identity with all women in the experience of being female."[43]

In a similar way, thousands of women were moved—their self-concepts changed. Those who had for too long submitted passively, though internally raging at the patronizing, poor care they received from their doctors, felt validated in the consciousness-raising process and became empowered by education, organizing experience, carrying out struggles, and winning victories. They will never be the same.

Those who came with a perspective other than the direct feminist one, who were involved in Third World liberation struggles, found a forum in the women's health movement. And if sometimes the debates were painful because of the ignorance or insensitivity they revealed, they were always fundamental because they exposed the most divisive of ideological constraints—attitudes of superiority based on race or class. We were forced to grapple with each other's prejudices and eventually by sharing experiences to understand our different positions and reach unity.

Bringing organized women into direct conflict with the holders of power in the medical establishment radicalized many. Some moved beyond reform and came to advocate revolutionary changes in the health care system and in American society itself.

Its thrusts into medical schools and other health institutions placed more women in positions of increased power. These women in turn are providing support for others who enter now.

Women who have been advocates, counselors, providers, administrators, and community organizers of health care institutions can act as links between their communities and these institutions. It is now possible to develop consumer projects in which health services are monitored. For example, the National Women's Health Network has published a guide for monitoring the HEW guidelines on sterilization in order to help community organizations develop activities to prevent abuses.[44] It may provide a model for penetrating the institutional structures themselves.

A massive body of literature attests to the prolific writings of women scholars on health, but what is most impressive is the national recognition that many have gained. The unquestionable stature of women researchers is sufficiently evident that funding sources have taken note. A recent example is provided by Helen Marieskind, who conducted the study on Caesarean sections at the request of HEW. Women's research findings and pertinent health information are broadly distributed to hundreds of thousands via the network of organizations.

It is precisely in the creation of organizations of national scope, such as the National Women's Health Network and the Reproductive Rights National Network, that the women's health movement has made a unique contribution.

A promising recent initiative has been the joining of forces with trade unions and the occupational health movement in the Coalition for the Reproductive Rights of Workers, which is concerned with the effects of chemicals, radiation, and other hazards on the reproductive systems of both women and men.

The movement showed that it could ultimately cut across class and ethnic lines when it focused on what was happening to the majority of women.

Where it will go, no one can predict. The danger of co-optation, ever present in this society, is great. Women may be satisfied to testify, impel legislation, influence those in power to grant abortion services and better contraceptives, assume more places in the medical hierarchy, and hold well-paying positions in foundations, federations, and the like. Or they may overcome their racism and their own comfortable class positions sufficiently to join workers, Third World people, and other progressive forces in the health industry and the general society for a sweeping restructuring that will empower the workers and patients.

The author wishes to thank the many sisters and brothers who participated in the struggles for women's, and ultimately people's, liberation; they make the history that is the subject of this chapter.

For many years, the collective Committee to End Sterilization Abuse (CESA) was my political home. Thanks, compañeras and compañeros, for deepening my understanding of reproductive-rights issues. The countless members of the National Women's Health Network and Center on Constitutional Rights, the Committee for Abortion Rights and Against Sterilization Abuse (CARASA), and the Reproductive Rights National Network (R_2N_2) continue to lead the way.

My friends Esta Armstrong, Rhonda Copelon, Adisa Douglas, Carola Greengard, Eddie Gonzalez, Linda Tschirhart Sanford, Susan Schechter, Barbara Seaman, Amy Schwartz, Karen Stamm, Nancy Stearns, and Nora Zamidow, and my daughters Laura and Jo Ellen Brainin all took time from their own valuable work to review and make helpful suggestions.

I give special thanks to Sheryl Burt Ruzek for her excellent analytical history *The Women's Health Movement* and to Sue Davis for her wise support and generous sharing of her writing skills. And finally, in memoriam, thanks to my dear friend Joan Kelly—feminist historian—for having been my friend and counselor.

part III

HEALTH WORKERS

6.

medical education:

NEW WINE IN OLD WINE SKINS

Rocio Huet-Cox

Medical education was buffeted by intense demands for change during much of the last two decades. Challenges came from civil rights activists and the women's movement, as well as from the government. Programs of preventive medicine were demanded of a system of medical education that moved only slowly to expand the scientific, technological, disease-oriented focus of the traditional model. Health was sought for *all* people, including the underserved; it was to be a right, not a privilege.

Such pressures led to changes in medical education. Family practice once again became a fixture in medicine and made primary care available to millions. The supply of physicians greatly increased. And the addition of numerous courses in ethics, behavioral science, sociology, and preventive and occupational medicine probably made future physicians somewhat more aware of the complexity of factors influencing an individual's health.

Yet did these changes really enable medical education to promote and maintain our health more effectively? Was the old model of medical education still largely intact? Did it prove resilient enough to alleviate people's mounting health needs? Or did it serve at times to frustrate them? Answering such questions requires looking at the model of medical education that has been preeminent ever since the publication of the famed Flexner report, at the beginning of the twentieth century.

MEDICAL EDUCATION FROM 1900 TO 1960

In 1908, Abraham Flexner was commissioned by the Carnegie Foundation for the Advancement of Teaching to study the quality of medical education at the approximately 130 medical schools. Before then, medicine in the United States had tended to be a "trade," medical education being conducted either under the apprenticeship system or in proprietary trade schools. Most schools had minimal requirements for admission and lacked affiliation with educational institutions. The implementation of the Flexner report swept away this traditional system. The basic structure of medical education changed. A new curriculum emphasized course and laboratory work in basic sciences in the first two years, and extensive clinical experience in the third and fourth. A thorough knowledge of the biomedical sciences became the basis of medical care.[1] Medical schools began to affiliate with universities. Only "high-quality" medical schools were granted accreditation, and half the existing medical schools closed.

The Flexner report insisted that the sine qua non of rational treatment and diagnosis was a solid grounding in the natural sciences. Surviving schools attained a new level of competence. Great strides were made in biomedical research. Yet these positive changes were paralleled by equally important negative consequences. Medical schools became standardized and uniform. Science in the medical school was set apart from science on the general campus. Medical schools were separated from other relevant disciplines in the university—economics, sociology, psychology, and others.[2] And medical schools largely ignored health care delivery outside their own schools and their own hospitals.

Flexner's report also aided a process already underway before the consolidation and elimination of medical schools. Between 1904 and 1915, 92 schools closed their doors or merged, 44 of them in the first six years after the appearance of the report and 48 in the next six. This resulted in a significant decrease in the output of practitioners.[3] By 1950, there were only 77 medical schools in the country.

The impact on black medical schooling was immediate. Cut off from sources of funding, partly because of Flexner's report, five of the seven disapproved medical schools closed. In 1910, there was one black doctor for every 2,883 black people in the United States (compared with one physician for every 684 people for the nation as a whole). By 1942, there was only one black physician for every

3,377 black people. Women fared little better. Flexner's recommendations contributed to keeping them at an average of less than 5 percent of all medical graduates from 1900 until World War II. Of the women's medical schools, all closed but one.[4]

The Flexner report served, in essence, to establish a highly durable model for medicine—disease oriented and mechanistic, centrally based in the hospital or office, and focused on the individual patient. In this model the sick or injured individual comes to the solo practitioner for a rational assessment of an illness. The physician then attempts to "cure" the patient with the diagnostic and therapeutic tools placed at his disposal by biomedical research and technology.

This model was deeply rooted in the Flexnerian paradigm of medical education, which changed slowly before the 1960s. By then, postgraduate study had been added to basic medical education, as a result of the rapid increase of scientific knowledge.[5] Basic research and research training was fueled by monetary support from the government and private foundations.[6] Burdened with so much biomedical knowledge, the undergraduate medical curriculum proved increasingly unable to incorporate more information, so the graduate years of medical education were extended markedly to allow for its absorption. An internship year was grafted onto the collegiate program, a pattern that had become nearly universal by the end of the 1920s. Residency training in medical specialties was appended in the 1930s, and by the end of the 1950s this practice was found almost everywhere.[7]

Behind this model was a changing context within which doctors worked. The pragmatic, highly technological, cure-oriented medical system developing rapidly through the early 1900s required hospitals and medical schools that replaced the solo practitioner as the center of the system. Flexner himself sensed the imminent need for a reorientation of the physician's role: "The physician's function is fast becoming social and preventive, rather than individual and curative. Upon him society relies to ascertain, and through measures essentially educational to enforce, the conditions that prevent disease and make positively for physical and moral well-being."[8] And yet not until the 1960s did American society begin to consider the restructuring of the U.S. health care system, including the powerful institutions of medical education.

PRESSURE FOR CHANGE IN MEDICAL EDUCATION IN THE 1960s AND 1970s

The reforms demanded in the health care field were interwoven with the popular quest for equality, freedom, and social change—

with the civil rights, women's liberation, and peace movements. Out of these movements grew the popular concept of health care as a right of all people, including those who had been historically deprived—blacks, Puerto Ricans, Mexican Americans, native Americans, the poor, women, the elderly. This concept was made evident by Cecil Sheps in the report of the Eighth Teaching Institute of the Association of American Medical Colleges:

> Certainly the interest of the public in health and in health programs is clear to everyone. It is based on the broad recognition that health is a vital national concern, not only because of the direct relation of health to productivity and problems of defense, but also because of our relatively new notions about human rights and human dignity. Thus, it is generally recognized by the Western countries that medical care should be available to all people, regardless of their ability to pay, bringing the best quality of care to them when they need it.[9]

Civil Rights Movement

The civil rights movement began exposing the institutionalized racism in this country. The health industry proved no exception. Demands were raised for more and better services for nonwhites, community participation in the planning and execution of health centers and hospitals, and the opportunity for nonwhites to enter the health industry as physicians or nurses rather than as the majority of the lower-echelon work force. In 1968–69, blacks, native Americans, Mexican Americans, and mainland Puerto Ricans together made up only 2.9 percent of the entering classes in medical schools, of which 2.7 percent were blacks. And the majority of these black students were attending Howard and Meharry, the only two black medical schools in the country left open after the Flexner report.[10]

Black, Puerto Rican, and Mexican-American neighborhood organizations concerned solely with health began developing at this time. The civil rights movement also started a massive hospital organizing drive for nonwhite workers.[11]

Women's Movement

The women's liberation movement originally began in the midsixties by exposing the oppression of women in a predominately male-dominated society. By the end of the sixties, several women's groups were taking on the sexism in the health care system. Although 70 percent of the nation's health workers were women in 1965, women constituted only about 9 percent of the entering classes of medical schools.[12] Feminists were demanding better and more health services for women—dignified care, legal abortions, and more women physicians, among other things.

These groups employed demonstrations, nonviolent resistance, grass-roots organizing, and wide-ranging educational efforts needed to counter the deep commitment of existing institutions to the protection and furthering of the institutions' interests.

Student Movements

Another group that organized to voice dissatisfaction with the medical care system involved people who were medical and nursing students in the sixties. Many attended college during the anti–Vietnam War and civil rights era. Some entered medicine with a desire to serve the public rather than to gain prestige or money. Many joined the Medical Committee for Human Rights and eventually other civil rights groups.

In 1965, sixty-five students from schools of medicine, nursing, dentistry, and social work formed a national group, the Student Health Organization (SHO).[13] No longer in existence, it advocated radical changes in medical curricula, the health care system, and society at large. These original sixty-five students and others who joined them objected to the inequities in health care. Through their early efforts, volunteer clinics to serve migrants, children, and ghetto inhabitants were established. The students organized federally funded community health projects obtained from the Office of Economic Opportunity and from Head Start. They demanded that medical schools respond more to the needs of the community. Medical schools, supported to a great extent by state funds, had a responsibility, they argued, to provide community service and to reach out to the communities in which they were located. And some suggested that community service be added as a fourth goal of medical schools, along with education, research, and individual patient care. Community service would imply a willingness on the part of the teaching hospital and the faculty of the affiliated medical school to develop an appropriate involvement in needed community health services.[14]

These students demanded that medical schools change the admissions policies that allowed almost no one except white males to become physicians. Cost alone was proving prohibitive; only children from wealthier families could pay for medical school. In 1961, 40 percent of all medical students came from the 12 percent of families with incomes of $10,000 or more a year.[15]

The more traditional American Medical Student Association (AMSA), originally founded as the Student American Medical Association (SAMA) in 1950, became more active in curricular reform and community involvement as a result of SHO. Leaders from SHO in 1969 moved into the then SAMA, and SAMA soon broke away from the AMA, reflecting its independence in its name change. AMSA advocated health care as a "right and not a privilege," involvement in curriculum committees, course work in fields outside of the biomedical sciences but essential to the practice of medicine, more elective time, and more preceptorship experiences. The dedication of *A Handbook for Change,* written in 1973 by members of AMSA and others and devoted to reforms in medical education and health care, reads as follows: "To our patients . . . forced to seek care from a generation of health professionals who have been inadequately prepared to meet the demands for health care in a rapidly changing society."[16]

Many other medical student organizations also reflected the idealism and activism of these earlier SHO students. Black, Chicano, and Puerto Rican health workers and students voiced their concerns about the absence of health services in these communities through their own organizations: the Student National Medical Association (SNMA), the National Chicano Health Organization (NCHO), with its successor La Raza Medical Association (LaRaMA), and Borriqua. These groups focused on improving the health of these minority populations by increasing the numbers of black, Chicano, and Puerto Rican physicians serving these minority peoples.

Despite the lure of wealth and prestige offered by the medical profession, these activist students did not forget their commitment to serving the public. They were influenced considerably by the larger movements for social change in this country. Joining with these groups, they repeatedly asked why a country as wealthy as the United States was not providing all of its people with adequate health care.

Health Status of the U.S. Population

Amid these movements for equality and social change, the federal government began making the development of a more rational and egalitarian health system a major priority. The Kennedy-Johnson administration was aware of the contrast between the expected application of biomedical technology and the reality of medical care. Infant mortality was still high and life expectancy low in the United States, relative to comparable industrial countries. The major centers of medical research and education were producing the high technology of medicine, but these advances either were not filtering down to the level of applied health care or were not as effective at fulfilling the country's health needs as had been hoped. Many questioned the possibility of correcting health deficiencies through improved medical care when the emerging major health problems in the country were related to environmental, occupational, and socioeconomic conditions. Many felt that medical education and research should focus on the prevention or reduction of those individual and societal factors involved in the manifestation of these diseases, rather than relying on the employment of highly sophisticated, expensive treatment techniques, such as open heart surgery and extensive cancer resection surgery, to overcome these major killers after individuals had been afflicted.[17] The government was beginning to feel a need to intervene more directly in the health care field.

President Johnson appointed a commission in 1964 to recommend methods for reducing the incidence of the major chronic killers through new research and through more complete utilization and distribution of existing medical knowledge. This commission on heart disease, cancer, and stroke reported in 1965:

> It is the conviction of the President's Commission that our government has a profound responsibility, which is not yet fully discharged, for leadership, stimulation, and support in the protection of the health of the American people. . . . The nation can well afford and the people can enthusiastically support substantially increased expenditures intended to save lives today and produce more lifesaving knowledge for tomorrow.[18]

Although many of the recommendations of this particular commission, which included a direct federal role in patient care and medical education, were not immediately enacted into law, the 1960s saw a great expansion of government intervention in the delivery of health services.

Government Intervention in Health Care

This intervention included the Medicare and Medicaid programs, regional medical programs, comprehensive health planning, and federally financed neighborhood health and mental health centers.[19] Government involvement also increased enormously in the area of medical education. A long series of legislative enactments affected federal funding for health professional education. During the forties and fifties, biomedical investigations were supported in the medical schools through large federal investments under amendments to the Public Health Service Act. These research grants were then the main federal investment in the health professional schools. As federal monies increased for research, schools altered their programs and faculty in accordance with the grant stipulations. The income for medical schools related to this source increased from 11 percent in 1946 to 42 percent in 1968. By 1968, some 33 percent of all faculty salaries were supported by the government's research and research training grants. Approximately 40 percent of the full-time medical faculty was receiving some federal research money.[20]

The first major interest the federal government showed in supporting health professional education directly came in 1963, with the Health Professions Education Assistance Act. This legislation offered matching grants for health school construction and loans for students in several of the professions. In 1965 it was amended to provide grants to five categories of schools that would increase enrollments, and guaranteed loans for low-income students. As more money was offered in these areas, federal monies for research in medical schools were decreasing. In 1968, the Health Manpower Act granted a flat nominal sum of money to each school and made additional funds dependent on increases in the student body or in the number of graduates. This law, which also authorized grants to assist schools in financial distress, was extended in 1970 through the Health Training Improvement Act.[21]

As the federal government was shifting its emphasis from research to education, Medicare and Medicaid were enacted in 1965. These programs affected medical schools because they provided federal money to pay for the health care of aged and indigent patients, many of whose medical expenses had earlier been absorbed by the medical schools, who treated them like charity patients. Schools could thus now direct those monies to areas other than patient care.

Health manpower continued to be the focus of legislative emphasis in the Comprehensive Health Manpower Training Act of 1971. Health professional schools were awarded annual operating grants, determined by the number of students enrolled per school—a "capitation" formula. This legislation also authorized traineeship and fellowship grants in family medicine. Funds for developing family practice departments, bonuses of $6,000 per student graduating in three years from medical school, and financial incentives for accepting and enrolling more minorities into medical schools were all offered by the federal government in the sixties and seventies.[22] The Health Professions Education Assistance Act of 1976 mandated the nation's medical schools, as a group, to reach the 50 percent level for first-year affiliated residencies in primary care by 1980. If the schools did not collectively reach this goal, each school would individually be responsible for meeting the quota at the risk of losing its capitation.[23]

Beginning in 1972, the Health Manpower Education Initiative Awards offered federal dollars for Area Health Education Centers (AHEC). The AHEC concept, attributed to the Carnegie Commission report of 1970, included the decentralization and regionalization of health professional education, to be achieved through joint partnerships for educational purposes between university health centers and area health education centers at a distance from the university centers. Medical students and residents would receive clinical training at these AHEC sites. The purpose of this strategy was to better distribute health care providers by geography and specialty through educational interventions.[24]

To further induce medical schools to deal more directly with the problem of geographic maldistribution of physicians, appropriations for National Health Service Corps scholarships, awarded directly to students in exchange for service obligations in underserved areas, were tied to capitation appropriations.[25]

Much of the government funding to increase the number of physicians graduating from medical schools resulted from the widely accepted belief that there was a shortage in health care personnel, especially physicians, at the beginning of the 1960s.[26] Many perceived this shortage, especially of primary care physicians, as critical to the nation's health. Equally critical was the geographic maldistribution of these health workers.

Shortage of Health Personnel

The perceived shortage of physicians was accentuated by the evolving nature of the U.S. population. Both the number and composition of the people in the United States had changed substantially since 1900. From a nation of 76 million inhabitants in 1900, this country had grown to 181 million in 1960. The proportion of individuals in the upper age group was increasing as well. From 1950 to 1965, the percentage of those sixty-five years of age and older rose from 8.1 percent to 9.4 percent, a modest but substantial increase in absolute numbers, given the rise in population.[27] Persons over sixty were at this time shown to require health care more frequently and for longer periods of time than younger people. With increases in life expectancy, individuals had an additional number of years in which they would need health care. The diseases of the older population also tended to be more chronic and less responsive to treatment.[28] With Medicare and Medicaid programs, the elderly as well as the poor—two previously deprived high-risk groups—began to use more health services.[29] This increased demand for health services was occurring at a time of decreased availability of general medical care.

Shortage of Primary Care Physicians

The number of general practitioners declined precipitously, from 50 percent of all M.D.'s in 1915 to less than 5 percent in 1960.[30] This was due to the trend toward specialization that swept medicine in the years after World War II. This trend was the result of many factors. With the phenomenal explosion in basic biomedical knowledge leading to the development of more sophisticated technology, many young physicians feared incompetence in many fields and therefore felt the need to specialize. These new physicians were being educated in medical schools in which federally supported research had become the central institutional activity; hospitals and medical schools were viewed as the source of all new information and the only home for truly "good" physicians. There was also increasing income in specialty practice due to higher reimbursement for specialists from health insurance programs and the increased use of expensive equipment and procedures by specialists.

One of the chief problems of specialization was the fragmentation of individual patient medical care. Continuity of care became an increasingly scarce commodity for persons with chronic and environment-linked health problems. Some observers at that time estimated that anywhere from 80 to 90 percent of all physician services were being rendered to the moderately or chronically ill who did not need the services of highly specialized physicians or the sophisticated resources of the modern hospital. Yet these individuals often sought specialists as the availability of primary care physicians decreased.[31]

Geographic Maldistribution

The geographic maldistribution of physicians only aggravated the issue of the perceived physician shortage. This distribution varied substantially from that of the population. The Middle Atlantic census region had almost twice as many physicians for its population as did the East South Central region. The majority of physicians were located in urban areas. For example, while New York had 199 M.D.'s and D.O.'s providing patient care per 100,000 population in 1967, Mississippi had only 69.[32] And in cities like New York and Boston, the majority of physicians were found in the middle- and upper-class sections, not in the ghettoes or barrios. As a result of this supposedly inadequate number of physicians graduating from U.S. medical schools in the 1950s, an increasing proportion of foreign medical graduates (FMGs) filled U.S. residency positions and obtained licensure in the U.S.[33] Many of these FMGs practiced in underserved areas in this country where U.S. graduates chose not to locate. There was some concern at this time not only about the "brain drain" from underdeveloped areas but also about the quality of the undergraduate medical education that some of these FMGs received; there thus existed a question concerning the quality of care that FMGs were delivering in the face of the shortage of U.S. graduates.

Rising Medical Education Costs

All of these factors contributed to the emphasis American society was placing on reforming the health care system. And the demands discussed here came at a time when costs were rising in the field of medical education, reflecting the rapidly rising expenditures for health care in this country. The burgeoning of biomedical research, the increasingly expensive facilities and faculty needed to educate future doctors, and the growing cost to medical schools and teaching hospitals of educating residents who were now demanding more reasonable compensation were all major financial issues that medical schools and their universities faced at this time.[34] The various programs of grants-in-aid for research, both federally and privately funded, provided a major component in the support of many faculties at the beginning of the sixties.[35] The problem of emphasis and balance among the three areas of teaching, research, and patient care was already giving rise to difficult questions concerning the objectives and needs of medical education at this time, and it was only exacerbated by these financial and societal pressures, which came from different directions and without coordination.[36]

REFORMS IN MEDICAL EDUCATION IN THE 1960s AND 1970s

How were medical schools to respond, if at all, to these demands and incentives for reforms in the medical system? Predictably, given the increased cost of medical education, the strongest single incentive given to medical faculties to change their programs was money, coming for the most part from the federal and state governments. Initially, the government focused on increasing the number of physicians. Medical schools responded in three ways: (1) by ex-

panding existing medical schools, (2) by creating new schools, and
(3) by decreasing the length of medical education in some schools.

Expansion of
Existing Medical Schools

Through the 1963 Health Professions Education Assistance Act, its
1965 amendments, and the 1971 Comprehensive Health Manpower Training Act, the federal government provided a significant
incentive to medical schools to increase their class size, despite the
long-standing assumption by the medical profession that larger
classes would mean lower standards.[37] Efforts to expand schools
were bearing fruit by 1968, when all but 8 of the established 91
schools had increased their enrollment. This increase continued in
the 1970s, reaching 65,189 in the academic year 1980–81 (compared with 30,288 students in 1960).[38] Claims of resulting lower
standards were refuted by Paul Sanazaro, who found no correlation
between class size in medical schools and performance on part 1 of
the national boards, attrition rate, or career choice. However, the
schools did have lower average costs per student.[39]

Creation of New Schools

Federal funds also provided support for the construction of new
medical schools. The number of medical schools increased from 86
in 1960 to 103 in 1970.[40] A total of 40 new schools have been
created since 1960, of which 75 percent are state owned. Of the
6,536 new first-year places established overall between 1965 and
1975, 66 percent were in state schools, while of the 2,049 new
first-year places created in new schools, 83 percent were in state
schools. It is evident that the increase in medical school enrollment
was significantly supported by state tax dollars. The federal government increased its institutional support greatly, from $93.4 million
in 1965 to $330.6 million in 1974, with the capitation program
accounting for 67 percent of the institutional awards made in
1974.[41] From 1967 to 1971, construction grants were also high,
$80–$100 million per year.[42]

Decrease in Length of
Medical Education

Federal bonuses of $6,000 for each student graduating from medical
school in three years were accepted by many medical schools, despite opposition. In 1973, a three-year medical school curriculum
was offered in 27 percent of the medical schools. In 1978, only 8

percent still offered it. Government financial incentives were the acknowledged greatest motivation. In the AAMC site visits to three-year medical schools, administrators frequently stated that "we went to the three-year program to gain additional funding, hire additional faculty, and gain political favor with our state legislator."[43] The majority of the faculty at these schools, for example, expressed very little concern for change: "Even among deans of four-year institutions, curriculum or educational program issues were not stated as positive factors in their consideration (to convert to three-year curriculum)."[44] Although the evaluations of student performance in clinical clerkships, tests of knowledge, clinical performance in the first postgraduate years, service chief ratings, and scores on part 3 of the National Board of Medical Examiner showed no significant differences between graduates of three-year and those of four-year medical schools, three-year medical school curricula had bloomed and withered by 1978.

The failure of these accelerated programs to spread to all medical schools and the gradual shift back to a four-year curriculum appear attributable to opposition to the three-year program within some medical school faculties despite federal funds. This opposition included the bias against graduates of three-year programs that directors of residency training programs often exhibited. In addition, there were the difficulties of faculties long accustomed to predetermined teaching and vacation schedules and now forced to readjust to new routines, and the workload of the students who now had only three years to complete an already overcrowded curriculum.[45]

A few medical schools responded to the public cry and governmental incentives for more physicians by eliminating the sharp separation between the college and the medical curricula. Promising high school or early college students were accepted into an integrated premedical-medical program. Johns Hopkins was the first to introduce one of these plans, offering in 1959 a five-year program beginning after two years of college. The other innovations of the sixties were six-year programs accepting graduating high school seniors, for the most part. Of the twelve such programs listed in the *1979–1980 AAMC Curriculum Directory,* eleven offered a six-year premedical-medical curriculum to a small group of students in addition to the regular four-year curriculum. Only the University of Missouri at Kansas City was listed as offering solely a six-year combined program.[46] These programs did reduce the length of time required for completion of the course of study, which was considered desirable for these very bright participants, who might otherwise have been discouraged by the eight years of formal training.[47] These programs also intended to eliminate the duplication of material and to make such subjects as humanities and social sciences part of the professional curriculum.[48] Data from Boston University's six-year integrated program provide evidence that the performance of concerned, qualified high school students on standardized examinations is at a superior level, and that it is consistent with the medical faculty's expectations of the eight-year graduate.[49]

Preceptorships

In response to the concern over the shortage and maldistribution of primary care physicians, preceptorships were resurrected as an educational device in the sixties and the seventies to encourage medical students to practice under the supervision of a community physician in a rural or other medically underserved area. The preoccupation of U.S. medical education with specialization had systematically excluded the career model of a community physician from the curricula of medical schools. In preceptorships, students treat patients in the office of the supervisory physician. There, students often learn to work with other health professionals such as nurse practitioners or physician's assistants.

Medical schools took advantage of the available monies, and by 1978 the 1971 Comprehensive Health Manpower Training Act had provided over $28 million to support preceptorship training in about seventy-five allopathic and osteopathic schools.[50] Now many medical schools in the United States offer students the chance to elect a community preceptorship, and many indeed require it of their students.[51]

Area Health Education Centers

Selective opportunities for medical students to have various statewide off-campus health-related experiences were increased significantly through Area Health Education Centers (AHECs). These were joint partnerships between university health centers and health education centers some distance from the university center. Between 1972 and 1979, eleven AHECs were awarded federal contracts totaling about $84 million. Not only were community preceptorships in underserved areas made available to medical students through AHECs, but the number of residency programs participating in primary care fields were increased in many state communities. This exposed residents to the possibilities of practicing in these communities.

There is evidence to date that primary care preceptorships actually influenced specialty selection or practice location, which had been the expectation when these preceptorship training programs were initiated. Such decisions, according to several authors, are already made before the preceptorship occurs.[52] Nevertheless, some authors have demonstrated a significant increment in student learning about the environment in which primary care is delivered. They argue then that the reason for continuing required preceptorships is to provide students with what may be the only experience that exposes and sensitizes them to many management issues and patient needs not so obvious in a tertiary care setting.[53]

Family Practice and Primary Care

A campaign was waged from 1946 to 1969 to increase the numbers of primary care physicians in the United States through the recognition of family practice as a specialty and by having family practice departments in medical schools. The prestige of the general practitioner had plummeted to its nadir after World War II; it started to recover in the 1960s, when public opinion was focused on social progress and the needs of the community. General practitioners began to press for the formal recognition of family practice as a specialty. Their efforts culminated in 1969, with standards for board certification.[54]

Legislators and educators felt that students would not be attracted to family practice and would specialize in other fields unless trained by family practitioners. Public funds were therefore made available to help support the rapid expansion of family practice programs in most medical schools.[55] With this government support, there were, by 1972, according to the 1972–73 AAMC directory of medical education, 23 independent departments of family practice in the 113 medical schools, 15 schools that linked family practice with community medicine, and 6 schools that had family practice as a subdepartment of internal medicine. It is difficult to determine how much of the curriculum in medical schools is actually taught by family medicine faculty; published curricula are often misleading. Topics previously listed under introductory courses, outpatient clinics, social medicine, epidemiology, and even public health are sometimes listed as family medicine even though they are not taught by that department. Undergraduate medical students began getting a brief exposure to family practice in the early years of school with something more substantial (of two to six weeks duration), as well as electives, in the final year or years.[56] In 1980, 47 medical schools required a family medicine clerkship lasting an average of six weeks.

Although it is too early to assess the impact of increased numbers of family practice programs and of family practitioners on the health status of the population, geographic maldistribution and lack of access to care continue. These problems do not seem to be improving simply with the training of more primary care physicians. And it has not been shown that family practice faculty alone in family practice departments teaching medical students can attract them to that specialty. Much evidence to date suggests this is untrue.[57] Many factors affect career choice, and in any assessment of the impact of curricular changes on this choice, the influence of external forces, such as public opinion, the indebtedness of students, and the rapidly increasing public prestige of family practice must be taken into account. Despite a lack of evidence showing the direct link between career choice and exposure to family practice, a large number of those involved in medical education did agree that sufficient exposure of students to primary care, enabling them to appreciate the nature and scope of primary care, was an educational experience that should continue to be part of the curriculum.[58]

Curriculum Changes

In response to public demands for physicians who could provide comprehensive, continuous care to people with chronic illnesses often related to environment, life-style, and occupation, medical students were exposed to previously ignored topics in medical education. These topics included alcoholism, community and preventive medicine, ethics, drug abuse, emergency medicine, geriatrics, nutrition, health care provision, and occupational medicine. In 1980, 89 schools reported having a formal program to promote interest in human values as they relate to medicine. Seven other schools were planning one. One hundred and three schools offer instruction in human values during the basic-science years, 56 do so during the clinical years, 77 provide special forums or seminars, and 48 offer human-values sensitivity training or experience. In the last three categories, 14 to 16 further schools are in stages of planning such a program.[59]

But there is very little information concerning the content of these courses or how much time is actually devoted throughout the undergraduate curriculum to this area. The amount of time given to preventive medicine, on the other hand, has been estimated. According to the *1979–1980 AAMC Curriculum Directory,* 95 of the 125 accredited medical schools require teaching time that can be identified as relating to preventive medicine, community medicine, or public health; 91 have departments related to preventive and community medicine with faculty. Yet it has been estimated that less than 1.5 percent of the total undergraduate medical curriculum is devoted to prevention.[60] Seventy schools have a requirement in the first or second year, 6 in the third or fourth years, and 19 in both.[61]

The addition of course work in ethical, behavioral, forensic, and preventive issues, among others, affecting the practice and art of medicine was certainly of note, since it seems that these previously ignored topics, which are very important to medicine, were now being emphasized. Through teaching in human values, students were being shown that such issues as the use of placebos and euthanasia were integral parts of medical practice and required thoughtful decisions that physicians acting in isolation could not make. Through teaching in preventive medicine and public health, future physicians were being better prepared to understand that the major health problems of our population are chronic, noninfectious diseases influenced significantly by environmental, behavioral, and occupational factors. But without more information about the amount of time devoted to these topics and about the content of the courses, and in the absence of any standard against which to judge the efficacy of the attempts to teach these topics, it is impossible to determine to what extent, if any, these efforts are addressing the needs out of which they had arisen. That 75 percent of the accredited medical schools have departments related to preventive medicine or public health would seem to signify an interest on the part of medical schools in this orientation to medicine. Yet the fact that less than 1.5 percent of the actual time in the curriculum is devoted to this area raises serious doubts about the commitment and ability of medical education to teach this different orientation.

In an attempt to respond to some of the medical students' demands for less fragmentation in their education, many medical schools began offering more clinical exposure in the first two years of medical school. No quantitative assessment of this trend in medical schools is available, but with few exceptions, the very rigid traditional division between the two years of preclinical years and two years of clinical studies had been reduced by the 1970s. In 1971, the majority of medical schools reported a 25 to 33 percent reduction in basic-science instruction time, along with the adoption of interdepartmental instruction.[62] Case Western Reserve University had been the first medical school to introduce interdepartmental instruction, as early as 1952.[63] More elective time was being offered in 1971 as well. Throughout the 1970s, the numbers of schools making these changes remained fairly stable. One of the more pervasive innovations in the 1970s was the adoption of a pass-fail system. And as of 1975, only 28 schools claimed to "rank" their students.[64] Many medical schools responded to students' demands for more self-determination in curriculum content by appointing student representatives to curriculum committees.

In 1976, according to the results of a national survey of medical schools in which 91 schools responded, approximately one-third of the medical schools claimed to have developed some form of independent-study program to respond to students' requests for more self-directed responsibility. Of the 31 schools with these self-defined independent-study programs, eleven stated that they used them in the basic sciences alone, while 17 schools had programs in both the basic-science and clinical portions of their curricula.[65] This percentage compares with a 58 percent positive response reported by 135 American and Canadian medical schools indicated in the *1974–1975 AAMC Curriculum Directory,* in which the following definition of independent study was used: "Independent Study refers to educational formats imposing neither specific course sequence nor prearranged time periods for student learning. Students develop their own learning programs but must satisfy faculty requirements." Schools were reporting that these programs were at least as effective as traditional programs when judged by the criterion of performance on the national boards.[66] Furthermore, well-prepared college students tended to find independent study more challenging and acceptable. Furkenstein has stated, "Harvard studies indicate that many very able students who have abandoned their plans for medical careers and now plan graduate studies in science or psychology did not enter medical school because they disapproved of being a medical student, not because they lacked admiration for the career of a physician."[67]

Enrollment of Minorities and Women

Spurred by the enactment of civil rights legislation, the provision of financial incentives to medical schools to increase minority enrollments, and the assistance available to students from low-income families, the number of minorities in medical training has increased substantially during the last two decades. Yet the approximate goal of 12 percent for minority enrollment set during the 1970s by the AAMC was never reached. And now the trend in minority enrollment is showing a leveling off, if not a slight drop. Minorities now constitute approximately 7 percent of the enrollment in medical schools, compared with less than 3 percent of all medical students in the 1960s.[68]

In addition, because of legislation forbidding sex discrimination and because of the changing role of individual and organized women, more women entered medical schools in the last two decades—from less than 9 percent in the sixties to approximately 25 percent in 1980.[69]

CONCLUSION

These, then, were the major concrete changes that occurred within the medical education system in the last two decades: enlarged enrollments, increasing percentages of low-income and minority students, the expansion of residency training in family practice and other primary care specialties, and wider exposure to relevant topics in medicine. What can we say about these changes in the context of the health needs spurring public outcry at that time? A central question is implicit in an assessment of the nature of these changes: Is the graduate of 1980 any better equipped than a 1960 graduate to influence positively the factors that cause ill health, after being trained in this "reformed" medical education system? Graduates of 1980 may be more attuned to the need for primary care. They may treat their patients more like human beings and not simply like disease entities. Younger physicians may be able to identify a few more specific environmental, occupational, and socioeconomic factors that contribute to ill health, having learned about them mainly in epidemiology courses. But have the 1980 graduates been taught the skills to aid their patients (both individually and collectively) in altering these factors?

The greater number of physicians being produced in 1980 are being trained in curricula that have been rearranged but that are essentially unchanged since 1960. Despite the increased flexibility, interdepartmental teaching, and limited exposure to disciplines outside the basic biomedical sciences in today's curriculum, medical students graduating in 1980 are still being taught to focus on a disease in the individual patient, as the graduates of 1920 and 1960 had been.

Up to 20 percent of the total cancer mortality may be associated with occupational hazards.[70] Yet how much does a young physician know or do about the health effects of the thousands of toxic synthetic chemicals in our environment? How much more effective are individual physicians today in helping patients alter their poor dietary habits, cigarette smoking, alcohol abuse, or severe emotional stresses? How much does a recently graduated physician know about nutrition? How many physicians think to oppose those who encourage smoking, drinking, and poor eating habits? How much more deeply committed as a group to serving the underserved are graduates of 1980 than are those of 1960? Geographic maldistribution of health care providers and lack of access for needy populations has continued in the last two decades despite increased numbers of physicians and family practitioners. Perhaps some of the new minority physicians graduating will practice in minority population areas, but how much can a few individuals alone do to alter our health statistics significantly?

Individual medical faculty may have desired to rectify some of the inequities and inadequacies of the medical care system by producing more and different practitioners who would collectively challenge this system. A few may have been deeply committed to altering the basic traditional model of medical education to produce a cadre of highly respected physicians better equipped to apply primarily the skills of preventive medicine rather than the highly sophisticated tools of curative medicine. But medical schools as a whole did not show this same commitment. They developed no major thrust in this direction. The focus of medical education continues to be the study of diseases of the individual patient isolated from the multitude of complex factors influencing ill health.

The federal government attempted to intervene in medical education much more in the sixties and seventies than ever before, in order to control the number of physicians, their specialties, their practice locations, and their medical paradigm for the benefit of improving the nation's health. Under the guise of cooperation and commitment to the public, medical schools accepted large amounts of taxpayers' dollars, while making no fundamental or permanent changes in the medical education system. Most observers would agree that liberal reforms in medical education did occur in the last two decades. Through these reforms medical schools assuaged demands that medical education accept a partial responsibility for the inequities and inadequacies of the health care system. It could be argued that had the medical schools not been cooperative in changing some aspects of the medical education structure, the public demand for a different type of practitioner would have been intensified. Mounting public pressure could have augmented support for a rational national health plan. Lasting basic changes in the training of health professionals and in service delivery might have been forced.

Instead, what we have today is a continuing problem of geographic maldistribution, rising costs of health care, poor health statistics for the medically indigent and minorities, a projected oversupply of physicians in some areas, and a government retreating from an active role in the medical education process and withdrawing support for social programs. In the last two decades, in short, medical institutions benefited substantially from federal monies but the public's health derived little lasting benefit.

The liberal reforms of the last two decades may have made future physicians a bit more humane than before, and one could argue that we are better off because of this. But are we really? Did we actually lose an opportunity to fundamentally change an inadequate system because we saw the possibility of some improvement without as much struggle?

The question for the future is whether we, as a nation, are willing to continue accepting small, potentially inconsequential changes in the medical education and health care system, or whether we are willing to challenge the powerful conservative institutions of medical education and to demand that they be responsive to our health needs. In large measure, those same medical institutions are supported through taxpayers' dollars. It is our health that is at stake. How many more decades can we wait?

7.

affirmative action
in medicine:

MONEY BECOMES THE ADMISSIONS
CRITERION OF THE 1980s

Hal Strelnick

Richard Younge

Integrating the nation's medical schools became a part of the civil rights agenda only in the late 1960s. Equal opportunity in medical education was not addressed for more than a decade after the 1954 Supreme Court decision that forbade segregated schools. The number of medical students attending segregated schools remained unchanged during this period. Although black people constituted 12 percent of the U.S. population, black students never filled more than 2.5 percent of all medical school places, most of them in the "black medical schools."

The health problems of recruits to Great Society programs, such as the Job Corps, revealed yet again the poor health status of minority communities. Earlier in the 1960s, congressional hearings on the programs sponsored by the Office of Economic Opportunity's (OEO) "War on Poverty" had provided evidence of inadequate health care for poor and minority people in the United States. The OEO-funded health centers established to address these problems and several urban medical schools were the objects of significant community pressure for minority professionals and stressed the need to desegregate health professional education. Some universities felt such pressure from their own students. Beyond the principles of equal opportunity, the demonstrated need for health care in poor and minority communities, a shortage of health workers to fulfill that need, and an ideology that tied economic development to the upward mobility of individuals provided a major impetus to integrate medical education. The underlying assumption has remained that equality and economic development would be achieved by individual efforts toward upward mobility.

A BRIEF HISTORY OF
RACISM IN MEDICINE

The roots of the problem of affirmative action for medical education actually reach back to an earlier era of social reform that redirected American medical education toward the reforms associated with Abraham Flexner's report to the Carnegie Foundation. The report's impact on foundation funding resulted in the closing of almost half of the medical schools in the United States, among them five of the seven schools educating predominately black physicians.[1] Only Meharry and Howard among the black medical schools survived this transition to the scientific training of highly specialized physicians. Today's shortage and maldistribution of primary care physicians are, in part, consequences of the Flexnerian reforms. These reforms profoundly changed the class background of those trained to become physicians, eliminating poorer part-time and night students and closing down proprietary "diploma mills" that "overproduced" doctors for a profit.[2] In the sixty years since Flexner, the proportion of medical students from working-class and poor families has been fixed like an indelible quota at 15 percent.[3] This heritage led to the sadly ironic situation that the physician-to-population ratio among black Americans in 1974, twenty years after *Brown* v. *Board of Education,* was actually worse than it had been in the 1940s.[4]

Medicine has not earned the exemplary professional status that it often claims in regard to its own history of racial discrimination. In 1948, one-third of all medical schools were officially closed to blacks, and quotas limited black enrollment at others. As recently as 1963, five American medical schools were still officially closed to blacks.[5] Not until 1964, the year when the Civil Rights Act was passed, did the American Medical Association prohibit racially discriminatory membership policies.[6] Not until 1969 did all of the nation's medical schools enroll more black students than did Howard and Meharry alone. Racial prejudice and institutional racism did not end with the 1960s. In 1980, in a poll conducted by the official journal of the Association of County Medical Societies, deans of American medical schools voted the nation's three predominantly minority medical schools (Howard, Meharry, and University of

Puerto Rico) the three worst in the nation.[7] In 1981, the Institute of Medicine published a study entitled *Health Care in the Context of Civil Rights,* which concluded "that race is associated with differences in the use of health services . . . that do not mirror differences in need" and that "a variety of forms of racial . . . segregation exist in American health care."[8] Although de jure discrimination has ended, individual and institutional de facto discrimination persists.

A BRIEF HISTORY OF AFFIRMATIVE ACTION

Affirmative action in medical education is rooted in larger political and social movements. FDR's Fair Employment Practices Commission was created in 1941, following a threatened march on Washington by A. Phillip Randolph and other black leaders. The presidential directive ordered an end to racial discrimination in federal hiring and empowered the commission to investigate compliance with the order.

Amid a renascent civil rights movement in the 1960s, President Lyndon Johnson extended equal employment coverage through Executive Orders 11246 and 11375. These prohibit discrimination in employment by all employers holding federal contracts and require affirmative action programs by all government contractors and subcontractors receiving contracts of more than $50,000 and employing more than fifty persons. Title VI of the Civil Rights Act of 1964 forbids discrimination against students on the basis of race, color, or national origin. Title VII, as amended by the Equal Employment Opportunity Act of 1972, forbids employment discrimination on the basis of race, color, national origin, religion, or sex by any employer of fifteen or more persons, public or private, whether or not he receives federal funds.

The first federal sex discrimination legislation, the Equal Pay Act of 1963, was also enacted in response to the civil rights movement. It requires equal pay for equal work regardless of sex. In 1972, this was extended to cover executive and professional employees, including college and university faculty.

PHILANTHROPY: THE MARK OF THE FOUNDATIONS

The mark of the Rockefeller Foundation on racial aspects of medical education continued long after its support of the findings of the Flexner report. Over $9 million went to Meharry Medical College between 1916 and 1960. Howard University Medical School received more than $500,000 between 1926 and 1936 before federal support began. The foundation also funded the first residencies and internships available to blacks, at Sydenham Hospital in New York City.[9] Other philanthropic support from the Julius Rosenwald Fund helped develop health centers for blacks at Provident Hospital in Chicago and Flint-Goodridge Hospital in New Orleans. After World War II black physicians around the Provident Hospital created the Provident Medical Associates, which evolved in a few years into the National Medical Fellowship, Inc., which has supported blacks and other ethnic minorities in all phases of preparation for medical education and specialty training. The Rockefeller Foundation responded to the National Medical Foundation's publication in 1952 of its progress report, *Negroes for Medicine,* by funding a study in 1955 on the status of integration in medicine. In the interim the Supreme Court made its unanimous landmark decision in *Brown* v. *Board of Education.*

Forces outside medicine dominated the movement for affirmative action within medicine in the 1960s. Private philanthropy, following the lead of the Rockefeller Foundation, gave support to scholarships; counseling and tutoring; improved science teaching in the predominantly black colleges; special premedical, postbaccalaureate, and summer programs; regional and national identification and referral systems; conferences; and eventually programs for secondary-school and precollege students.[10] As the decade progressed, the federal government displaced the private foundations as the major source of funding. Many of the diverse federal grants programs borrow their underlying ideologies and paradigms from these privately funded pilots. This unofficial partnership between the federal government and foundations continues today largely under the aegis of the Robert Wood Johnson Foundation, the nation's second-richest foundation and the most involved with health and medical care.

THE RESPONSE OF ACADEMIC MEDICINE

While individual medical schools developed and participated in these experiments, not until 1970 did academic medicine officially respond to the civil rights movement. As this movement reached higher education, a task force consisting of the Association of American Medical Colleges (AAMC) and a consortium representing the AMA, the American Hospital Association, and the National Medical Association announced in April 1970 an objective of 12 percent "representative" minority enrollment in American medical schools by 1975.[11] The AAMC included blacks, Hispanics, and native Americans in its minority enrollment goal.* The 12 percent figure, however, was roughly the percentage of blacks alone in the U.S. population in 1970. (The combined percentage was about 16 percent.)

Later figures show that American medical schools fell far below this modest, 12 percent goal. Specifically, minority enrollment increased from about 2.5 percent in the academic year 1968–69 to a peak of 8.2 percent in 1974–75. Since then the figure has leveled off at 8 percent, as admissions only replace graduates and withdrawals.

The 1970 AAMC report made several additional recommendations: substantial increases in and coordination of financial aid to minorities; the creation of an "educational opportunity bank" and a network of regional centers to provide health career counseling for minority students; and expansion of the AAMC's Office of Minority Affairs, established in 1969 with grants from the U.S. Office of Economic Opportunity. Seven years later, only the last goal was achieved, according to an HEW-commissioned evaluation.[12] This was largely due to a $1.5 million OEO grant, which the AAMC received to administer some fifty programs for minority students from 1969 to 1973.

A 1978 AAMC report suggested that minorities would have to wait until the year 2000 for parity in medical schools.[13] Although the report lamented the withdrawal of federal support for minorities, both fiscal and philosophical, it focused on the various steps (and, therefore, "hurdles") that minority students encounter as individuals along the path to becoming physicians. The report largely laid blame elsewhere for the failure of medical schools to achieve their own objectives.

REGENTS OF THE UNIVERSITY OF CALIFORNIA *V.* BAKKE

The AAMC report was published during the same month that the Supreme Court announced its *Bakke* decision. The decision was claimed as a victory both by proponents and by opponents of affirmative action, reflecting the lack of unanimity of the Court itself.

---

*Asian minority groups were not among the population included in the AAMC affirmative action programs, because they are not generally underrepresented in the health professions relative to their proportions in the general population. However, they do suffer discrimination and racism in the health care system, as in other aspects of American life. When not otherwise designated, minority-group data in this article include blacks, Hispanics (specifically, mainland Puerto Ricans and Mexican-American Chicanos), and native Americans, reflecting the AAMC data.

No single opinion represented a majority of the justices, and six separate opinions were published. This division of the Court led to two separate five-to-four majorities. The first ordered that Allan Bakke be admitted to the medical school at the University of California at Davis and found its affirmative action program illegal. In the second five-to-four majority, the Court held that some forms of race-conscious admissions procedures are constitutional.

In 1973 and again in 1974, Allan Bakke, a white male with an engineering degree, applied to the UC-Davis medical school and was rejected. He then brought suit in a California state court, arguing that minority candidates with lower grades and test scores were admitted under its special admissions program and that he was being discriminated against because of his race when he was prevented from competing for sixteen seats reserved for "disadvantaged" applicants. He alleged that the school's dual-track admissions program violated the equal-protection clause of the Fourteenth Amendment of the U.S. Constitution, a comparable portion of the California constitution, and Title VI of the Civil Rights Act of 1964. The California state and supreme courts agreed. When the case reached the U.S. Supreme Court, blocs of four justices each voted to sustain and to reverse the lower courts' ruling. Justice Powell agreed with each bloc on different points for different reasons, thus creating the separate majorities.

The Supreme Court has clearly held that under the Fourteenth Amendment and Title VI, race-conscious remedies may be employed where judicial, legislative, or administrative bodies have made findings of past discrimination. The question at stake in *Bakke* was when *voluntary* measures intended to remedy the present effects of past discrimination may take race into account. Justice Powell's opinion, narrower than that of the four justices he joined in the second majority, found admissions efforts using racial categories acceptable only (1) to overcome demonstrated racial bias of standardized tests or grading systems, (2) to produce sufficient doctors who serve primarily certain racial or ethnic communities, and/or (3) to promote student body diversity. Had the medical school advanced any of these arguments (which it did not), the decision might not have been split. An admissions program that would meet Justice Powell's constitutional standard would be "flexible enough to consider all pertinent elements in light of the particular qualifications of each applicant, and to place them on the same footing for consideration, although not necessarily according them the same weight." Thus, race or ethnicity can be considered as one criterion among many for admissions decisions.[14]

Over sixty amicus curiae briefs were filed with the Supreme Court before its decision. Several of these pointed out that facts and arguments favorable to minority interests were not being presented by either Bakke or the university, such as those later itemized by Justice Powell. Some students at UC-Davis even accused the university of arguing its case in such a way as to insure that its affirmative action program would be declared unconstitutional.

THE STATE OF AFFIRMATIVE ACTION IN MEDICAL EDUCATION

What gave rise to charges of reverse discrimination, and what was the impact of the *Bakke* decision? From 1950–51 until 1968–69, black enrollment at the nation's medical schools remained below 2.5 percent, reaching its nadir in 1965–66 at 2.0 percent. Beginning in 1968–69, it started to rise, reaching its zenith in 1974–75, when black enrollment reached 6.3 percent. The total underrepresented minority enrollment reached its zenith in 1974–75 and 1975–76, when 8.2 percent of medical students were black, Chicano, mainland Puerto Rican, or American Indian. Minority students are not evenly distributed among the schools. In 1974–75, only 17.6 percent of all black medical students attended predominantly black schools, compared with 30 percent as recently as 1968–69. By 1979–80, the predominantly black schools (including Morehouse) were again enrolling almost 30 percent of all the new black students.

Absolute numbers are more positive, showing an almost fivefold increase in the total number of underrepresented minority students during the decade of the 1970s, when total enrollment almost doubled. However, the percentage of minority applicants accepted has dropped while the number of applicants has stabilized.

Since the *Bakke* decision little has changed. As of this writing, three classes have been admitted; though showing increased percentages of minorities over those in 1978–79, they remain nearly identical to those of most other years of the decade (except 1974–75). However, it appears that these minorities are increasingly concentrated at fewer schools. In 1976–77, the ten best and the ten worst schools enrolled an average of 18.2 percent and 1.4 percent minority students, respectively; in 1980–81, the best had climbed to 21.2 percent, the worst had fallen to 0.45 percent. The *Bakke* decision thus appears to have been read like a Rorschach test. Institutions committed to affirmative action have continued their pursuit of equality, but their numbers have shrunk; those with little or no commitments have given up their pretense. Progressive and regressive institutional admission patterns have been shown to extend to women and across disciplines into dental and pharmacy schools. Minority enrollment also affects what is actually taught.

The attention paid to ethnic and racial and class differences in disease patterns, health attitudes, and risk factors in the medical school curriculum has been shown to be proportional to minority enrollments despite their importance to all practitioners.

THE FEDERAL ROLE

The schools are not the only party responsible for this apparent limit on the participation of minorities in medicine. The federal government has reflected the changing political atmosphere in its initial support of and recent withdrawal from affirmative action.

The financial barriers to becoming a physician should be obvious. After completing college, students must be prepared for four additional years of study, almost never under conditions that allow part-time work. The expense of training serves not only as an economic but also as a psychological deterrent, compounded by intense competition for admission, lower teacher expectations, and racial admissions bias, both real and perceived. From the beginning of their education in primary and secondary schools through their attendance in college, the poor have less of their own resources to spend on their education, and less government money is spent on them.[15] Faced with financial problems that pose a major barrier to a medical education, minority groups have turned to the federal government for financial support. While the federal response has had a consistently positive impact on minority enrollment in undergraduate education, its impact on medical education has been inconsistent.[16]

In 1952, the President's Commission on the Health Needs of the Nation called attention to shortages in health care personnel and recommended federal aid for medicine, which the Surgeon General's Consultant Group on Medical Education reiterated in 1958. The dramatic launching of Sputnik precipitated the first federal venture into direct student assistance with the National Defense Education Act (1958), the precedent for all subsequent student aid. In 1963, the Kennedy administration enacted a student loan program and a construction-grant program for medical and other health professions, the Health Professions Education Assistance Act (Public Law 88-129). The law was amended in 1964 and 1965 (when Medicare and Medicaid were passed) to extend the student loan program, encourage medical school expansion through a system of grants based on the number of students in a school (called "capitation"), and establish the Health Professions Scholarship program.

The Health Manpower Act of 1968 (Public Law 90-490) integrated all of the previous legislation. From 1964 to 1970, more than

$800 million was appropriated under this legislation, 17 percent going to student financial aid.

In 1971 the Comprehensive Health Manpower Training Act extended the loan and scholarship programs and added loan forgiveness for serving in shortage areas. Efforts to influence specialty choice and geographic distribution and to increase the proportion of minority students were made through special project grants to schools. This included support for projects designed for "identifying, recruiting, and selecting individuals from disadvantaged backgrounds." These programs were to facilitate entry of disadvantaged students, provide counseling and other services to retain them, provide preadmission programs, and publicize sources of financial aid.

Almost immediately after the passage of this legislation, a reexamination of federal health manpower policy began. The "doctor shortage" came to be understood as a maldistribution of physicians by specialty and geography. But the reassessment still did not address language and cultural barriers to health care. Nor did it consider the evidence that low-income students traditionally choose primary care practices (even without incentives or obligation) or that professionals of all racial and ethnic groups serve largely their own communities.[17]

After five years a consensus emerged that resulted in the Health Professions Education Assistance Act (HPEAA) of 1976 (Public Law 94-484). As amended in 1977, its major student financial assistance programs include the following: National Health Service Corps (NHSC) scholarships, Health Professions Student Loans (HPSL), Scholarships for Exceptional Financial Need (EFN), and Health Education Assistance Loans (HEAL).

The goal of direct student financial assistance has been to "increase access of students from all income levels to health professional careers" and thus to stimulate applications that would then allow the schools to be more selective and improve quality.[18] From 1965 to 1973, a total of $295.3 million was allocated for loans and scholarships to the health professions schools for students with "exceptional financial need." Linking access to increased competition did inflate grades and test scores, but it actually reduced the representation of low-income students between 1963 and 1967.[19] It proved a windfall for affluent students and for the schools.

Between 1970–71 and 1974–75, successful political pressure for higher minority enrollments dramatically increased funding of the scholarship and loan programs and produced a "filter-down" effect of additional aid to minority students. For example, in 1971, 40 percent of blacks, 34 percent of native Americans, 27 percent of those with Spanish surnames, and 26 percent of Asians received federal scholarships, compared with 22 percent for all medical students.[20] As a result, the proportion of medical students from low-income backgrounds increased 25 percent and the proportion from families with incomes over $25,000 decreased 28 percent during this five-year period.[21]

In the mid-1970s the backlash set in. Between the academic years 1973–74 and 1975–76, combined support for affirmative action through the Bureau of Health Manpower decreased almost $103 million. A study assessing affirmative action efforts for DHEW noted a direct correspondence between federal funding and minority enrollment:

> . . . minority first-year enrollment has followed the same pattern of change as the levels of Bureau of Health Manpower funding except for an apparent one year delay. The sharp increase in BHM support in 1973–74 was reflected in increased minority student enrollment during the 1974–75 academic year. Similarly, the drop in BHM funding to below the Fiscal Year 1973 level appeared to result in a significant drop in the number of nonrepeating first-year minority students enrolled in U.S. medical schools. Thus, the substantial changes in the two most recent Fiscal Years, after a generally increasing trend of funds support, appears to have had major effects on the enrollment levels of minority students in medical education.[22]

Decreasing capitation and financial aid and increasing inflation have made schools even more reluctant to admit low-income and minority students. Minority programs, as usual, were on "soft money" and lacked institutional support. The headlines appropriately began reading, "Money Becoming Admissions Criterion."[23]

Over the last decade total expenses have risen far more quickly than loans or scholarships, so increasing amounts must be paid from student and family resources. Tuition in some schools is more than $10,000 per year. At the same time, while the number of students who must share these resources has risen, the scholarship programs concentrate the total available support among fewer students.

While the NHSC scholarship program has not always succeeded in targeting its resources to those with greatest financial need, it has attempted to refine the criteria for awarding scholarships to those most likely to serve in underserved communities. Despite criteria blind to race, sex, and financial need which it inherited from a *Bakke*-sensitive Congress, the NHSC scholarship program has succeeded in targeting and supporting minority medical students in excess of their proportion of the total enrollment. According to a former chief medical officer of the NHSC, "No minority applicant has ever been turned down." The effort, then, by the Reagan administration to eliminate the NHSC scholarship program altogether will have a potentially devastating effect on minority enrollments—an impact dwarfing that of the *Bakke* decision without so much as a footnote, let alone a headline.

A rationale for the Reagan administration's reduction of federal support for medical education comes from the prediction of a "doctor glut" by the Graduate Medical Education National Advisory Committee (GMENAC). This committee, impaneled by the HPEAA of 1976, was to advise the secretary of DHEW (now DHHS) on the number of physicians needed in the United States, their appropriate specialty distribution, the means for improving their geographic distribution, the appropriate finance mechanisms for graduate medical education, and the strategies for implementing the recommendations. Their final, seven-volume report was submitted to Secretary Patricia Harris in September 1980. In it, the committee predicted an excess of 70,000 physicians by 1990 and of 145,000 by 2000.[24]

Of the forty recommendations of the GMENAC report, only that dealing with the predicted physician excess has received much attention. Its recommendations most pertinent to the question of minority enrollments were, in fact, incorporated in the report's cover letter from its chairperson, Dr. Alvin R. Tarlov, who wrote that GMENAC sought to achieve "a balance between supply and requirements of physicians in the 1990's, while assuring that programs to increase the representation of minority groups in medicine are advanced to broaden the applicant pool with respect to socioeconomic status, age, sex, and race. . . ."[25] Recommendation No. 26 specifically addressed affirmative action:

> Greater diversity among the medical students should be accomplished by promoting more flexibility in the requirements for admission; by broadening the characteristics of the applicant pool with respect to socioeconomic status, age, sex, and race by providing loans and scholarships to help achieve these goals; and by emphasizing, as role models, women and underrepresented minority faculty members.[26]

After the Reagan election victory in November 1980, Secretary Harris, the first black and first woman secretary of DHHS, rejected the unanimous recommendation of GMENAC to extend its charter or establish a successor. Washington observers believe that she thought that GMENAC would hurt affirmative action in a political climate in which only one of its forty recommendations was heard.

The Reagan administration ignored the report's recommendations (which call for an increased federal role) and capitalized on its prediction of a doctor surplus to justify cutbacks in medical education in general. Federal intervention, they argued, is the problem, not the solution to the nation's health needs. Arguments raised during the Nixon administration resurfaced, questioning the legitimacy of public support for medical education at all when physicians are assured such large incomes.

The Omnibus Budget Reconciliation Act of 1981 (Public Law 97-35) largely adopted the Reagan administration's cutbacks, making only cosmetic modifications. For example, while National Health Service Corps scholarships were not eliminated, no funds were appropriated for the 550 new positions authorized. All capitation grants to health professional schools were ended. In 1982, the Reagan administration wanted additional reductions, asking for the elimination of the Exceptional Financial Need scholarships for the poorest 2 percent of the medical students, the National Direct Student Loans, the Health Professional Student Loans, and graduate and professional eligibility for Guaranteed Student Loans. The latter alone supported 72 percent of medical students, and all three loan programs accounted for $228 million in medical student borrowing in 1980–81. Medical students were expected to finance their training with Health Education Assistance Loans (HEAL), at 3.5 percent above the current treasury rate (about 19.5 percent), and Auxiliary Loans to Assist Students (ALAS), at 14 percent interest, without federal subsidies during school years. The mean debt for medical students is expected to exceed $25,000 by 1983 if these measures are passed. Combined with inflated tuitions, the prospect of such indebtedness will have a profound impact not only on the number of underrepresented minorities but also on the specialty choice and practice location of all medical graduates, exacerbating the already acute specialty and geographic maldistribution of physicians in the United States.

A REVIEW OF THE PROGRAMS SUPPORTING AFFIRMATIVE ACTION IN MEDICAL EDUCATION

Programs supporting affirmative action have largely shared an underlying assumption that progress will come in correcting the "deficits" in individuals rather than in institutional or systemic racism. A series of myths, couched in the terms of "liberal" social science, have served as the rationale for these programs. The eight dominant myths, which we have empirically challenged at length elsewhere, are the following:[27]

1) blacks and other minority students have lower aspirations and less motivation than whites do;

2) blacks have a higher attrition rate in colleges in health careers than whites do;

3) recruitment of minorities to medicine should begin in high school or earlier;

4) the pool of college undergraduates and minority applicants is not large enough to achieve representative minority enrollment in medicine;

5) in order to admit more minority students, medical schools will have to lower their standards;

6) there has been a uniform and comprehensive effort to recruit and retain minority students and faculty in U.S. medical schools, that is, everything that can be done has been done;

7) there is no evidence that minority members would better serve the health needs of the nation than whites would; and

8) the federal government is doing everything in its power to support affirmative action in medicine.

These myths provide an ideological framework in which to examine efforts to address the minority individual's "hurdles" on the road to becoming a physician.

Decreasing Attrition along the Educational Pathway

Several barriers face students progressing toward careers in medicine.[28] Preventing minority students from dropping out en route from primary school to medical school has been the goal of many programs, based on the premise that proportional representation can be achieved by increasing the pool of qualified applicants.[29] Many urban and rural primary and secondary schools with high minority enrollment frequently cannot provide students with the skills to succeed in college. These schools lack the financial base to provide good academic training. Often, minority students receive inappropriate counseling and take vocational instead of science courses. Failure to advance from college to medical school has also been attributed to low degree aspirations,[30] to lack of social integration, such as contacts with faculty members,[31] and to inadequate finances.[32]

Programs that have been developed to recruit primary and secondary students to medical careers have focused on academic enrichment, the identification of physician aspirants, and their encouragement by providing role models. These programs have provided academic enrichment in the sciences in order to insure that minority students have the prerequisites for medical school admission.

Precollege Programs

The National Scholarship Service and Fund for Negro Students (NSSFNS) observed in 1948 that poor preparation of blacks in high school prevented them from attending college and ultimately medical school.[33] The proportion of blacks completing high school has risen from one-third to three-fourths since the NSSFNS report.[34] The number of black high school graduates has increased, but the problem for minority students remains that the high school diploma does not guarantee adequate preparation.

After its study, the NSSFNS began an academic enrichment program for junior high school students in Harlem. In 1963, the program served as a model for one sponsored by the Provident Clinical Society of Brooklyn. This group of black health professionals developed a program to encourage minority students in a Bedford-Stuyvesant junior high school to stay in school. Members of the clinical society served as big brothers (and sisters) to the students during their high school years. The students were invited to visit the members' offices in order to observe medical or dental practice. Of the thirty-six students who participated, 89 percent finished high school and 80 percent entered college. The program demonstrated that long-term support and guidance can increase the proportion of minority children who finish high school and enter college.[35]

Similar programs have been developed in Atlanta,[36] Arizona,[37] and Texas.[38] Programs directed at secondary and primary students have, for the most part, been small in scope. They have attempted to improve the quality of the education of a few, select students and to stimulate their interest in health careers. They have not altered the underlying problem; many inner-city and rural schools do not provide minority students with good academic training.

College Level Programs

Some minority students who start college wanting to become physicians change their minds before graduating. Between 1970 and 1976, proportionately more black, Latin, and native American freshmen than white freshmen wanted to become physicians. Fewer of them actually went on to become medical school applicants.[39] Attrition during the college years contributes to minority underrepresentation in medicine.[40] Many programs attempt to stimulate and maintain minority undergraduate interest in careers in medicine.

Students in predominantly black schools represent a large pool of potential applicants. Several programs in the 1960s attempted to improve their science teaching and to provide their students with summer experiences at the larger, stronger schools. The Harvard Health Careers Summer Program began in 1969. Students from black colleges in the South spent eight weeks at Harvard doing intensive work in sciences. Students also spent a few days a week working in a clinical setting.[41]

The Woodrow Wilson Teaching Internship program began in 1963, sending graduate fellows to teach for one year at black colleges in the South. This approach sought to improve science teaching at these schools.[42]

Medical schools have been active in undergraduate premedical recruitment programs. During the academic year 1974–75, ninety-seven schools responded to a survey about their recruitment activities. Three-quarters of them said that they sponsored visits for undergraduates. One-third had summer recruitment programs designed to introduce prospective applicants to medical careers, the medical school, and to enhance their science skills.[43] Many of these programs are funded by Health Career Opportunity Grants which were cut 14 percent in 1981.

Changing the Medical School Admissions Process

During the 1960s and 1970s, medical schools came under increasing pressure to change how they chose their students. Medical schools sought to diversify the sociocultural mix of their students, and to select students who would opt for primary care specialties. Admissions committees also faced an increasing number of applicants with ever higher GPAs and MCAT scores. Attempts to modify admissions criteria led to the development of a new MCAT and to the exploration of various noncognitive measures to predict medical student and physician performance, and to wider, greater representation of minority-group members, students, and community representatives on admission committees.

The MCAT

The Medical College Admission Test (MCAT), developed in the late 1940s, has posed an important barrier to minority applicants. Originally designed to predict which applicants would complete their medical education, the MCAT did not predict academic achievement in medical school, residency, or medical practice.[44] The MCAT has been criticized for stressing recall of information rather than ability to reason and use information.

Minorities and students from lower socioeconomic classes consistently had lower MCAT scores. Race was a strong predictor of low scores. Black students from all socioeconomic groups scored lower on the old MCAT than did whites.[45] This finding supported the contention that the MCAT was racially and culturally biased.

The AAMC established the Medical College Admissions Assessment Program (MCAAP) in 1972. It recommended the development of a test to replace the MCAT.[46] The new MCAT, first administered in 1979, stresses problem solving and ability to recognize relevant data. It deemphasizes knowledge of facts, and attempts to measure skills relevant to the medical school basic-science curriculum and to clinical medical practice.[47] Minority-group representatives contributed to and reviewed the development of the new MCAT. Minority students continue to score below whites on the new MCAT. Simply changing a standardized test cannot compensate for a legacy of unequal educational opportunity.

Med-MAR

Other changes in the admissions process include the Medical Minority Applicant Registry (Med-MAR). Introduced in 1969, this program circulates basic biographical information about underrepresented minority applicants to admissions officers at all U.S. medical schools.[48] Students may identify themselves as belonging to an underrepresented minority when they take the MCAT, or by contacting the AAMC. The schools receive a Med-MAR listing twice a year and may initiate further communication with the students. Since 1969, the AAMC has also published *Minority Student Opportunities in United States Medical Schools* every other year. Each medical school may disseminate information concerning its minority recruitment and retention programs in this publication.

New Admissions Criteria

Personality traits used in conjunction with cognitive variables can predict medical school performance.[49] Compassion, sensitivity, and moral judgment contribute to one's qualification to be a physician. These attributes are not measured by MCATs and grade point averages. Research done at the University of Maryland shows that for minority students, a positive self-concept, realistic self-appraisal, long-range goals, leadership experience, community service, and preparation to deal with racism strongly predict academic success.[50]

The admissions interview provides information about an applicant's noncognitive qualifications. Most medical schools rely heavily on MCAT scores, GPA, and the interview in making their decision.[51] The Simulated Minority Admissions Exercise (SMAE), developed by the AAMC, attempts to reduce bias in the interview.[52]

Admissions Committees

Schools involving minority-group members on admissions committees have been most successful recruiting minority students.[53] A survey of medical school admissions committees found that among the seventy-three schools responding, 55 percent had at least one minority member. Of 853 committee members surveyed, 5.0 percent were black, 0.7 percent Puerto Rican, and 0.4 percent Mexican American.[54]

Ninety schools responded to a pre-Bakke survey on affirmative action programs in 1977.[55] Sixteen percent had separate committees to consider minority applicants. Seventy-five percent of the schools said that they had modified their admissions criteria to increase the number of underrepresented minority students, but most of the schools declined to state how they modified their admissions criteria.

Increasing First-Year Positions

The Carnegie Commission recommended in 1970 that the number of medical school positions be increased and that schools develop plans to recruit minorities and women in conjunction with expansion plans.[56] Because the number of first-year positions increased, no fewer white males are admitted now although more minorities and women have been entering medical school.[57]

Retention — The Medical School Years

The potential minority physician, having negotiated the educational pathway from elementary school to medical school acceptance, still faces formidable obstacles. The medical school retention rate for underrepresented minority students today is about the same as it was for majority students twenty years ago. Attrition at medical school begins before the first day of classes. Between 1970 and 1976, 319 minority students who were accepted to medical school never enrolled.[58]

Many medical schools offer pre-enrollment summer programs for minority students.[59] The pre-enrollment programs that have been developed have several objectives in common. The programs are generally open to all students, but they are used predominantly by minority students. They provide the student with an orientation to the medical school environment, and introduce the students to the first-year curriculum and faculty. "The programs anticipate the worst and the best. The worst being the medical school environment, and the best being the strength of the students."[60] The first-year basic-science curriculum may be lightened by the inclusion of some preliminary work in anatomy or in other courses during the summer. Perhaps most important, the summer programs provide students with an opportunity to begin to form networks of social and academic support.

Social Supports

Minority students in predominantly white institutions experience social and academic stress. An unpublished 1973 survey of students at the University of North Carolina School of Medicine was cited in a study of stress and health.[61] The school's insensitivity to black students' cultural backgrounds, financial problems, lack of black role models, negative faculty attitudes toward minority students, and poor undergraduate preparation were common problems. Minority students had higher perceived stress, and they felt that they had fewer sources of social support. This perceived lack of support clearly indicates the importance of peer networks.

Women and minority students are often excluded from part of the social process by which one learns to be a physician, what has been called medical professionalization. The criticism that minority students are distant, hard to teach, or not self-critical may result from their exclusion from this informal but important aspect of medical education.

Organizations of minority medical students have helped to establish support networks at schools that have enough minority students to form a group. Student organizations whose membership is predominantly nonminority have also been strong advocates for programs to recruit and retain minority students. The Student National Medical Association, the American Medical Student Association, ASPIRA, and La Raza Medical Association each have health careers opportunity grants that provide instruction and counseling for minority students in premedical programs and medical school.[62]

During the late 1960s, community groups demanded that medical schools train more minority students. The College of Medicine and Dentistry of New Jersey at Newark is an example of a school that has successfully recruited and retained minority students. Since the school's opening, following the urban uprising of 1968, its Board of Concerned Citizens has influenced the policies of the school with respect to minority students, faculty, and employees.[63] Many minority students at CMDNJ-Newark feel that community support has played a vital role in maintaining affirmative action programs at the school.

Administrative Supports

Offices of minority student affairs have been established at about half of the medical schools. They may be involved in recruitment programs, the admission process, and securing financial aid. They can provide an important source of personal and social support for students, but an AAMC study of eight schools revealed that the existence of an office of minority affairs is neither necessary nor sufficient for a successful minority recruitment and retention program.[64]

Positions in the offices of minority affairs often provide the few administrative and faculty positions held by minorities in many medical schools. While students identify lack of appropriate role models as a serious problem, medical schools have not succeeded at recruiting minority faculty members.[65] Like medical students, minority faculty are concentrated at three schools. Forty-five percent of the underrepresented minority faculty members are at Howard, Meharry, and the University of Puerto Rico.[66] Underrepresented minorities hold about 7.7% of all medical school faculty positions. Few minorities hold basic-science, full-time clinical, or senior academic positions.[67]

Medical schools expanded their curriculum to include information on the social factors that influence the work of physicians and the health of their patients. A survey of U.S. medical schools in 1976 showed that curriculum emphasis on minority health issues correlated with minority enrollment and retention.[68] Minority students may be attracted to schools that offer such courses, or their presence at a school may reveal the need to include minority health issues in the curriculum. Informal teaching about minority and women's experiences in the health care system still occurs during the clinical years on the hospital wards as time-honored stereotypes pass from teacher to student.

Programs to change faculty and majority student attitudes about underrepresented minority students have seldom been reported.[69] Surveys of black and white students and administrators at predominantly white institutions revealed divergent perceptions of factors that make a particular school attractive to black applicants, and of the types of problems that women and minorities face on campus.[70]

The potential for misunderstanding exists because blacks view whites' attitudes opposite to the way whites view themselves. Schools have not attempted programs to enable students, faculty, and administrators to clarify their expectations of and attitudes toward one another. One report of a medical school's tutorial program for students who failed basic-science courses began to address this issue.[71] Students and faculty explicitly stated their attitudes, assumptions, and expectations about each other instead of assuming that they knew what the other group was thinking. Only then did effective teaching and learning begin to take place.

FINANCING AFFIRMATIVE ACTION — THE FOUNDATIONS

Foundations have participated in expanding opportunities for minority students seeking careers in medicine. Their contributions for the support of programs for minorities peaked in 1972, at $9.5 million. The total grants reported in 1977 declined to $1.2 million, the lowest level of support during the 1970s.[72]

The Macy Foundation supported a wide range of minority recruitment and retention programs. These programs included recruitment activities by medical schools, basic-science enrichment programs for high school students, support of offices for minority student affairs, and the Haverford College Post-Baccalaureate program. The Macy Foundation also supported the AAMC task force that wrote the report *Expanding Educational Opportunities in Medicine for Blacks and Other Minority Students.* The Ford, Rockefeller, Sloan, Grant, and van Ameringen foundations have also funded similar minority support programs.

Two sources of private money for direct student aid are National Medical Fellowships and the Robert Wood Johnson Foundation. National Medical Fellowships began in 1946 as a program to support specialty training for black physicians.[73] The NMF has distributed over $16 million to more than 4,000 physicians and medical students during the past thirty-five years. As its foundation support has declined, NMF has come to rely more on corporations and past scholarship recipients for support.

In 1972, the Robert Wood Johnson Foundation committed $3.5 million for four years to medical, dental, and osteopathic schools to underwrite loan and scholarship awards for minority and women students. This total of $14 million provided less than 5 percent of the student aid funds from all sources during those four years.[74] The RWJF supported a guaranteed student aid program that began in 1977 and provided loans to students who could obtain no other

sources of financial aid. This $30 million program guaranteed loans
for 8,000 students. In April 1981, the RWJF announced the end of
this program.[75]

FINANCING AFFIRMATIVE ACTION — THE FEDERAL ROLE

The first federal project grants to influence specialty choice and
geographic distribution of physicians and to increase the proportion
of minority students were awarded under the Comprehensive
Health Manpower Training Act of 1971. Health Career Opportunities (HCOP) grants supported projects to identify, recruit, and select
individuals from disadvantaged backgrounds. The Health Professions Education Assistance Act of 1976 continued to authorize
HCOP grants through fiscal 1980. Between 1972 and 1979, 236
projects received $72 million.[76] Grant recipients included medical
schools and undergraduate institutions, undergraduate science enrichment programs, community groups, and minority medical professional organizations. The programs supported by these grants
provide medical career counseling to secondary and undergraduate
students, financial aid, and other support services for medical students.

Minority students rely heavily on scholarship aid to finance their
education. Federal scholarship programs have an enormous impact
on minority recruitment and retention. The Carnegie Commission
and the AAMC Task Force both recommended expanded federal
support of undergraduate education in order to reduce defections
from the medical education pathway. Sixty-six percent of blacks
and 53 percent of other underrepresented minorities, compared
with 32.8 percent of whites, begin medical school in debt.[77] A
national survey of 7,261 medical students in 1974–75 revealed that
those who applied for financial assistance were disproportionately
underrepresented minorities, married, and from rural communities.[78]

Cutbacks of federal aid to medical schools and for medical students have clear implications for affirmative action programs. Phas-
ing out need-based scholarship and loan programs in the face of
rising tuition establishes the policy that medical education is only
for those who can afford it. Even the predominantly black schools
may have to favor those students who can afford to pay their own
way. The Reagan administration's budget completely eliminated
capitation grants to medical schools in fiscal year 1982, an $84
million reduction, despite the GMENAC report that recommends a
continuation of loan and scholarship programs to increase the number of minority and women physicians.[79] Medical schools say that

affirmative action is expensive because recruitment and retention programs face elimination as the schools lose federal support. The DHHS has already observed the consequences of federal aid cutbacks on affirmative action in its 1977 report, quoted above, when first year enrollments fell a year after earlier budget cuts.[80]

CONCLUSIONS

The programs to increase the number of minority physicians that were directed at primary-school, secondary-school, and premedical college students succeeded in increasing the absolute number of minority medical students. They have not sustained the rate of increase or the percentage of minority medical students. The number of minority students rose as these programs identified, tutored, and supported individuals progressing along the educational pathway. Inadequate primary- and secondary-school systems produce more minority students than all the programs combined can help. These programs clearly help some students get into medical school, but they have not changed the education system. This has limited their success.

Some significant structural changes in medical education have occurred. The changes in the MCAT and admissions criteria can improve the chances of some minority applicants but cannot compensate for a legacy of inferior education. The curricular changes produce a more roundly educated physician but probably do not contribute much to reducing minority attrition.

Reforms in medical education during the 1960s and 1970s that aimed at representative enrollments for racial and ethnic minorities sought to correct "deficits" in individuals. They have not, on the whole, addressed the institutional and systemic roots of minority underrepresentation. Affirmative action in medicine is still largely seen as a benefit for individuals and not for the larger community despite ample evidence that training minority physicians helps meet the nation's health manpower needs and that the curricular changes described above benefit all medical students. Successful affirmative action seems to depend on a critical mass of minority students and faculty involved in the admissions and retention process, thus posing a sticky chicken-and-egg question: Without minority students and faculty, how can an institution succeed in recruiting minority students and faculty? The content of the medical curriculum reflects institutional commitments to affirmative action yet the sociocultural factors in medicine are important for all clinicians and should be taught at all medical schools, not just at those with large minority enrollments. Most affirmative action programs have relied too heavily on "soft money"—external public and private funding

—and have not been institutionalized. As federal commitments to medical education and research wane, and as tuition skyrockets and "money becomes an admissions criterion," medical schools will be hard pressed to maintain those commitments to minorities that they have had. Expensive, high-risk minority students will not be in demand.

The federal role has been a complex one, both aggravating the problem of access through increased competition and providing financial support to individual students, experimental programs, and institutions. Its "soft money" has allowed institutions to tack on programs (with their not insignificant overhead) without requiring significant institutional change. The future of vital federal financial aid is in great doubt. As prospects of a doctor surplus overtake the continuing specialty and geographic maldistribution as the major health manpower problem, minority students will find less and less support for their special financial and personal needs. The plateau that minority enrollment has reached since its zenith, in 1975, will give way to a clear decline and representative enrollment postponed well beyond the year 2000.

The *Bakke* decision itself has proven to be an institutional Rorschach test open to interpretation along the lines of institutional interests and commitments. *Bakke* proved less of a landmark decision than one marking the closing of an era.

The many experimental programs of the 1960s and 1970s are not without value, although mainly descriptive studies of them exist, making no analytic comparisons of their effectiveness. While studies on individual students abound, few institutional factors have been examined in assessing which approaches succeed and which fail in recruiting, admitting, retaining, and graduating minority medical students. This will certainly be fertile ground for research as limited funding and conservative policies make cost effectiveness the major criterion for continued support. We suspect that programs that strengthen minority students' social support networks, emphasize their noncognitive strengths, and benefit all—not just minority students—will prove most effective.

IMPLICATIONS

The GMENAC report called the period from 1955 to 1980 "The Era of Debate and Funding of Health Manpower." During these years, a "pipeline" of scholarship recipients holding service obligations was established that will be producing doctors for ten years to come. These physicians have obligations to serve in America's health manpower shortage areas, but the funding limits on the NHSC and the difficulties of private practice in such communities promise to perpetuate the discontinuous care to which poor communities have been forced to adapt. A disproportionate number of these graduates will be black, Latino, and native American. While many of them may desire to settle in the communities in which they serve, the economic constraints and practice burdens that the current system imposes are likely to shorten their stays. Thus, a program designed to provide comprehensive and continuous care to underserved communities will ultimately reproduce the discontinuities of the emergency wards and clinics that it was to replace.

Despite the growth in the absolute numbers of majority and minority physicians and the predictions of a doctor surplus in the GMENAC report, low-income and predominantly minority communities will still suffer from shortages of health resources and will continue to depend upon indifferent and impersonal institutional care. Public support for community health and migrant health centers has diminished, further exacerbating the problems of underserved communities. Some minority physicians who have completed their postgraduate training and are seeking work in such underserved communities are already reporting that primary care positions are not available unless major relocations are considered. This problem of a contracting job market for minority physicians who have planned to serve "their people" may further disillusion minority physicians as well as "their" communities, the indifference of the market being easily interpreted as just another manifestation of racism.

Although it might have been expected that medical faculties would begin to reflect the growing numbers (but not percentages) of minority physicians, this has not occurred. The presence of minorities on medical faculties has not kept up with their general growth during the decade. With the waning federal support for medical education in general, faculty opportunities for minority scientists and academic physicians will certainly decrease. This will have the secondary effect of providing fewer advocates and role models within the medical schools—roles already shown to be essentials of successful affirmative action programs. Thus, a vicious downward spiral is reinitiated.

Lack of minority faculty combined with growing numbers of minority interns, residents, and fellows poses special problems of racism. In the apprenticeship educational model so characteristic of specialty and subspecialty training, evaluation and advancement become almost entirely dependent upon the subjective opinions of senior house staff and attending physicians. While much has been written about the minority medical student, little study has been made of minority house staff. As the current structure of postgraduate training isolates individuals from all but their specialty peer group, minority residents who have depended upon their peers for coping with college and medical school may face special problems.

The very limited success of the affirmative action effort in medicine suggests the limited extent to which the public agenda for equal opportunity may be imposed upon largely private institutional imperatives for meritocracy. Even public universities employ the banner of "academic freedom" as insulation against legal demands for equity. With the *Bakke* case, medical education quite innocently became the battleground for the legal confrontation between American ideologies of meritocracy and equal opportunity. Those changes that did take place in medical education, however, came largely from forces outside of academic medicine—from the civil rights movement, the courts, and federal and state governments. Many of these changes do not seem to be permanent structural changes in medicine and medical education likely to weather escalating costs and the waning of public support. Whether the increased number of minority physicians will prove to be a critical mass for change remains to be seen. Even were all of these physicians to serve in shortage areas, the economic exigencies that created the maldistribution would not yet be addressed.

Affirmative action in medical education never sought to reorganize institutional priorities to serve the public's need but rather tried to groom individuals from minority backgrounds to the schools' needs. Efforts were made to give *individuals* equal opportunity without challenging the legitimacy of the power structure. The marketplace remained the appropriate and legitimate distributor of resources and power, requiring only assurances of "equal opportunity" to remedy inequities and engage the disenfranchised. All these represent the limits of reformism.

The broader lessons to be drawn from this experience include the following:

> 1) private and academic institutions are well protected against attempts to impose a public agenda on them through regulations and incentives that do not at the same time change its power structure and priorities;
>
> 2) lasting change is most likely to come from broader forces outside a given institution or discipline;
>
> 3) lasting change is unlikely to come from an emphasis on individual achievement and programs designed to "improve" individuals to suit institutional needs; rather, structural change implies that institutions have changed to suit the needs of individuals;
>
> 4) efforts for change that address only race or ethnicity, without also grappling with the impact of class and the

economic consequences of race and ethnicity, are likely to effect change that is only "skin deep"; and

5) institutional responses vary considerably with the specific history and conditions of each, rich in contradictions, that make the efforts of committed individuals strategically irreplaceable.

Finally, until changes in the larger society take place that remedy the structural impact of race and class on everything from infant mortality to life expectancy and that color every aspect of American life in between, representative minority enrollments in U.S. medical schools alone will be mere tokenism. Sadly, today, even this very modest goal remains remote, and the American health care system is the poorer for it. Unfortunately, these circumstances will not change until the health care system and society as a whole are organized around meeting the needs of people rather than the marketplace.

8.

the national health service corps and health personnel innovations:

BEYOND POORHOUSE MEDICINE

Fitzhugh Mullan

The story of the American town with no doctor has become a cliché. The problem is a real one and has stimulated enterprising communities all over the country to rent billboards, buy ads in medical journals, hire head-hunting placement agencies, and pay the way of local students to go to medical school in the hopes they will return to lay on hands in their hometown.

The malady is not confined to the countryside. The exodus of physicians from inner-city neighborhoods over the past decades has been profound. In many urban areas patients have only the choice of the county or municipal hospital or of Medicaid mills for their health care. After 5 P.M. and on weekends, the emergency room is their only option. Many institutions—public hospitals not least among them—have likewise had difficulty recruiting and retaining adequate physician staff. County and city health facilities, nursing homes, prisons, state hospitals, and homes for the retarded have all experienced difficulties finding doctors to meet their medical needs.

Much has been written about the "health care crisis" and the "manpower shortage" of the last twenty years. The data and charts from these many commentaries are helpful in understanding the present situation, but they do not tell the whole story. The origins of the current circumstances are deeply rooted in this nation's social history, going back to the beginning of this century. In order to understand the present situation, one must begin with a look at the evolution of medical services since the time of Abraham Flexner.

THE FLEXNER LEGACY

Flexner's report,[1] published in 1910, is well known for its enormous impact on medical education, as has been discussed in the chapter on medical education. Its influence has by no means been limited to medical education, but has borne heavily on the entire delivery of health services in the United States. While Flexner's comments were directed primarily at medical education itself, the upheaval that those changes brought about altered the direction of medical practice from that time on.[2] Flexner's report severely criticized the quality of medical education, pointing out that numerous schools then operative had poor facilities and a threadbare faculty. These institutions aimed to produce doctors quickly, paying little attention to the rapidly accumulating body of modern, scientific information. They were diploma mills, and Flexner recommended that they be closed down. He was a firm believer in the German scientific tradition as embodied in the then new Johns Hopkins University. By way of conclusion, the report suggested that only schools of medicine based in universities were adequate to the challenge of producing physicians.

The American Medical Association (AMA) and major American philanthropic organizations closed ranks behind Flexner, and over the following two decades the number of active medical schools in the United States was halved. Although the absolute number of physicians practicing in the United States during this time did not fall, the physician-to-population ratio decreased significantly, dropping from 149 per 100,000 population in 1909 to 125 per 100,000 in 1930—a decrease of 10 percent.[3] From that point until 1965, the physician-to-population ratio in the country remained relatively fixed. By 1965, however, both medical care and society's expectations had changed to such an extent that the numbers of physicians produced by the post-Flexner medical schools were increasingly insufficient to meet the nation's needs.

The second, quiet legacy of Flexner's work was not to become apparent until many years after the report. By joining medical education to basic science in as formal a way as it did, the report set the stage for the development of specialty medicine. Obviously, Flexner alone cannot be credited with responsibility for the rapid shift away from general practice that occurred in the middle of the twentieth century, but the principles that his report enunciated laid the groundwork for the explosive growth of specialty and subspe-

cialty medicine that, mediated by the medical schools, occurred in
the period following World War II. In the years between 1950 and
1963, the profile of private practitioners shifted from two-thirds in
general practice to two-thirds in specialty practice. Far fewer general physicians were available to treat the public than had previously been the case. The resultant implications for patient care were
considerable and contributed, perhaps even more than the absolute
number of physicians, to the population's perception of a medical
crisis. But both the number of physicians and their style of practice
is in many ways traceable to the wisdom *and* the astigmatism of
Flexner and his followers.

The American Medical Association, as prime spokesman for organized physicians, was content with the static physician-to-population ratio. It was generally opposed to any significant increases in
the pool of available physicians. Doctors' salaries were good, and
conventional wisdom argued that a greater supply of doctors would
diminish the income of individual physicians. The AMA actually
had a policy known informally as professional birth control.[4]

Even though the physician-to-population ratio in the United
States did not, contrary to popular belief, take a dramatic downturn
during the 1950s, there developed a sense that something was different. What had changed was the public perception of what was
needed in the way of physicians. Citizen groups, communities,
politicians, and ultimately physicians themselves increasingly
raised their voices to ask why America had become such a physi-
cian-poor society. The reasons for the emerging problems were
multiple and additive over time. By 1960, medicine had a great deal
more to offer the average patient than it had in the time of Flexner.
The population had responded by calling on the medical system far
more than it had previously. Whereas in 1930 the average American
saw a physician little more than twice a year, annual doctor visits
had reached 4.5 per person by 1964.[5] During the same period,
hospital admissions rose from 56 to 145 per 1,000 population, and
average hospital days from .9 to 1.3 per person per year. Clearly,
health care was a more important part of the agenda of the average
American in the 1960s than it had been three decades earlier.

Not merely did the advance of technology increase utilization of
medical services. The population itself was evolving in directions
that made medical care a more important factor. The growing age,
affluence, and level of education of Americans all changed in a way
that made the demands for medical services greater. The increasingly urban population likewise drew doctors to cities and made
heavy demands on their time.

When these developments are combined with a fixed pool of
physicians with a greatly diminished number of generalists, the

reasons for the "crisis" cease to be obscure. A set number of increasingly technical physicians were treating a relatively older and more urban population for an ever expanding variety of ailments. In a system that was unregulated with respect to physician charges or location, the result was a marked accentuation of the distributional inequities already present. The medically rich got richer, while the medically poor tended to become poorer. Medical disenfranchisement became a reality for many citizens, rural and urban.

THE GROWING DEMAND
FOR CHANGE

In the country's communities, the physician shortage was in no way academic. The billboards, the medical-journal ads, the steady stream of letters to members of Congress, legislators, the AMA, and anybody in authority who would listen were testimony to the problem. By current standards these were not sophisticated lobbies with dues-paying members and offices in Washington. Rather, they were hat-in-hand attempts by individual communities to fill a void in their communal life.

Two political movements of the mid-1960s were also to have a long-term influence on the definition of the physician shortage. These movements would contribute to the specific concept of medical underservice as related to poverty. The two were the civil rights and the student health movements.

By 1964, the civil rights movement in the South had focused its attention on school integration and voter registration. The summer of 1964—the "Mississippi Freedom Summer"—saw hundreds of northern white students go south to staff the projects organized by the Student Non-Violent Coordinating Committee (SNCC) and the Congress of Federated Organizations (COFO). In an effort to provide medical support for the civil rights activities, a number of physicians of liberal and activist persuasion from around the country hastily banded together as the Medical Committee for Human Rights (MCHR). Working with Mississippi-based black doctors, they sent rotating teams of physicians, nurses, and medical students to Mississippi to provide whatever medical support they could. Since civil rights workers were dispersed all over the state and since the actual medical capabilities of the itinerant MCHR teams were limited, they developed a concept—really a tactic—known as "medical presence." This meant a visible turning out at demonstrations, rallies, and marches. The idea was that the activists would be heartened and strengthened by the presence of medical personnel and that potential antagonists, including the police, might be discouraged by the same presence. Moreover, if violence should erupt, the medical workers would be there to provide first aid and perform triage. Therefore, it was obligatory that white coats, doctor bags, and red crosses be made evident at public events as much of the time as possible. Medical presence remained an important function for health care workers and students throughout the civil rights demonstrations in the South and, in later years, in the North. The concept was adopted wholesale by the antiwar movement, in which many of the same individuals later participated.

By 1965, the role of medical personnel in the civil rights movement had matured. MCHR opened a permanent office in Jackson, Mississippi, and assigned volunteer students and nurses to ongoing medical projects in outlying counties. Most of these programs challenged barriers to access to medical care, such as segregated hospitals and racist physicians. Health associations were established and classes in first aid and sex education were provided.[6] Significantly, health care and the right to health care had emerged as important issues for the civil rights movement. As the movement spread and as the national awareness of urban decay became more acute following the urban rebellion of the late 1960s, the provision of health services remained a prominent rallying point for activists and an item of negotiation in confrontations with federal, state, and municipal governments.

During the same period, and often stimulated by the civil rights movement, a growing concern emerged among medical students about the inequities in the medical care in the United States. An interdisciplinary group of students, many of whom were veterans of the civil rights movement, came together in 1965 as the Student Health Organization (SHO).[7] Chapters sprang up around the country, reaching a high point in 1968, when more than 500 students attended the annual national meeting of the SHO. Using student-run lecture series and a spate of local and regional publications, the SHO focused its attention on health care for the poor. Much of the students' energy went into curricular reform at the various schools, which, in many cases, spurred the formation of departments of community medicine. The SHO featured activism and experiential learning. The students organized term-time, community-based health projects as well as more extensive summer projects funded with federal grants that they obtained from the Office of Economic Opportunity and from Project Head Start.

The generation of student leaders that passed through medical school in the latter part of the 1960s, as well as a number of students from other health disciplines, became involved with the health care crisis in general and the absence of services in poor communities in particular. The spirit of idealism, change, and, at times, militancy was infectious. The activists of that time did not fall victim to the

Cadillac-and-country-club elitism of traditional medical practice, nor were they dazzled by the enticements of the high-technology laboratory. Rather they were determined to reverse the growing inequities in health care that they inherited. They felt, reasonably enough, that a nation that could put people on the moon could provide decent medical services for all of its citizens. That was the challenge of the next decade.

Although the civil rights movement and the student health movement gave a certain direction and verve to the debate about the physician shortage, they were by no means the only groups speaking in strong language by the end of the 1960s. In October of 1970, the Carnegie Commission on Higher Education issued a report called *Higher Education and the Nation's Health: Policies for Medical and Dental Education.* [8] The report called for an expansion of the number of places of medical school by 50 percent, for a dramatic increase in the number of nonphysician providers, for an increase in general medical (as opposed to specialty) training, and for the creation of a National Health Service Corps.

NEW LEGISLATION

The mid-1960s were a watershed period for new health legislation. Titles XVIII and XIX of the Social Security Act (Medicare and Medicaid) became law in 1965. Although these programs did nothing to change the numbers of health practitioners, they did alleviate some of the problems of paying for medical care that the old and poor traditionally suffered. From the practitioners' standpoint, Medicare and Medicaid provided reimbursement for patients who had previously been "deadbeats" in the eyes of the profession. These people, to be sure, faced other barriers to access to medical care, but Medicare and Medicaid substantially reduced the financial impediments to their receiving service. Paradoxically, however, Medicare and Medicaid aggravated the general perception of the doctor shortage, because the new programs, without adding practitioners to the work force, stimulated the use of medical services. As a result, traditionally well-served populations as well as newly enfranchised ones experienced mounting difficulties in obtaining physicians' services.

A second area of innovation was the Office of Economic Opportunity's (OEO) Neighborhood Health Centers. Although the Economic Opportunity Act of 1964 was not by any means designed as a piece of health legislation, it quickly became apparent to the OEO leadership that the absence of health care was a significant problem for the poor of the nation. In 1965, three demonstration neighborhood health centers designed to provide comprehensive, one-door health services for disadvantaged neighborhoods were funded. The neighborhood health centers multiplied rapidly during the Johnson administration and tenaciously held their own during the Nixon and Ford years. With the dismantling of the OEO in 1973, the neighborhood centers, significantly, were not closed but were transferred to the Public Health Services as Community Health Centers (CHCs). The program has continued and grown, with appropriations reaching a highpoint of $325 million in 1981. During the same period, the Migrant Health Program was enacted. Initiated by the Migrant Health Act of 1967, this program has provided similar services targeted to seasonal farm workers and migrants. Underserved children have also benefited from the Children and Youth (C&Y) and Maternal and Infant (M&I) care programs that were added to the existing Maternal and Child Health legislation.

From 1973 on, these programs were administratively housed in the Bureau of Community Health Services of the Public Health Service and were managed in a coordinated fashion. Nonetheless, all of these programs had difficulties recruiting and retaining a sufficient number of physicians to meet their needs. Not only did project administrators often have difficulty finding physicians to staff their clinics, but they also had nagging problems with the quality of physicians available to them. Although some American-trained practitioners were comfortable with or interested in practicing in community-run and community-oriented clinics in poor neighborhoods, many were not. As a result, clinic directors often had to resort to part-time physicians, foreign-trained physicians, and short-term physicians who worked temporarily for the clinic while establishing their own practices elsewhere.

Once again the critical period of the mid-1960s saw developments that would begin to address the health manpower problem itself. The first stirring of a federal response to the problem came with the Health Professions Education Assistance Act of 1963, which was followed by further legislation in 1965, 1968, 1971, and 1976. These statutes provided for assistance for medical school construction, student loans, and, ultimately, capitation payments— per capita grants of unrestricted monies to schools, on the basis of the number of students enrolled in the school. The incentives were obvious and effective, especially when combined with a rapidly increasing biomedical-research budget brokered by the National Institutes of Health. The period from the mid-1960s on was an auspicious one for medical school growth: it saw an increase in the number of schools, from 86 in 1960 to 122 in 1978, and a jump in the total medical student enrollment, from 30,000 to 60,000 over the same period.[9] The medical baby boom thus produced has now become apparent in the ranks of active practitioners. In 1979 there were 178 physicians per 100,000 population (compared with the Flexnerian 130), and it is projected that by 1990 there will be more than 220 physicians for the same population.[10]

During the 1970s, once again with the help of federal grants, significant strides were made in the training of nonphysician providers. Although rules governing licensure and certification vary from state to state, it is estimated that 1,800 nurse practitioners, 12,500 physician's assistants, and 2,300 nurse-midwives are currently practicing throughout the United States, many of them in underserved areas. The importance of the nonphysician provider movement can be seen not only in the number of trained professionals that it produces but also in the challenge that it presents to traditional and often ossified patterns of training and practice in medicine. Nonphysician providers have established an impressive record of competence and service during their short history. Objections to nonphysician providers are frequently those of physicians with a pecuniary interest in preventing competition. Rather than promoting new practitioners, subspecialty societies and state licensing authorities have frequently impeded the growth of this movement. Although more voices will surely be raised against them as the medical marketplace becomes more crowded with physicians, the clinical appropriateness and the cost-effectiveness of these professionals argues strongly for their continued growth and development as providers of health care services.

THE ENACTMENT OF THE NATIONAL HEALTH SERVICE CORPS

The most specific federal program designed to deal with the doctor shortage in underserved areas was not enacted until 1970. The Emergency Health Personnel Act was reluctantly signed into law by Richard Nixon on New Year's Eve of that year.[11] The act founded the National Health Service Corps (NHSC), a concept that had been discussed in Washington for some time and that had been the subject of intense behind-the-scenes politicking for two years before its enactment. The idea was a simple one. The first provision of the act stated:

> It shall be the function of an identifiable unit within the (Public Health) Service to improve the delivery of health services to persons living in communities and areas of the United States where health personnel and services are inadequate to meet the health needs of residents of such communities and areas.[12]

Its passage marked the first time that the U.S. Public Health Service had been given a mandate to provide health services to the general population. Its activities had previously been limited to the care of specific populations defined by law, such as American Indians, merchant seamen, and federal prisoners. The 1971 appropriation for the NHSC was only $3 million, but the presence of the program greatly expanded the potential federal role in the delivery of health services in the country as a whole.

Although the NHSC came to occupy a pivotal role in the coordinated activities of the health services programs enacted in the 1960s, the NHSC did not originate as part of the Great Society. Its passage occurred not in the halcyon days of the War on Poverty but midway through Nixon's first administration and well into the Vietnam War. Its enactment under these conditions was testimony to the bipartisan belief that the doctor shortage was a grim and intractable problem that merited federal intervention. In spite of considerable backroom wrangling about the nature of NHSC, the final congressional votes in favor of the new law were overwhelmingly favorable. This consensus was, and would remain, a tremendous asset of the program for most of the decade that followed. The unanimity of congressional support for the program, however, camouflaged a basic divergence in political philosophy about health care that existed in the Congress and in the nation. Some, for instance, saw the new program as a remedial action by the federal government, a finger in the otherwise strong dike of American health care. Rural and conservative congressmen, many of whom had doctorless communities in their districts, tended toward this view. Others, with a more progressive and urban analysis, were persuaded that the predominant fee-for-service system in the United States would never provide equitable services to the less fortunate in the population. To them the NHSC represented a first step toward a permanent federal doctor corps that would insure equality in services for the entire population. Some even saw it as the first, tentative American experiment in socialized medicine. As the program developed and expanded, in their vision, the National Health Service Corps would become, simply, the National Health Service.

In 1970, politicians and health policymakers from all points on the political spectrum could endorse the concept of the NHSC in good conscience. Within that consensus, however, were the seeds of future difficulty. For example, in the Emergency Health Personnel Act of 1970, as in all subsequent versions of the legislation, there was a troublesome and basically schizophrenic directive as to how to charge patients treated by NHSC personnel. The law stated:

> Any person who receives a service provided under this section shall be charged for such service at a rate established by the Secretary, pursuant to regulations, to recover the reasonable cost of providing such services; except that if such a person is determined under regulations of the Secretary to be unable to pay such charge, the Secretary may provide for the furnishing of such service at a reduced rate or without charge.[13]

In other words, clinics were to establish fee-for-service practices, but they were also to treat everybody regardless of his or her ability to pay. This concept satisfied the pundits of various political persuasions, but it proved very difficult to put into operation. Over the years various program administrators managed this provision in ways that emphasized either fee-for-service medicine or the provision of services without regard to ability to pay. Either way, there were always members of Congress and members of the public complaining that the intent of the program had been abused and twisted. From the outset, then, the NHSC offered something for everyone—which was at once its strength and its weakness.

THE GROWING YEARS

The NHSC grew slowly at first. Twenty placements were made in sixteen communities around the United States in January of 1972, followed by 162 more in that summer. Most of the first group were physicians, although the law allowed for the employment of all types of health care providers. The initial communities served by the program were largely self-nominated. Prerequisites to NHSC support included the demonstration of a need for health services (usually through testimonials from local residents and authorities) and a degree of community organization that would suggest the ability to act as a responsible agent for the practice. When placements were actually made, a memorandum of agreement between the community board and the NHSC was signed defining the commitments on both sides. Some degree of community governance of the National Health Service Corps practice was deemed important by program administrators from the start, since the program was actually a partnership between the government and a locality. This principle was not defined in law, but it did appear in program regulations written and rewritten over the years. The types of community groups with which the corps did business were, as might be imagined, highly variable, ranging from those organized by Rotarians and businessmen in small towns to groups composed of racial, ethnic, or antiwar activists in other communities.

According to the NHSC concept, the community was to share the responsibility of establishing a clinic. The NHSC's main contribution to the community was the health professional, and it was not only a federal expectation but also a clear necessity that the community provide an office, office staff, and whatever other resources were necessary for the particular clinic. This invited a high degree of local creativity: there were clinics housed in trailers, homes, hospitals, and churches as well as in former bars, convents, schools, and automobile dealerships. Communities raised funds to support their clinics in a multiplicity of ways, which included cake bakes and raffles, land sales, private and religious philanthropy, and the use of local taxes and grant funds. Much of this local organizing proved sufficient to the task of establishing and, with the cash flow generated by the doctor, maintaining the NHSC practices. In some cases the efforts were insufficient, unsuccessful, or simply bogged down in local politics or community infighting. The more hustle and initiative already present, the more successful communities were in establishing NHSC sites. The larger, more disorganized, and more alienated a community or neighborhood was, the less likely it was to be able to make use of the corps. In general the model worked well in small, rural communities with a preexisting civic infrastructure and less well in the densely populated, transient, and often fragmented inner city.

County medical and dental societies also played a potentially important role in the development of corps sites. The law required that the program obtain "recommendations from state medical, dental and other health associations." The administration interpreted this to mean that the approval of the local professional society had to be obtained before NHSC personnel could be placed. This led to a number of instances in which county medical or dental societies, either out of fear of competition or out of ideological opposition to any federal presence in health, blocked the formation of a corps site despite community wishes and needs. Rarely, if ever, were organized professional groups instrumental in the initiation of NHSC practices. Subsequent versions of the law formally limited the role of local medical and dental societies to "review and comment" on proposed NHSC placements. In the main, organized dentistry proved to be far more self-interested and obstructionist in regard to the NHSC than did organized medicine, dispatching thousands of pieces of correspondence to members of Congress over the years and frequently adopting anti-NHSC resolutions at their local, state, and national conclaves.

The program grew slowly but steadily during its early years, increasing in size from 20 doctors in 1971 to almost 600 by 1976. Amendments to the initial law were passed in 1972. They defined the program more precisely and authorized the National Health Service Corps Scholarship Program (first called the Public Health/ National Health Service Corps Scholarship Program). The scholarship concept was not a whim but the logical extension of analyses by the Democrat-controlled health committees of Congress. Two specific recognitions governed their thinking and their lawmaking. First, capitation grants to medical schools were beginning to show results in increasing the number of physicians entering practice. Although these grants had in no way been designed to produce doctors for the poor, it had been hoped that the new physicians would diffuse themselves throughout the country, with the result that chronically underserved areas would benefit from their services. It soon became apparent that this was not happening. Capitation money simply was not buying doctors for the poor. Second, the size of the National Health Service Corps would never be very great as long as it relied exclusively on the recruitment of volunteer health professionals at modest, PHS wages. Even in the Vietnam era, when the military draft was still in place, the competitive position of the corps was not great. If the NHSC was to be more than a demonstration program with several hundred physicians, a more reliable source of supply had to be found.

The close relationship between the scholarship program and traditional programs of student aid created a tension that was to be an ingredient of the program from the outset. Students and financial-aid officers, naturally enough, tended to look on NHSC scholarships as a mechanism to finance the cost of medical education. Indeed, the term *scholarship* is itself a misnomer, because it implies financial support in return for academic performance. The NHSC scholarships, of course, were designed for a different purpose and though they did pay the academic way of students, they were explicitly intended to be means of producing a specific and very special cadre of health practitioners. The scholarship program, in fact, was more akin to the training of military pilots where a group of young people were given a set of special skills at government expense to perform a public mission for a set period of time. After that time the skills remained with the individual, to be used in any way that he or she saw fit.

Although the NHSC labored hard over the years to run the program as a strategy for service delivery rather than as a student aid mechanism, potential points of confusion and disagreement repeatedly emerged. Some students became upset because community experience, public-service work, and specialty preference rather than grades were used for selection. Schools, subscribing to the student aid notion, did little to alter their curricula to accommodate the needs of students destined to work in community-based, primary care practices. Certain members of Congress have themselves frequently added to the confusion by responding to complaints about cutbacks in student loans and assistance funds by pointing to the NHSC scholarship as a substitute. As the scholarship program developed and scholarship graduates joined the NHSC as practitioners, the differences between traditional student aid and the scholarship program became clearer and a number of actions were taken to reinforce the principles of service delivery.

The scholarship program grew annually in budget and in awards. The largest number of new awards (3,347) came in the 1979–80 cycle, and at the high point, in 1980, 9 percent of the nation's medical students were receiving NHSC scholarships, as $75 million was spent on the program that year. The scholarship program was destined to become a very important part of the service delivery agenda for the federal government and a critical element in the health care of traditionally underserved communities.

1976 AND BEYOND

The year 1976 stands out as a turning point for the National Health Service Corps. Whatever various legislators and policymakers had envisioned for the NHSC, the Nixon and Ford administrations, in keeping with their free-enterprise philosophy, managed the program grudgingly. Program development was concentrated in rural areas using a solo practitioner, fee-for-service model for most corps sites. In spite of the enabling language in the law, virtually no NHSC practitioners had been placed in other Public Health Service programs, such as the Community or Migrant Health centers or with units of state or local government. The NHSC had 590 professionals in the field by 1976, most of whom were physicians. In total, they represented a tiny fraction of the nation's medical manpower —less than one-sixth of one percent of America's doctors.

The Carter administration saw the NHSC in a much more aggressive light. Dr. Julius Richmond, the assistant secretary for health and surgeon general, talked frequently about the mission of the Public Health Service in general and about the NHSC in particular as providing "equity" in health services for all Americans.[14] The number of students already in the scholarship pipeline was significant, and Joseph Califano, the HEW secretary, was eager to plot a strategy that would, through the increased use of scholarships, produce an NHSC with a field strength of 15,000 by the year 1990. There was little expectation among the administration leaders that the private sector would play any significant role in meeting the problems of the underserved. In their judgment, the answer lay in an NHSC that would staff clinics sponsored by federal, state, and municipal governments as well as such traditionally poorly served institutions as prisons, jails, state mental hospitals, and public general hospitals. While the level of funding for the corps and the scholarship program did increase during the Carter years, Califano's ambitious policies were not pursued after his departure. Fiscal constraints, medical school resistance, and growing opposition from organized medicine gave the post-Califano period in the NHSC a kind of Alice-in-Wonderland quality—everybody thought the corps was a great idea but nobody wanted to defend the program or pay for it.

The integration of the NHSC with other service delivery programs of the Public Health Service, however, was quietly but forcefully implemented after 1976. Although CHCs and the NHSC were authorized by different statutes, neither law precluded the complementary use of the two programs. Many communities that had received an NHSC physician had, in fact, difficulty providing adequate facilities and nonmedical support for the practice. Other communities that had obtained CHC grants had well-equipped, well-staffed offices but found it hard to recruit a competent physician. The coordinated use of the manpower program (the NHSC) and the grant program (CHC) made excellent sense from both a pragmatic and a policy perspective and was pursued vigorously after 1976. This strategy resulted in a far wider choice of placements for NHSC professionals, which improved the ability to recruit volunteer (that is, nonscholarship) providers as well as offering all NHSC practitioners a spectrum of placement that would not have been available under the limited-placement model previously in place.

The "integrated" strategy proved to be controversial, however, because it challenged the right wing of the consensus that had supported the corps. Many rural and conservative congressmen were far less enthusiastic about CHCs than they were about the NHSC, and the strengthening of the CHC Program by the NHSC was not part of their agenda. They argued further that the corps had always been designed to be a fee-for-service, "private practice type" program quite different—in their view—from CHCs. Their pique had no basis in law. Nowhere in the statutes of either program were these arguments borne out. The Carter administration's management of the NHSC took no more liberties with the law than the preceding administration had taken, albeit in differing ways. The integrated strategy made the sum of the two programs more effective than they would have been if managed separately; it was a bold step in an aggressive plan to treat the needy.

The new law passed in 1976 was helpful in regard to urban placements. It broadened the definition of a Health Manpower

Shortage Area (HMSA), a concept that had first been introduced in the amendments of 1972. In order to apply for NHSC providers, an area had to be formally certified as a HMSA by the Bureau of Health Manpower. Certification was made on the basis of a physician-to-population ratio in excess of 1 to 3,500. (Before 1976 the ratio had had to be greater than 1 to 4,000.) These guidelines were written in such a way, however, that entire counties or cities were rated as a unit. This made most urban areas that had pockets of heavy physician concentration ineligible for NHSC assistance, even if they also had neighborhoods bereft of physicians. The 1976 law expanded the scoring system, incorporating additional factors and making smaller units, such as trade areas and census tracts, eligible for designation as HMSAs. This rendered many more urban areas eligible to receive corps practitioners.

Both because of the designation problem and because of the low priority that the Nixon-Ford administration gave urban health, the NHSC made very few urban assignments prior to 1976. The situation was complicated by the fact that most of the urban placements that were made resulted in failure. The solo, fee-for-service model simply did not work in the inner city. The few trials that were attempted were not large enough, secure enough, or well enough staffed to survive in the tough environment of the ghetto or barrio. The CHC model—with an adequate building, ample support staff, and enough practitioners to rotate coverage and meet specialty expectations—proved to be far more successful in the urban environment. Armed with the new designation criteria, the integrated strategy, and the Carter administration's commitment to cities, the NHSC expanded its urban placements rapidly after 1976. By 1980 almost 40 percent of all corps placements were in urban areas.

Another development that made the period following 1976 one of rapid change was the maturation of the scholarship program. Seventy-four scholarship graduates were placed in practice in 1976. That number climbed to 480 in 1978 and to almost 800 in 1980. During these years the vigorous recruitment of volunteer (nonobligated) practitioners continued; in 1978 and 1979 an additional 500 volunteer professionals were recruited, almost 300 of whom were physicians. As a result the size of the corps grew rapidly, to 2,100 by 1980.

The scholarship program presented challenges that had not been envisioned during the early years. To begin with, the bureaucracy treated the new scholarship program as a mere extension of previous student aid programs. Through the initial years of the scholarship activity, when the major job of the program was the regular disbursement of checks, this made little difference. But as scholarship recipients reached the point of fulfilling their obligation, it became increasingly apparent that little had been done to prepare them for the specific job they were undertaking.

NHSC took this problem to heart in 1977, when it initiated a series of activities for students beginning as soon as they received scholarship awards. This undertaking was called "acclimation" and consisted of publications, summer and elective preceptorships at corps sites, annual conferences at schools with large numbers of scholarship students, and a network of scholarship "advocates" at schools that had smaller numbers of recipients. The purpose of these activities was to keep NHSC students and residents in deferment abreast of developments in the program and to encourage their interest in and enthusiasm for community medicine while they approached their period of service.

The scholarship program has raised many questions about the basic professional strategy of the government. Some have argued that the use of the scholarship mechanism to generate manpower for the NHSC was a corruption of the program and that the only professionals whom the NHSC should place are those who select the corps over all other practice possibilities. Certainly a scholarship mechanism produces numbers of practitioners who arrive at the point of service with some ambivalence. In fact through 1980 approximately 30 percent of the scholarship recipients defaulted on their service commitment. That is, three out of every ten graduates of the scholarship program chose to pay back costs that they had incurred under the lenient terms of the law rather than fulfill their obligation. Some, perhaps, had calculated from the outset that the scholarship could be, in effect, a low-interest loan; for others the sense of personal or professional commitment had changed in the three to seven years between the time of the award and the time of the service payback. Indisputably, the scholarship approach has predictable imprecision built into its selection process.

Moreover, the placement of scholarship recipients in communities proved to be quite different from the placement of volunteer professionals, since those in the latter group essentially chose their community from those available and served with self-generated enthusiasm. Every attempt was made to treat scholarship graduates in a similar fashion, except that the ultimate decision about placement remained with the NHSC rather than the individual. Several different systems of regional allocation and site selection were employed over the years. All of them attempted to give individual practitioners and their families maximal choice of placement while, at the same time, redistributing providers along predetermined lines on the basis of the number of HMSAs in a region or a state. Armed with the scholarship, the corps ultimately could assign predictable numbers of professionals to a given locale or region. It could, in fact, redistribute manpower. This capability enabled the NHSC to fulfill the most basic intent of the law—the placement of providers in communities that previously had been unable to obtain doctors. The placement of scholarship graduates has at times resulted in unhappy professionals or disappointed communities, but it has produced a quantity, quality, and predictability of providers for underserved people that had not been possible before. This has been an enormously important achievement.

NEW DIRECTIONS

During the period 1976–80, there occurred a number of internal changes in the management of the corps that paralleled the growth of the program. These efforts were aimed at developing a greater cohesiveness and sense of professional identity in the NHSC. Prior to that time the regional offices of the Department of Health, Education, and Welfare (now the Department of Health and Human Services) held periodic orientation conferences for new NHSC members. The conferences, however, were random events with no standard agenda or fixed meeting date. Many NHSC providers went to work with no orientation at all. Starting in 1977, orientation conferences were standardized in format and coordinated by headquarters in Rockville, Maryland, at which speakers like Sen. Edward Kennedy and Surgeon General Richmond were selected to give the keynote speeches. In the belief that a clear understanding of the corps' role as a national program would make it easier to labor in isolated and sometimes alien settings, the orientations were aimed to give the new practitioners a sense of mission and pride in their work. Clinical conferences with a somewhat more regional focus but a similar purpose were instituted in the winter months in such a way that NHSC members attended two conferences in their first year and one conference every year thereafter.

The regional offices were key to the NHSC, since they were responsible for site development, placement, and ongoing support. These offices were staffed by career Public Health Service employees, most of whom were not health professionals and few of whom had ever lived or worked in underserved settings. A clear gap in perception and experience separated the providers in the communities from the support staff in the regional offices. In order to lessen this gap, "clinical coordinators"—usually veteran NHSC practitioners—were recruited to work on the regional office staff. These individuals dealt with the numerous clinical issues that arose, ranging from licensure problems and hospital privileges to physical and psychological problems among the providers themselves.

The clinical coordinators provided a host of services, not all of which had been anticipated. They established links with medical schools and medical centers for referral, consultation, and continuing medical education for the field staff. They helped to arrange miniresidencies and refresher courses for doctors called on to provide services for which they had received insufficient training. They represented the corps at state boards and local and regional professional societies. From time to time they were called on to make tough clinical judgments—involving mental health, family well-being, and community relations—and occasionally they spelled doctors who needed vacation time.

During this period there was increased pressure for tighter management of all community health programs, including the NHSC. Productivity standards were introduced that required of every physician a minimum of 4,200 patient encounters a year. NHSC sites were made responsible for filing periodic management statements called the Bureau's Common Reporting Requirements (BCRRs), which reported financial and demographic information on the practice as well as aggregated clinical data. Many corps sites, especially those with a small and simple front office, complained bitterly about the reporting burden. Many corps providers resented the productivity standards as an intrusion into their mode of practice. The message coming from Washington, however, was clear. The NHSC, growing as it was, could not command continued budgetary increases with the simple claim that it did good works. It had to demonstrate programmatic efficiency and accountability.

An important question for the corps had always been its retention rate. It was one thing to supply doctors to shortage areas on a rotational, short-term basis; it was quite another to provide long-term or permanent solutions to the problems of underserved communities. From the beginning it had been the hope of the program's supporters that, once placed, corps providers would remain in their communities. Some saw this as a permanent federal role, whereas others hoped that after an initial period of support corps practitioners would convert to private practice and remain indefinitely. Early on, however, it became apparent that the permanent placement depended to a large degree on the types of communities selected. Generally, the more unattractive, poor, or isolated a community was, the less likely it was to retain a physician beyond a limited tour of duty. Therefore, if the program attempted to place practitioners in the most underserved communities, it diminished the likelihood of a good retention rate. Then too, the probability of a conversion to private practice was diminished by a policy of placement in the poorest communities, which were least likely to be able to support a private practice. Recognizing this, the corps leaders from the mid-1970s on encouraged practitioners to consider career opportunities in the Public Health Service. NHSC providers were invited to renew their assignments following an initial tour of duty with an understanding that they would continue in their community so long as the practice was warranted and their performance was good. Conversion to private practice was encouraged, but its limitations were clearly recognized and sites were not designed with private conversion as the foremost consideration.

The result of the changes in program management as well as of the emphasis on career commitment was a significant rise in the retention rate over the years. In 1974, 14 percent of all corps professionals who had finished their first tour of duty chose to extend their term as federal employees in their respective communities, and none converted to private practice. The figures increased steadily; in 1980, 35 percent extended their service in the corps while 4 percent remained as private practitioners in their communities, yielding a total retention rate of 39 percent. This 39 percent, of course, cannot be interpreted as a guaranteed lifetime of service to the community in question, but it does represent more than the third of the professionals whom the NHSC had placed in communities who remained voluntarily for longer portions of their careers and provided services to traditionally underserved people. Most observers considered this a significant accomplishment, whereas those worried about the growth of a federal doctor corps considered it anathema.

THE 1980s

Will the current decade see a continued increase in the availability of physicians and health services for underserved people? Certainly, the raw data suggest that there are going to be many more physicians in practice in the future than there have been in the past. The Flexnerian state of affairs, it would seem, has been left behind forever. There can be little argument that the United States has come far in redressing the physician deficit caused by a fixed ratio of physicians during a long period of increasing medical and technical capability. There is, and will be, intense debate as to what the proper physician-to-patient ratio should be at this point in our medical and economic history. A first cannon was fired in that battle by the publication in 1980 of the Graduate Medical Education National Advisory Committee (GMENAC) report, which projects that there will be a physician "surplus" of 70,000 by 1990 and of 145,000 by the year 2000.[15] Although the GMENAC conclusions are by no means accepted by all parties, the report makes a methodical case that *in the aggregate* we will soon have at least enough doctors to care for our population. The question left unanswered is how

these physicians will distribute themselves and whether traditionally underserved areas will share in this new bounty. Even GME-
NAC itself is not sanguine on this point, predicting a continued
maldistribution of providers and calling for continued federal
efforts in this area.

Others have argued that the marketplace will take care of virtually all the problems of medical services. A group of researchers
from the Rand Corporation studied the trends in the location of
board-certified specialists between 1960 and 1977 and concluded
that a diffusion of specialists is under way to towns of smaller and
smaller size.[16] Proponents of a diminished federal effort have seized
on these data and used them to argue that the problem is curing
itself. There are major problems with this reasoning. The board-
certified specialists counted in the Rand study often replaced uncer-
tified GPs who served the same communities, producing no net gain
in manpower for small towns. Specialist care (and the Rand study
counted dermatologists and urologists as well as internists and
pediatricians) does not necessarily represent an appropriate or cost-
effective form of service delivery. Finally, these calculations ignore
the economic barriers to services that exist in many communities
and for many individuals. Documenting an increased supply of
physicians and some evidence of their migration away from urban
centers does not provide any assurances that traditionally underserved people will be cared for. Even the Rand study itself con-
cludes, "Finally, continuation or expansion of the National Health
Service Corps will most certainly increase the number of physicians
in non-metropolitan areas that otherwise would not attract physicians."[17]

Fiscal and political conservatism, nonetheless, have played an
increasingly prominent part in the political process that governs the
fate of the federal manpower initiatives. In this climate, the loose
consensus that had supported the NHSC has come under increasing
stress. Though still a small appropriation by government standards,
the NHSC and the scholarship program combined had a budget of
almost $145 million in 1981. Having 2,000 providers in communi-
ties around the country and more than 8,000 students on award or
in deferment, the corps was no longer a demonstration program.
Calculations using the retention rates described above as well as the
anticipated availability of scholarship graduates would have
brought the NHSC to a level of 5,000 practitioners by the mid-
1980s. These projections have caused considerable problems for
advocates of a limited program or of no program at all. Since the
government has already paid for, or is in the process of paying for,
the education of most of these individuals, it would be an embar-
rassment to fiscal conservatives to excuse scholarship recipients

from service. On the other hand, the employment of these future graduates creates a larger corps and a larger budgetary outlay in support of the program.

The strategy of the Reagan administration has been twofold. First, it has eliminated new scholarship awards so that the pipeline will dry up in the future years. Second, it has kept the NHSC at a level of 2,000 or fewer professionals in the field, in order to minimize its cost and its impact. The mainstay of this strategy, however, has been the Private Practice Option (PPO). The PPO first appeared in the 1976 law as an alternative-placement system to be used at the discretion of the secretary of the Department of Health and Human Services. It allowed the scholarship graduate to serve the period of obligation in a nonfederal capacity (private practice or salaried practice), provided that it was in a "priority" shortage area and that the individual made at least the same salary that he or she would make as a member of the NHSC. The Carter administration spent little effort implementing the PPO, feeling that it was diversionary to the main intent of the program. In 1980, budgetary pressures were such that the PPO was attempted on a limited basis, and a small number of scholarship recipients selected it. In 1981, virtually all restrictions on the PPO were relaxed, and the NHSC promoted private placements in a variety of ways. These developments, combined with the uncertain future of the program itself, caused better than 30 percent of the scholarship graduates to opt for the PPO. While budget cutters and free-market ideologues have applauded this development, others are concerned that the broad use of the PPO will severely curtail the effectiveness of the NHSC. The inclination, obviously, will be for scholarship graduates to situate private practices in the most lucrative parts of the counties or trade areas that are designated as underserved. Some practices will be established in proximity to already operative CHCs and NHSC sites, tending to draw away their paying patients and leaving the community-based programs in a weakened condition. PPO practitioners are obliged to sign documents indicating the location of their shortage area practice and agreeing to see all patients regardless of ability to pay. However, it remains the job of the NHSC to monitor these agreements—a difficult job with adequate resources and a virtually impossible one with a curtailed budget.

The NHSC enters the 1980s well equipped to do the job for which it was established. Whether its resources continue to be targeted carefully on the problem remains to be seen. Certainly the political alliance that built the NHSC is no longer intact, and the immediate future of the program is in the hands of some of its sharpest critics.

THE BALANCE SHEET

There can be little question that the access to services as well as the absolute health status of poor and disadvantaged Americans are better now than they were in 1960. The infant mortality rate has decreased and longevity has increased for the population as a whole. More specifically, there is increasing evidence that the health of the underserved has improved. Per capita physician visits for the poor and near poor have risen, while infant mortality among minorities has fallen significantly. Although large gaps remain between the health indices of the poor and the rich, the poor have at the least kept pace with general improvements in health care and, in some instances, have narrowed the gap. From the manpower perspective, it is evident that health practitioners are accessible in hundreds of communities where none were before. The NHSC by itself has provided more than 10,000 person-years of service to shortage communities since 1971. The complex of community-oriented health programs (including Medicaid and Medicare) has provided a degree of medical enfranchisement that was but a vague hope before 1960. This movement has provided not only health services for the poor but also employment, career development, and a galvanizing effect in poor communities. The founders of the early neighborhood health centers unabashedly saw their mission as stimulating employment and community organizing in addition to delivering health care. Over the years that tradition has been carried on in thousands of communities where these health programs have been active. Very often the board of a National Health Service Corps site or a community health center has become involved in other civic and political activities, and, as often as not, their providers have become spokesmen for their causes.

Looked at from the perspective of the professions, the community health movement has had a significant impact. Tens of thousands of physicians, dentists, nurse practitioners, and physician's assistants have worked in shortage areas, often in clinics that are governed by the community. While many have served only for short periods of time, others have stayed and built careers in programs such as the NHSC, the Indian Health Service, community health centers, and public hospitals. They are now able to articulate the needs and the challenges of community medical practice in a way that previous generations of charity doctors never could. Slowly these individuals are assuming more significant leadership roles in government, public institutions, and academe. Moreover their experience, their practice, and their world view enable them to serve as role models for younger professionals and students—a phenomenon that did not exist as late as the mid-1960s, when community-oriented SHO students found very few practicing clinicians to emulate. Finally, many more women, minorities, and non-physician providers are in practice today than was the case even ten years ago. Many of these individuals have worked or are working in underserved areas.

On the other side of the ledger, there are still problems. Foremost among them is the basic nature of the system. No matter how well-intentioned or how generously funded programs such as the National Health Service Corps are, they are ultimately fingers in the dike. The predominant mode of health service delivery in this country remains private practice. Government-subsidized or -stimulated programs to care for people for whom the private system functions inadequately are addenda to the prevalent mode and, as such, do not constitute a coherent system of their own. That is and will remain a severe detriment to accomplishing the goal of equitable care for all. The directives that governed the NHSC—even under the Carter administration—exemplify this point. On any given day the NHSC was supposed to serve the most underserved but to charge on a fee-for-service basis; treat the needy but in no way compete with the private sector; and retain mature, veteran practitioners in communities but not become a permanent medical service. The mission was intriguing but impossible.

Within the community health programs, there remain considerable problems with the quality and accountability of the providers. Even though I am persuaded that the absolute number of physicians serving the poor and the relative number of *committed* physicians serving the poor have both increased, there are still large numbers of practitioners who work in underserved areas on a stopgap basis, grudgingly fulfilling a scholarship obligation or indifferently earning a living while building a private practice elsewhere. By no means do shortage areas have a monopoly on uncommitted physicians, but it cannot be argued that the development of humane and rational programs such as the NHSC and CHCs has alleviated the time-honored problem of health professionals disdaining to work with brown, black, poor, isolated, and institutionalized people.

Moreover, the United States still lacks a real ethos of community medicine. The providers who work in the Indian Health Service, the NHSC, CHCs, and public general hospitals, for instance, do not see themselves as part of a common movement. They identify, perhaps, with their program or their clinic, but they have been neither educated nor professionally socialized to think of themselves as front-line practitioners of community medicine. There exist no journals, professional organizations, or learned societies that speak to them as a group. In academe, community medicine is not taught as a clinical discipline or encouraged as a career option. Much needs to be done to unite the disparate elements of clinical community medicine in order to make it the permanent and creditable part of the American medical system that it should be.

READING THE TEA LEAVES

What can be concluded from all this history?

First, it is impossible to escape the conclusion that the health care of geographically or economically marginal populations is tied to the economy of the nation. Like personal philanthropy, American governmental largesse is acutely sensitive to the state of the economy; this surmise, however, does not lead to simple axioms about the fate of socially progressive health programs. If the times are flush and the economy is robust, as it seemed to be in the mid-1960s, strategies designed to buffer the population against the capriciousness of the "marketplace" will flourish. If, on the other hand, the economy is in desperately bad shape—as in the Great Depression—people's perception of social programs change, and a much greater part of the populace will look to the government for relief. Under these circumstances social programs would be brought into being at a great rate, as was the case in the 1930s. When the economy is mixed, as it was through the latter part of the 1970s and promises to be in the 1980s, the situation is not propitious for governmental initiatives to equalize service delivery. The middle class is struggling to make it in the private sector and is minimally responsive to the needs of the less fortunate. The programs that have been designed for assistance to the least able thus come under scrutiny and attack. This is likely to be the immediate fate of programs designed for health services to underserved people.

There can be little argument that the National Health Service Corps and its fellow health manpower programs of the past two decades have been reformist and incremental in nature. The most sanguine of observers could count the NHSC as no more than a laboratory for possible future federal initiatives in the deployment of medical personnel. By no stretch of the imagination is the NHSC a National Health Service. The question can reasonably be asked, therefore, whether equity in services would not be better served in the long run if there were no such intermediate efforts—efforts that, it could be argued, serve to mollify legitimate political tensions and dissipate popular grievances that would ultimately lead to a major and permanent change in the way health services are distributed in the United States. My own response to that question is that incrementalism in the development of all social services is an inescapable part of the history and fabric of this country. The legacy of the

Progressives and the "muckrakers," of the Social Security Administration and the Children's Bureau, as well as of the initiatives of the
1960s is powerfully that of gradualism—reform built on reform like
a coral reef. I share the frustrations of many who do not feel that
this evolution has always produced the human-service systems or
the simple social justice that we—as a nation—are capable of, but
it is *our* history and a compelling one at that. The National Health
Service Corps is very much in this tradition, and it is moot to
conjecture that it should have—or could have—been otherwise.

There is also a highly practical argument in favor of the manpower reforms as they have developed in recent years. The United
States lacks a strong tradition of public medicine for a program such
as the NHSC to build on. The Veterans Administration and the
military medical programs serve specific beneficiaries and not the
public as a whole and therefore offer relatively little guidance to the
NHSC. Learning how to recruit, educate, place, and support public
practitioners of health care amid a system that—in rhetoric, at least
—is still overwhelmingly private is an enormously complex task.
The history of the NHSC, the scholarship program, and the CHCs
has been difficult, at times uneven, and replete with potent opponents, but the experience gained by a generation of program administrators, community leaders, and practitioners has been
invaluable. It would be hard to imagine the United States moving
toward a National Health Service without the internship in the
system that thousands of critical individuals have had working the
highways of community health services since 1965. That experience will not be for nought.

All that said, the United States has advanced over the last twenty
years in being able to articulate and treat the health care problems
of the nation's underserved. The challenge of the immediate future
is to maintain and, where possible, to augment those efforts in an
atmosphere that is likely to be hostile. That endeavor will be aided
considerably by communities and individuals who have been medically enfranchised over this period and who will not easily allow
themselves to be made subjects of poorhouse medicine once again.

9.

new health
professionals:

CHANGING THE HIERARCHY

Molly Backup
John Molinaro

For most Americans, taking a trip to "the doctor" has always meant seeing a physician with an M.D. degree. Sick people were diagnosed and managed by doctors and cared for by nurses.

During the 1960s, however, medical practitioners who were *not* M.D.'s were introduced to new roles in the health care system. Nurse clinicians appeared in cardiac care units, managing cardiac emergencies in the doctor's absence. Nurse-midwives began to obtain delivery privileges at hospitals. Physician's assistant (PA) and nurse practitioner (NP) training programs were established, and people going to the doctor's office now sometimes saw a PA or NP.

The influx of such "new health practitioners"* was hailed as innovative—and as a potential solution to the problem of the overspecialization and the maldistribution of physicians.

Different groups had different dreams for PAs and NPs and different problems they hoped to solve. Organized medicine wanted

---

*"Midlevel" health workers have been part of the health care system for centuries. Today, health workers with skills and training in community health, mental health, nutrition, health education, and a large number of other fields serve in highly valuable roles in what could also be referred to as "midlevel" jobs. This chapter is limited to a discussion of midlevel clinical practitioners but recognizes that they make up only a part of the midlevel health work force.

to relieve the doctor shortage without losing control over the health care system. Advocates of the free-enterprise system needed to demonstrate that it could meet the demands for care. Consumers wanted more access to care and would not tolerate disparities in care in rural and inner-city areas. Patients hoped for a health worker who would be less far removed and who would treat them with more understanding and respect. Women and minorities demanded to enter the system as health professionals and to receive better care as patients. Health workers and ex-military corpsmen were increasingly militant in their demands for upward mobility and jobs. Both nurses and medics were already functioning in expanded roles and wanted recognition and legal sanction. The government and consumers were concerned about escalating costs. Individual physicians wanted to ease their workload. Institutions needed to become less dependent on foreign trained physicians, who, once they gained citizenship, were less controllable and were already seen as "midlevels" with the added disadvantage of being foreign. And individual students saw an alternative to medical school's many years of study, high tuition, technological focus, and elite graduates. New health practitioners were seen as a possible solution to all of these problems. Supported by various groups with differing goals, the new health practitioner often became the focus of struggles within the health care system, being hailed as the response to, or castigated as the diffusion of, the calls for change.

Actually, midlevel practitioners are anything but new to the United States. The archives of the Newark, New Jersey, Public Health Department contain a 1913 reference to "Teachers of Infant Hygiene"—nurses who were trained to perform well-child examinations and to manage routine illnesses of children in the city's pediatric clinics. As recently as the early 1900s, midwives delivered a majority of the babies born in the United States. Those with formal training had a better maternal mortality record than the national average (including mothers attended by obstetricians).[1] The New York State Obstetrical Society argued in 1902 that "obstetrics would never be elevated to its rightful place so long as midwives were permitted to practice"; and the economic loss to obstetricians from midwife-attended births was estimated to be greater than $5 million annually.[2] After decades of legislative battles and public pressure, the involvement of midwives declined. In 1970, they attended only one-half of one percent of all births in the United States.

What was "new" was not that such health workers were delivering health care. Nonphysician healers and practitioners had been the rule rather than the exception throughout the 1800s. As late as

1864, not one state in the Union had a law requiring a license to practice medicine. In the early 1900s, however, organized medicine, concerned with falling fees, increasing competition, and a lack of professional status, began a drive to limit the right to deliver medical care to university-trained M.D.'s only. With the Flexner report and subsequent developments, virtually all schools that trained women, minority, and working-class medical students were shut down. Midwives, "Teachers of Infant Hygiene," and other midlevel health practitioners were all but driven out of the U.S. health care system.

By the 1960s, however, the call for "new health practitioners" was heard again, and this time organized medicine was supporting the idea. But why had a health system without midlevel practitioners become unacceptable to the public by the 1960s? How were new health practitioners to solve the problems? And what was the result?

WHY MIDLEVELS?

The two most often cited reasons for the development of new health professionals are the shortage of physicians and the need to curtail rising health care costs. The annual number of medical school graduates had not risen significantly since 1900, when with a population of 80 million the number of graduating doctors in the United States totaled 5,214. In 1950 there were 5,553 graduates and in 1960 there were 7,081, for a population of almost 180 million.[3] It was generally recognized that "if it were not for the foreign graduates, we would be totally decompensated."[4] It exacerbated the shortage that only 21 percent of the physicians in 1970 characterized themselves as general practitioners, as opposed to 83 percent in 1931. With the maldistribution of physicians, so that few were available in rural and inner-city areas, the problem was becoming a crisis. At the same time the costs of medical education and medical care were escalating rapidly.

In this situation, state and federal authorities became interested in new health professionals who would be cheaper to train, who would ease the maldistribution by geographic area and by specialty, and who would save money for their patients and the insuring government or business. Some hospital administrators sought to create a less costly and a salaried employee who would be more controllable; the American Hospital Association has been one of the earliest and staunchest supporters of physician's assistants. Those who supported the free-enterprise system sought ways of supporting fee-for-service medicine. "We must consider ways in which still increasing demands for services can be met," one of them wrote, adding that PAs and NPs "are less distasteful than another alternative, which is that of giving up the free enterprise system."[5]

The executive vice-president of the AMA, in suggesting that R.N.'s could be trained as PAs, was even more explicit in seeing them as supporters of profit-oriented health care: "Such nurses, since they might be paid on a fee-for-service basis, might become 'new advocates' for that payment method."[6] Organized medicine was supportive of the programs to train PAs. "The most vexing problem to be faced is the shortage of physicians, which will continue through most of the 1970's," it was noted in the AMA's *Journal*. "The only available alternative is the training and supervised deployment of 'physician substitutes.' "[7] Another medical publication summed up the problem: "Clearly, if something isn't done, the whole American system of medical practice will be in serious trouble with forces other than those within the medical profession itself dictating the mechanisms by which medical care is provided in the future."[8] The training programs were often placed in medical colleges, perhaps in order to maintain control in the hands of the medical profession.[9]

Organizationally, nurse practitioners were less controllable. Nursing schools and the nursing professional organizations held themselves apart from organized medicine. When the American Nurses' Association was approached in 1970 by the AMA to help recruit nurses to train as physician's assistants, it rejected the request. An editorial in a 1970 issue of the journal of the American Nurses' Association referred to the request as "raiding nursing to solve a doctor shortage." Since then, nursing schools and the ANA have sought to develop their own version of new health professionals—the nurse practitioner—whose training and philosophy reflected nursing and not medicine. Support for the nurse practitioner concept from organized medicine has been limited in some ways because of this added independence, but the tradition of nurses carrying out doctors' orders has partly offset this. There were ways to retain control over both emerging groups, and support from physicians, although it was qualified, grew.[10]

As medicine became more and more technical, physicians with years of training jumped at the idea of an assistant. They hoped to relieve the demands of mundane tasks so that they could concentrate on specialized areas. Hiring an employee was not as threatening as forming a partnership with another physician, and it provided greater income.

Most important, both organized medicine and the government were responding to patients' demands and social unrest in supporting new health professionals. Both were aware that patients and community members were dissatisfied with their access to and with the quality of health care. Criticisms abounded of impersonal clinics, which offered no explanation of tests or treatment; which lacked counseling, health education, and preventive services; and which had a different specialist for each disease, with no one to oversee the care and discuss it with the patient and family. Criticism of foreign medical graduates (FMGs) from both patients and other doctors also increased as the U.S. medical care system grew more and more dependent upon graduates of schools outside the country to provide care in hospitals. In 1963 there were 30,000 FMGs in the United States; in 1977 there were 86,000. This was an increase from 11 percent of all practicing physicians in 1963 to 20 percent in 1977. In 1969, 32 percent of all interns and residents were FMGs.[11] Some of the criticism of FMGs was openly racist, but some was based on a desire to have care delivered by someone of similar cultural and language background.

Patients and community members were not the only ones demanding change. Health workers grew increasingly frustrated with the rigid hierarchy in health care jobs. Competent people, especially nurses, became burned out or dead-ended; unionization grew commonplace. Hospital workers became increasingly militant and expressed their dissatisfactions through strikes when their demands were ignored. Opening up a midlevel category of health workers allowed mobility and the appearance of decreasing the rigidity of the hierarchy while still not challenging the hierarchy itself. The more career-oriented and vocal critics could be siphoned off into the new level without upsetting the basic structure.

The women's liberation movement also encouraged nurses and other women health workers to seek an expanded role. As nurse practitioners and physician's assistants, they entered areas of medicine previously dominated by male physicians. At the same time, patients were openly requesting female health care practitioners. Women in NP and PA programs could meet this demand and possibly avert some of the criticism of M.D.'s.

Medics returning from Vietnam, very medically skilled but underemployed or unemployed, added to the unrest. Others, such as coronary care nurses or public health nurses, had already developed skills in diagnosis and treatment that were not legally recognized. New career options would both relieve the doctor shortage and provide a safety valve for some of the pent-up resentment.

Finally, the first tentative steps in the separately evolving PA and NP programs built on each other. Organized nursing, seeing the creation and rapid success of PAs, was encouraged to proceed with its version of the NP, and PA programs used the "expanded role nurse" (such as the rural visiting nurse and coronary care nurse clinician) as a model for their development. The acceptance by patients and by organized medicine of a primary care generalist may have been significant in the concurrent development of family practice as a board-certified specialty for physicians. If patients were open to nonphysician generalist health care practitioners, surely they would accept a physician in family practice.

P A s   A N D   N P s

The first PA program was started in the 1960s with a class composed entirely of military medics, and being the first, it received a great deal of attention. Today, many people still perceive PAs as largely male ex-corpsmen. In fact, over 40 percent of all PAs are women, and only a minority have any previous military experience.

Nursing schools had historically felt that "nursing theory" was a vital and unique part of health care, one that doctors did not provide. Nurse practitioners were envisioned as individuals who would learn and use nursing skills but combine these with additional medical training and become clinicians, with both the medical and the nursing perspectives. That view has remained more of an ideal than a reality, as many nurse practitioners have found that the split between nursing and medicine was due more to the inherent structure of the system than to a lack of theoretical training. Appreciating the value of and knowing how to provide health education, counseling, nutrition advice, and psychosocial support could not overcome the problems of lack of time with patients or inadequate resources.

The first programs to train NPs and PAs reflected the philosophies of their founders and their particular concept of what a new health practitioner should be. PAs, to some of their earliest supporters, would be technical assistants to the physician, suturing wounds, casting fractures, working in emergency rooms. Nurse practitioners, in the eyes of the ANA, would continue to be nurses practicing nursing, but they would now also diagnose and manage patients' illnesses. In the earliest days, these generalizations were largely true. With time, they have become less so, as realities of the health care system altered the original ideas and spawned a new health practitioner who was an amalgam of all the different concepts.

Although NPs and PAs function in nearly identical roles in the health system, the two groups continue to maintain separate legal and professional identities. The American Nurses' Association, in defining a registered nurse in 1955, specifically exempted all acts of diagnosis and prescription from the practice of nursing. Diagnosis and prescription, however, are exactly what practitioner training involves. Physician's assistants adopted the AMA's definitions of themselves, which specified that services would be provided only under the supervision and direction (and control) of a licensed physician.

Both definitions focused on avoiding confrontation over the issue of the legal right to practice medicine. PAs say they practice only with the doctor in charge; NPs say they do not practice medicine at all. This denial of any desire to compete with M.D.'s for independent medical practice was instrumental in securing organized medicine's support in the early stages of the development of the new profession. Now, however, the reality of how NPs and PAs actually do practice—as opposed to their official definitions—has caused some uneasiness among physicians.

While the debate continued over who did what, there was general agreement that midlevel practitioners were having a positive impact on the system. In 1963, federal funds were approved for the training of nonphysician health professionals. In 1967, a national advisory commission recommended that the government give "high priority to . . . experimental programs which train and utilize new categories of health professional."[12] By the early 1970s, the number of programs training new health practitioners had increased exponentially.

The earliest PA programs relied on innovative funding from private and federal government sources, including the Office of Economic Opportunity, the Department of Defense, the Model Cities program, the Veterans Administration, the U.S. Public Health Service, the Department of Labor, the National Institutes of Health, private foundations, unions, and even pharmaceutical companies. Prior to 1971, federal funding totaled $30 million but was not coordinated under any one program. In fact, 1,000 federal agencies were dealing with the idea of physician's assistants in the late 1960s.

The first PA program, at Duke University, was started largely through the innovation of Eugene Stead, then chairman of medicine. He was able to obtain early funding from varied sources; in 1972, DHEW took over funding of PA programs on a federal level, and Duke was one of several schools to be awarded a multiyear contract. The nature of the program has changed significantly over the years, so that it no longer primarily trains corpsmen in surgical areas, but rather trains women and men from varied backgrounds, largely in primary care.

While Duke is acclaimed as the grandfather of PA programs, there were several other early programs whose initial development and direction were only minimally related to the program at Duke. The Child Health Associate Program, started by an R.N. and M.D.

team, originally trained public health nurses from rural Colorado for four months in chronic and episodic pediatric care. It is now a three-year PA program and includes some training in adult care as well.

The Johns Hopkins School of Health Services, under grants from the Robert Wood Johnson Foundation and the National Association for the Endowment of the Humanities, began training health associates in 1972. A majority of these students were women. Students with backgrounds in the arts and humanities were given as much priority in admission as those with health experience or a scientific background.

An even further departure from the traditional medical school model of training mainly upper-middle-class white students with funds from wealthy private sources was seen at the Long Island University–Brooklyn Hospital program, which started with money from the Bruner Foundation, the Model Cities program, and student stipends from District 1199 of the Hospital Workers' Union. The first class, in 1970, was all-minority. Significant changes have occurred, including a shift to a student body that is now only 30 percent minority.

In 1969, the first of several Medex programs started in Seattle. These programs, several of which have recently closed, were all geared toward training medics, mainly those who had served in Vietnam, through the late 1960s and early 1970s. The varied backgrounds and directions of these early programs reflect the divergent goals and personalities of those involved.

The large boost to these programs came in 1971 with the passage of the Comprehensive Health Manpower Training Act. Suddenly, medical schools were scrambling to develop primary care programs, including family practice residencies, PA programs, and NP programs in order to be eligible for federal funds. Under public pressure, Congress mandated primary care training and made significant federal monies dependent upon this prerequisite. Interestingly, some of the more elite institutions (such as Yale) were able to avoid training family practitioners (who were not eligible for hospital privileges at the Yale New Haven Hospital) by training nurse practitioners and physician's assistants. PA and NP programs counted as primary care programs and thus fulfilled the requirement without forcing a change in the affiliated hospital's restrictive policies on granting privileges. Scores of family practice residency programs were started with this primary care money, but PA and NP programs also got a significant boost in institutions where they may otherwise have been less acceptable. The National Health Service Corps (NHSC) was also established, providing scholarships to medical and allied-health students, including nurse practitioners, and requiring service in underserved areas on graduation. While PAs were not included in the scholarship program, many PAs have found employment in the NHSC. Since 1971, $70 million in federal funds have been channeled into physician's assistant training through the Health Resources Administration in the Department of Health and Human Services (formerly the Department of Health, Education, and Welfare).

Initially, some programs stressed surgical skills, but most soon emphasized the training of assistants to the primary care physician. Some have now expanded to include training in both primary care and specialty areas, and others have developed as postgraduate programs in specific areas such as surgery, occupational medicine, or emergency medicine. The physician's assistants are defined by the programs, by their professional organization (the American Academy of Physician Assistants), and by law as dependent practitioners who are responsible to a physician. In practice, interdependence is common. AMA and American Academy of Family Practice support for PAs has been tied to clear statements by the profession in favor of a dependent role. It is here that PAs and NPs differ most.

PA practice is regulated by state laws and not by any federal regulations (other than those governing use of controlled substances and federal third-party reimbursement). Only New Jersey outlaws the physician's assistant. Specifics in state laws vary, but all require that the PA function under the supervision of a licensed physician.

One of the major legislative problems for PAs is their inability to obtain reimbursement for services for Medicare clients. Other laws, such as those establishing NHSC scholarship eligibility requirements, have left out PAs either through oversight or through lobbying by special-interest groups. Functions already claimed by optometrists or X-ray technicians that would otherwise fall within the range of tasks that a physician can delegate to a physician's assistant may be ambiguously defined in other laws, and thus be excluded from PA practice.

Despite some recent changes, a higher percentage of PAs than M.D.'s are female, minorities, or of lower-class background, as a statement by the Association of Physician Assistant Programs acknowledged:

> Our experience indicates that students entering PA training are somewhat older and tend to have greater financial responsibilities than students in medical, osteopathic, dental and nursing schools. It has also been demonstrated that most PA students are from lower socioeconomic background than the above students.[13]

Initially, PAs were largely male, but now over 40 percent of all graduating physician's assistants are female. Early figures showed that approximately 13 percent of the PAs were minorities, but that percentage has since decreased significantly. Only a handful of schools continue to graduate the majority of minority PAs. Though a sophisticated analysis of class backgrounds is not available, previous education and prior work experience are probably valid indicators. Previous experience as a medical corpsman is decreasing in frequency (probably indicating a decrease in working- or middle-class students); college experience has increased significantly (probably indicating an increase in middle- and upper-class backgrounds). The greater emphasis on previous academic experience may limit the minority and working-class applicant pool. Since M.D.'s are more likely to practice in an area and with patients similar to their own background, this may limit the future deployment of PAs into some of the medically underserved areas where they are needed.

The personal values of PAs may also be substantially different from those of M.D.'s. Their future is not clearly defined as profitable and full of personal glory. The desire to serve, to do something worthwhile, and to be willing to risk something is at least present. The average student is also older and has experienced work before entering the training program.

The development of nurse practitioner programs in many ways parallels the development of PA programs. The nurse practitioners had forerunners. Coronary care nurses who knew how to defibrillate patients in cardiac arrest in the early 1960s finally gained approval to treat them first and then call for orders. Public health nurses had an expanded role in home visits in northern California as early as 1962. The Frontier Nursing Service in Kentucky had nurses acting as practitioners decades ago. These nurses have been able to "grandfather" into the profession by challenging the nurse practitioner certifying exam. While practical experience and passing a written exam has been a way to certification as an NP or PA, this option is being closed off. In the future, the only way to be certified will be to graduate from an approved school.

Although the overlap between NPs and PAs is significant (and some programs qualify as both PA and NP programs), a clear separation is being maintained. This seems artificial and related more to the external politics of the sponsoring organizations than to any substantive difference. A medical school may train both NPs and PAs who will eventually qualify to perform the same functions, and yet the students do not share lectures.

Prior to increased federal funding in 1971, there existed only a handful of nurse practitioner programs, with scattered funding.

There are now approximately 220 NP programs, with 15,000 graduates.

NP programs come in two forms: those that grant a master's degree, and those that grant a certificate. In some ways, this distinction parallels the training of the R.N. who has received a baccalaureate and the certified R.N. (also a registered nurse, but usually with a two- or three-year college program). Certificate NPs are significantly less likely to hold a previous degree or be ANA members; are more likely to have worked previously in a health center or community organization, and to work in primary care; and are slightly more likely to be minority. Some 97 percent of NPs are female, and 90 percent are white.[14] Clearly, NPs are more likely to be female than are M.D.'s or PAs, and are even slightly more likely to be minority than are M.D.'s but slightly less so than are PAs.

Legislation governing NPs is on a state level and has not always required major changes. As long as the function of nurse practitioners is seen as that of nursing, existing state nurse practice acts suffice. Amendments to those acts have been the major approach to expanding the scope of nursing. Idaho first passed such an amendment in 1971. Prescriptive practice rights have been more thorny and have reopened the debate over physician supervision as opposed to independence.

OUTCOME

There are now 11,000 physician's assistants and 15,000 nurse practitioners in the United States.[15] The number of births attended by midwives is again on the rise. The distribution of PAs and NPs is different from that of M.D.'s. The majority of them work in primary care and in medically underserved areas, although increasing numbers are now in hospital positions previously staffed by foreign medical graduates. In 1978, the distribution of PAs in practice settings was as follows: solo practice, 18 percent; group practice, 17 percent; hospital, 24 percent; nonhospital clinic, 23 percent; and military, 18 percent. A higher percentage of PAs than of M.D.'s work in rural areas. Thus, they are providing high-quality primary care to those who need it. The distribution of civilian PAs by community size is as follows: less than 10,000, 25 percent; 10,000–50,000, 21 percent; 50,000–250,000, 18 percent; and 250,000, 36 percent.[16] A 1976 Institute of Medicine report on primary care found that "while only 12.8% of all physicians were practicing in non-urban areas . . . 33% of PAs were . . . and 71% of PAs and 69% of NPs . . . were practicing in primary care settings."[17] With rising costs of institutionalized health care, recent trends show rapid increases in the employment of PAs and NPs in hospitals, prisons,

HMOs, and other institutional settings that face the problems of containing costs and of attracting and keeping high-quality physicians.

The quality of care and the patient acceptance of new health professionals is high. A ten-year retrospective study in the *Annals of Internal Medicine* summarizing twenty-one studies of care provided by PAs and NPs in a wide range of pediatric- and adult-hospital, urban- and rural-clinic settings concluded that "Nurse Practitioners and Physician Assistants provide office based care that is indistinguishable from physician care."[18] Another study of quality, published in *Medical Care,* reported, "Both non physician providers perform at an acceptable level of quality when physicians' compliance with the same quality criteria are employed as a standard of reference for the kinds of conditions they are trained to treat."[19] The *Annals of Internal Medicine* study, it should be noted, summarized data collected in many studies of rural and inner-city underserved areas—"Satisfaction with Medical Care in a Low Income Population," "Physician Extenders in Walk-In Clinic," "Evaluation of Physician Assistants in Rural Primary Care"—and thus indicates that high-quality care and patient satisfaction are found in the areas where they are needed most and where the suggestion of second-class care would be strongest.

Patient acceptance of new health professionals is high among all social classes:

> Satisfaction with care was equal to or greater than satisfaction resulting from care given by physicians. As a measure of acceptance, these studies indicate a high level of satisfaction with these nonphysicians as providers of ambulatory primary care. . . .[20]

Acceptance is highest in the lower socioeconomic groups and in medically underserved areas. A 1974 study of Medex (a type of PA) in the *Journal of the American Medical Association* found "that patients with firsthand experience accept physician's assistants."

> Patients rate the physician's assistants highly in terms of technical competence (89%), professional manner (86%), and report improvements in the quality of care (71%) and access to services (79%), since the physician's assistants began working. Eighty-seven percent of the patients who received physical examinations from physician's assistants were very satisfied . . . patients in the low access group rated Medex impact higher, . . . showed greater confidence in the

Medex, . . . and perceived Medex to be more competent, confident, courteous, and respectful than their counterparts in the high access group.[21]

PAs and NPs are more accessible to patients and are considered to be less elitist than the usual physician. Their class background is lower, and a higher percentage of women is found among them than among physicians. They provide patients with more education and counseling. They spend slightly longer with each patient and have training and background that emphasize the involvement of patients in their own care. They thus tend to demystify medical care and to empower patients. Despite its problems, the movement to physician's assistants and nurse practitioners is at least potentially progressive. It is not inherently "supportive of the present system."[22]

The cost of training nurse practitioners and physician's assistants is clearly less than that of training a medical doctor. The estimated cost of producing a board-eligible family physician is $112,000; that of producing a PA is $15,000.[23] And while the actual cost of an office visit may remain the same whether the patient sees a NHP or an M.D., the cost of providing care goes down. Whether the saving is passed on to the patient or the insurer is another matter, but less money is being expended on care of equal quality. This should, in theory, help keep the cost of institutional or private medicine down.

NHPs tend to order fewer inappropriate expensive tests and provide more preventive services, potentially saving still more. Since NHPs are less expensive to utilize, the salary for a primary care NHP being as little as one-third that of an M.D., reimbursement for their services from insurance companies and from Medicare and Medicaid could be set at a percentage of what is reimbursed for the same service by a physician. The federal government would save millions of dollars without lowering the quality of care. "Practices that employ nonphysician providers offer similar overall proportions of basic and complex care, greater proportions of preventive and health maintenance care, a lower proportion of hospital based care," one study found.[24] Another offered an estimate: "Total medical care costs were approximately 40% of those costs generated by physicians managing similar patients. . . ."[25]

And, perhaps most important, medical underservice itself causes high health care costs. Children grow up with health problems that would be preventable with quality primary care but that are irreversible and costly in adult life. The elderly in underserved areas reach terminal stages in illnesses that could be much less serious with ongoing care. NHPs, simply by providing basic primary care to those who would otherwise be without it, could make a major contribution to lowering health care costs. New health professionals clearly give high-quality care, work in underserved areas, and are well accepted by patients.

However, there are some unsolved problems. PA and NP programs are now emphasizing prior undergraduate degrees and thus may decrease working-class and minority applications. Tuition is rising astronomically (now $8,000 per year at many schools), eliminating most candidates. Many PAs and NPs who have been working in medically underserved areas through the National Health Service Corps are facing the loss of their jobs because of the proposed budget cuts. If funding for programs like the NHSC is reduced, it will be harder for new health practitioners to find employment in the areas they were created to serve. Perhaps most ironically, the fears of a shortage crisis in the 1960s have begun to change to fears of a surplus of medical providers. When the shortage was at its greatest, several new approaches to increasing the availability of medical care were started simultaneously. Medical schools were expanded, PA and NP programs were founded, and family practice was introduced as a board-certified specialty. The net effect of all of these developments has been to create a much larger total supply of providers than any of the founders of the separate approaches appreciated. Now each group is seeking to define itself as the major route to greater availability of care. The American Academy of Family Practice passed a resolution at its 1981 house of delegates meeting urging a reevaluation of the need for physician extenders and support for them only in a dependent status.

The Medical Society of the State of New York (MSSNY)—New York is the state with the largest number of PAs—has been actively opposing physician's assistants for years. Its health manpower committee reported in 1978 as follows:

> . . . the MSSNY at its House of Delegates Session in 1976 voted to abort the Physician's Assistant program. . . . We should also . . . disseminate information to all members of MSSNY, the Legislature, and to the Governor . . . that the Physician's Assistant program be phased out.[26]

To carry out the above philosophy, the malpractice insurance company started and controlled by the MSSNY tried to raise the rates 71 percent for PAs in addition to the percentage rate increase for M.D.'s in an attempt to limit the practice of PAs who are not under constant direct supervision by a physician. It did this despite the absence of actuarial evidence to justify the raise.

A dependent practitioner who can add to the income of the practice is one thing when there is a physician shortage. But when there is an oversupply of physicians and when competition for patients results, there will be more and more pressure to make PAs and NPs more dependent upon physicians:

> While quality of care arguments may be advanced on both sides of this controversy, it is likely that the real determinant will be economic advantage . . . an increasing supply of physicians will ultimately result in even these (independent) physician extenders assuming a dependent role.[27]

Current practices may thus be curtailed unless new strategies are developed.

The *Report of the Graduate Medical Education National Advisory Commission,* commissioned by the Department of Health and Human Services, recommends the continuation of PA and NP programs at the current rate and the undertaking of studies to determine the future need for training of medical professionals. But this may not be heeded if the self-protecting pressures from organized medicine are stronger than the forces for the rational planning of high-quality care. Funding already approved for PA programs in 1982 has been decreased. Proposals from the administration and Congress cut funding by a half for 1983. Similar cuts are proposed in NP training funds. With such withdrawals of federal funding, it is likely that several programs will close. And if the past is any guide, the largely minority programs and less prestigious institutions will probably suffer first. If financial cuts are accompanied by accusations of poor quality by organized medicine, PAs and NPs may be molded more and more in the image of the M.D. to counter such charges. The less elitist, more patient-oriented alternative provided by new health practitioners could be lost in the attempt to survive. Some of these trends are already apparent.

Alternative funding is not a viable solution. Private contributions cannot match the amounts given by the federal government in the past, and the competition for the private money that is available is becoming more intense. Since private donors are concentrating their funds in the areas of their self-interest, any grants will probably have major strings attached.

New health professionals could seek out areas of medicine that will continue to have shortages, such as geriatrics, or turn more toward counseling, education, and prevention. Yet these are often

the first services to be cut, and PAs and NPs have not been organized in a way that could allow them successfully to fight to keep
jobs or services. Most are not in unions. Their professional organizations have not looked at the issue, and their separate existence has
discouraged close communication and has reduced their local clout
even further.

In short, the value of PAs and NPs is now threatened. Although
they are clearly less expensive to train and utilize than physicians,
the savings are not always passed on to the consumer. Instead, they
may be absorbed by the institution or employing doctor. And the
climate is very different from what it was when NHPs were first
being conceived of and supported by the federal government, organized medicine, and consumers.

While there is still a maldistribution of physicians (there are over
1,800 federally designated areas with primary care health manpower shortages), there has been a 60 percent increase in the number of physicians since 1960, and family practice residency
programs have increased from 15 to 342 since 1969.[28]

The political pressure groups of the 1960s that forced many
concessions have changed and are less organized. PAs and NPs must
recognize this and begin to reorganize their own coalitions. It may
not remain in the interest of the forces that sponsored the coalition
of NHPs to continue to advocate their existence. But it will remain
in the interest of the PAs, NPs, and the patients they serve to have
that relationship continue. If NHPs can surmount the professional
jealousies that keep them apart and if both groups can unite with
their patients, a powerful coalition may emerge. Relying on organized medicine or the federal government did not work for midwives or other nonphysician practitioners in the past. It is not likely
to work now.

CONCLUSION

New health practitioners were resurrected in the 1960s and 1970s
because of support from organized medicine and the federal government in response to growing disenchantment with the health
care system. As such, new health practitioners are indeed, in one
sense, "sorcerer's apprentices, created to do the bidding of organized medicine."[29] However, NHPs have begun to challenge the
medical hierarchy enough to elicit cries of alarm from their sorcer-
ers: "PA's are a sorcerer's apprentice turned loose . . .";[30] "and
because of their function in the area of medicine, they are a danger
worse than the chiropractic";[31] "clearly the uncertainty about the
PA's autonomy . . . represents a threat to the professional preeminence and the personal practices of physicians."[32]

The future role of new health practitioners depends less on why they were created in the first place and more on what services they may provide within an evolving health care system.

Users of the health care system had wanted a "doctor" who was closer to their own background, more familiar with their community, and less mystifying and elite. Health planners looked for a more appropriately trained professional who was less expensive and more easily persuaded to function in areas that were underserved. Health care workers wanted a chance to broaden their skills and involvement in the system. And finally, organized medicine wanted a new corps of health workers that would defuse consumer militancy, curtail rising costs (and thus lessen the chance of government interference), and perform tasks that doctors did not want to do but that nevertheless needed to be done. New health practitioners have met all of these requirements. Which goals they will continue to meet in the future will depend on the broader politics of the health care system.

It may well be that a single way of training (and inevitably selecting and socializing) all medical school graduates will not serve the needs of every community in this country equally well. The board of a rural community-run clinic that one of the authors previously worked for voted unanimously to hire a PA with an M.D. consultant instead of an M.D. because they felt that PAs were more likely than M.D.'s to possess all the qualities they wanted in a local provider.

With a variety of motivations, class backgrounds, socialization patterns, training, and philosophy, the different midlevel health workers now emerging bring qualities that some patients may prefer. There is no evidence to suggest that good prenatal and obstetrical care can be given only by obstetricians, or that all primary care is practiced "better" by physicians, particularly when one takes a broad view of health. A practitioner with adequate clinical skills who remains in a community for many years may be providing "better" care than a series of highly skilled clinicians who come and go at frequent intervals. A World Health Organization study of feldshers, the midlevel health workers in the USSR, and of what their role implies about the use of PAs in this country raised this question: ". . . do we in fact need more MDs as presently produced, or do we need to redefine what we mean in terms of actual service when we address a professional as a 'doctor'?"[33]

Delivering health care requires a combination of skills, of which clinical diagnosis and therapy is only one. While physicians have developed this skill the most, and can serve as a model for other health practitioners in this way, other health workers have emphasized equally important health skills. Supporting the existence of more than one type of health practitioner ensures that these other skills will remain part of health care.

Nurse practitioners and physician's assistants may be able to add more to health care than just the services they directly provide. Medical students trained alongside new health practitioners have questioned the necessity and value of spending hours in the pathology lab doing frozen sections while the new health practitioner students learn how to appropriately refer and counsel patients with breast masses. Physicians with high-level technical skills recognize patient acceptance of and even preference for an approachable practitioner who relates to their medical, social, and psychological concerns. If the example can influence the training and practice of physicians as well, new health practitioners can have a major impact.

We do not know how patients will best be served in the future health care system, but "it may be that New Health Professionals eventually will replace general practice physicians, or create a separate rung in the hierarchy of health care providers, or carve out a distinct set of NHP services in primary care."[34] Other countries train diverse types of providers: "doctors" who provide a majority of the primary care and "professors" who function largely in academic medical centers and provide tertiary care. Moreover, as we find out what midlevel practitioners need to learn, we may find out what primary care M.D.'s do *not* need to know. Front-line medical care may require more of a background in community and social medicine and in public health and less of the detailed pathophysiology that all medical and osteopathy students are required to learn. PA and NP schools are exploring how much of the medical school curriculum can be altered or deleted and still produce a competent health professional.

The major issue to be addressed, then, is not whether midlevel health workers should exist but how they should relate to the health hierarchy and what forces will shape their future development. If new health practitioners become totally absorbed into the existing health system and stake their future on acceptance by the establishment, they will undoubtedly represent little in the way of progressive change. If PAs and NPs continue to focus their professional agenda on turf battles among themselves instead of uniting with patients and each other around common goals, they may both follow the path of the "Teachers of Infant Hygiene." Since they are at the focal point of the crisis in the medical system—working where doctors will not, providing patient-oriented services not given priority by mainstream medicine—there exists the other option, of using that position to work for change. The rural or inner-city clinics that hired a new health provider because they originally could not get a doctor can still unite with the NP or PA and their patients to demand the continuing availability of high-quality medical care, whose absence was in fact the original problem. Then, the role of the new health practitioner shifts from that of defusing the initial demand for a doctor who was not available to becoming an ally in the broader struggle in favor of access to relevant, high-quality care. The NP or PA who is less mystifying to patients and takes more time to discuss patient concerns can potentially provoke demands for *more* such responsiveness, rather than co-opting those demands.

Midlevel health workers are clearly a link between the public and the elite of the medical hierarchy. From this position, nurses, PAs, NPs, and other midlevel workers either can seek to ally with their patients and with lower-rung health workers to challenge the top of the hierarchy or they can be absorbed upward. Recent history is particularly relevant.

The Flexner report of 1910 successfully paved the way for the elimination of all but one type of practitioner, who came to dominate health policy decisions. The health care crisis of the 1960s was a consequence of this emphasis. We are once again faced with a growing range of options, along with new calls to narrow the training and scope of health professionals. Rather than repeat history, we should continue to support the existence of more than one type of health practitioner. This diversity can encourage the development of a health care system that provides not only crisis intervention care to a privileged sector but also total health care for everyone.

part **IV**

CONTROL OF HEALTH CARE

10.

community participation and control:

OR CONTROL OF COMMUNITY PARTICIPATION

John W. Hatch

Eugenia Eng

"I'm a proud man, always worked until the accident. I quit going out there [the county hospital] because they treated me so bad. Had to wait for hours and then the doctors changed every time and didn't seem to know what to do. The Lord was with me."

—Black Laborer,
Arizona

"They gave Grandpa a gringo diet. Now, I don't know, but it seems like they should know better."

—Mexican-American Community Aide,
New Mexico

"Hypertension is the main problem here. They've never screened, and you know they don't try to tell people what to do to manage the problem. I don't know why. They are just like the hustlers on the corner except they wear white coats."

—Black Community Council Member,
Chicago

INTRODUCTION

After a decade and a half of limited efforts toward involving the poor and the modest-income consumer in health care, the poor still suffer disproportionately from illness and injury,[1] and the physician still exercises the greatest control over the health care establishment. However, change has occurred. An analysis of U.S. legislative efforts in the 1960s to address the health problems of the poor and grass roots discontent sheds light on why the reforms, though quite limited, have had a meaningful impact on the quality of care and on who controls it. Community participation and control has been central to these efforts, for they raise the fundamental issues concerning the priorities, effectiveness, and accountability of services. They involved a novel and bold experiment that was remarkably successful—though, disappointingly, left unfinished.

COMMUNITY PARTICIPATION FOR WHAT REASON?

Being poor in America has not always been considered a social problem. At one time, the tired, the hungry, the poor, and the downtrodden masses were welcome. The fabric of American communities, both rural and urban, was sturdily woven with different ways of coping and with the hope for a better life. Community participation and control was a vital part of this fabric, functioning through organizations ranging from Chinatown credit unions to black burial societies. The earliest mutual aid society in the black community was organized in Philadelphia in 1787 to support its members in sickness and to benefit the surviving spouse and children of the deceased. The largest black-owned insurance company of today traces its origins to a similar mutual aid society.

Communities, then and now, are more than collections of individuals. Their members are part of a social system; they perform social roles and are bound to one another directly or indirectly by a network of rights and obligations.[2] Social order is found to varying degrees among communities in terms of formal and informal leadership and decision-making patterns. Members can exert influence on the social order because they are able to participate in decision-making either directly as leaders or indirectly as constituencies. This is community participation and control—the power to determine how best to maximize human potential and survival, and to act on it. Participation of poor and near-poor communities in efforts designed to free them from whatever barrier separated them from the good life experienced by the majority of Americans was not a social, political, or economic issue in the past. It is that today. Why? Because being poor has become a social problem.

With the advent of industrialization, urbanization, migration, and the Great Depression, traditional ways of eliciting community participation and control began to unravel. The continuing movement of American people from rural to urban communities accelerated dramatically during World War II: black people from the rural South and Puerto Rican people from the Island moved to northern urban centers, and Americans of Mexican ancestry from predominately agricultural areas of the Southwest and West migrated to urban centers in those regions. Within little more than a generation, these minority peoples had shifted from overwhelmingly rural and agrarian to metropolitan, usually inner-city lifestyles. Conflict and competition for living space, jobs, and cultural values in the cities contributed to white middle-class flight, sponsored by the federal government, to the presumed tranquillity of suburban living. Massive amounts of federal dollars were allocated to build the roads and finance the homes for these willing refugees from the turmoil of urban development.

Urbanization exacted an almost unmeasurable toll from the urban newcomers. Changing technology in agriculture and extractive industries responsible for sustaining the movement of people to urban places also resulted in a rapid decline in the demand for an unskilled, rural labor force.[3] The social and psychological costs have been staggering. Individuals and families from environments in which they understood and adhered to clearly defined norms and values were within a matter of hours transported to places where they faced many options and had few indicators as to which ones would best serve their personal interest.

The accompanying disarray may not have been greater than that experienced by earlier immigrants, but the nation's sense of social responsibility had sharpened. Youth especially learned quickly that old country values would not meet the survival needs of the new environment, and were forced to assume the burden of integrating the old country culture with the broader American culture. Urbanologists described the high rates of family instability, the ineffective schools, and the declining quality of the inner-city housing pool, as well as such personally destructive patterns of behavior as drug addiction, increasing levels of crime against individuals, and dependency.[4] Some warned that American culture could not be maintained if the nation's cities were allowed to disintegrate.

Theorists began to search for causes and to formulate strategies for the rehabilitation of urban communities. A vanguard of articulate and vocal civic leaders, academicians, and human-service professionals argued that the new urban conditions required massive governmental intervention. At first, such views lacked mass public support. The new urban dwellers, according to the conventional wisdom, would spend a generation adapting and then follow the pattern of upward and outward mobility established by dislocated European peasants who had immigrated several decades earlier. Slowly, however, the general applicability of that model was questioned. There was no longer a ready market for unskilled labor, because the structure of the job market was shifting from heavy-industrial to high-technology and skilled-service areas. Lower tax rates coupled with improved roadways and a growing population base were attracting business to outer metropolitan fringe areas.

In addition, the structure of basic survival support systems had shifted from reliance on ethnic mutual aid societies and ward politicians to professionally staffed, bureaucratically structured human-service conglomerates. Externally controlled services later compromised the development of a strong sense of community identity that complements the development of social controls and the exercise of political power.[5] It is in this context that the centralization of health and human services was justified on the grounds that quality and efficiency would be enhanced notwithstanding complaints from many inner-city residents who felt that these changes would result in reduced services to their communities. Access to health care was further limited by the movement of physicians and other providers to locations closer to their middle- and upper-middle-class clientele. However, service location and costs barriers could not explain the increasing rates of infant mortality in low-income census tracts within and adjacent to high-quality and publicly provided infant and maternal care facilities.[6] Being poor became a medical care problem as well as a social problem.

Prior to the Watts rebellion in 1965, Americans often appeared to equate poverty with geographic isolation, technological obsolescence, and poor education. Race entered into this equation through the added dimension of prejudice when the poor were black, had Spanish surnames, or came from other low-income ethnic groups. Compensatory efforts were designed to reduce the barriers that these factors imposed; the reality of social alienation was meanwhile ignored.

The Watts riots were unexpected, since the social, political, and economic conditions in this Los Angeles suburb appeared to be much better than those found in the South and in the older inner-city neighborhoods of the Northeast. The occurrence of the Watts disorder, more than any other event in America, strengthened the argument of those who saw the failure of community as a major factor in limiting certain populations from full participation in American society. Oscar Lewis's study of low-income Mexican

Americans and Puerto Rican Americans and Kenneth Clark's work with black Americans in Harlem provided a conceptual framework in which problems of poverty were seen as involving alienation from the core norms, values, and experiences necessary to successful functioning in mainstream America.[7]

Watts also provided the stimulus for the rapid expansion of health programs as a major component of the War on Poverty. The dramatic description of the difficulties experienced by Watts residents in seeking health care alerted liberal health professionals to the role they could play in improving the condition of neglected populations. Health care was an attractive poverty issue. Unlike job training, education, and other services provided by the federal government, its benefits would be highly visible and immediately available to every person in the community. Nor was health care as controversial or threatening to local politicians and human-service organizations.

Watts helped remind the nation that good health care is indeed a right for every American, not a privilege. Few professionals, however, viewed health status and the quality of care from the perspective of community development. The linkage between poor health and social alienation was not commonly understood, but as it became better known, the issue of community participation and control became pivotal.

COMMUNITY PARTICIPATION IN WHAT WAY?

A number of factors during the past two decades contributed to the national awareness that the absence of community participation and control affects the social and the medical care problems of America. America's international role after World War II and the wide-ranging competition with the Soviet Union during the cold war provided the stimulus to identify more sharply those areas of American life incompatible with the image of a just, free, and open society.

The presence in Washington, D.C., of black and brown persons representing governments that this nation wished to influence contributed to the removal of the most blatant forms of color segregation from that city. American ethnic and racial minorities, rightly sensing the opportunity for change, intensified their efforts to overcome those barriers to personal freedoms and economic benefits that were being projected to other nations as guaranteed to all by the American economic and political systems.

This moral position was flawed by the fact that black Americans still faced the crudest forms of race-caste segregation in the South, and discrimination in other parts of the nation. These incongruencies were being transmitted internationally, especially to Third World nations, by Soviet propagandists and their allies. During the early 1960s the hardest forms of societal resistance—such as police using dogs, fire hoses, and electric cattle prods and beating unarmed women and children who were peacefully protesting for the right to ride a public bus or to eat a sandwich at a dime-store lunch counter—gained sympathy and support from many nations of the world.

These acts of protest required community organization, public-relations skills, and massive support from citizens of many backgrounds, but it was essentially a black grass-roots movement. Within a year after the 1964 march on Washington, civil rights legislation, including the Voting Rights Act, was passed by Congress. Though black people had not reached the "Promised Land,"* they were headed in the right direction.

Although displaced black tenant farmers and laborers from plantations and small towns in the South were the more hard pressed for the necessities of life, urban youth adopted far more militant action to confront the high unemployment. Their own lack of personal focus, their psychological readiness to take whatever action seemed necessary, made them the most volatile element among blacks during that period. They were in the vanguard of violent rebellion in Watts and other low-income inner-city communities across the nation.

This complex set of forces—economic, social, demographic, national, and international attitudes and values—set the stage for the involvement of low- and modest-income citizens in a national crusade against poverty. The strategy of community participation and control in the 1960s was still very much an experimental notion. Implementing it varied in such small-scale pilot programs in cities as New York's HARYOU Act and Boston's South End Planning Council. The relative successes of programs like those strengthened experiments to revitalize broad levels of participation and higher degrees of expectation for accountability among poor communities.

The Economic Opportunity Act of 1964 was a landmark reform. Not only was it the single largest government-directed attack on poverty in American history, but it also included an innovation of

---

*The phrase is from the black spiritual "I'm Bound for the Promised Land" and is understood to refer to a land where freedom and justice would prevail and where conditions for spiritual and physical survival would not be difficult. This concept was influenced by the biblical account of Moses and the Hebrews and their exodus from Egypt in search of sanctuary. Martin Luther King was frequently referred to as the Moses who was leading his people out of the wilderness (i.e., years of slavery, injustice, and hard times) into a more hopeful period.

surpassing importance.[8] The concepts of community action and community participation were mandated by the federal government in a first attempt at involving the poor in planning and implementing programs that affect them—in education, therefore, recreation, labor, and health. Title II, Section 202(a), of the Economic Opportunity Act reads as follows:

> The term "community action programs" means a program:
> (1) which mobilizes and utilizes resources, public or private, or any urban or rural, or combined urban and rural geographical area (referred to in this part as a "community"), including but not limited to a state, metropolitan area, county, city, town, multi-city unit, or multi-county unit in an attack on poverty;
> (2) which provides services, assistance and other activities of sufficient scope and size to give promise of progress toward elimination of poverty or a cause or causes of poverty through developing employment opportunities, improving human performance, motivation and productivity, or bettering conditions under which people live, learn, and work;
> (3) which is developed, conducted, and administered with the maximum feasible participation of residents of the areas and members of the groups served;
> (4) which is conducted, administered, or coordinated by a public or private nonprofit agency (rather than a political party), or a combination thereof.

Through "maximum feasible participation," issues of policy and control were to be examined and reshaped by those outside the mainstream establishment. Poor communities were provided with direct financial linkage to the federal government through community participation and control. This particular piece of legislation focused on the revolutionary aspects of the War on Poverty,[9] and the Office of Economic Opportunity (OEO) became the strategic headquarters located in the executive branch.

At that time most agency boards were composed of persons of middle- and upper-income status who lived outside the community in which the agency was located. Staff persons, with few exceptions, were college educated. Not surprisingly, many community residents viewed local agencies as paternalistic and not inclined to support active-protest strategies such as rent strikes, picketing, and boycotts.

The new OEO-sponsored organizations, often staffed and directed by community people who did not have college degrees, began to assume administrative and staff responsibility for such basic neighborhood services as child day care, after-school programs, employment counseling, crisis management and referral, and other activities formerly carried out by professionally trained workers. In response to these reforms, many traditional agencies began to include low- and modest-income community representatives on their boards of directors and acted to broaden qualifications for employment to include non-degree holders. In some situations these tasks were well planned, and resulted in improved services to clients through broader coverage and more appropriate use of professional staff. Nonetheless, in a pioneering operation of national scope, uniformly high quality of service was difficult to achieve. Community participation and control was still in the experimental stage.

OEO disbursed $800 million to hundreds of communities within its first eight months of operation. Tufts University Medical School was the first to receive funding specifically for health, and it developed an urban neighborhood health center in Columbia Point in Boston and a rural comprehensive health center in Mound Bayou, Mississippi, known as the Tufts-Delta project.[10]

These two programs had very strong links to the medical school that founded them. The money given by OEO to Tufts to fund its operations came in the form of research and demonstration grants. Columbia Point and Mound Bayou were in essence demonstration projects designed not only to provide service to low-income communities but also to give insight into various key questions: What community participation and control strategies can be integrated into the delivery of medical services? What should be the nature of community boards? How much power should they have? How should the roles of board members be defined? What kind of jobs are appropriate for community people in a health center? What should be the structure of an ambulatory care service when improved care to low- and modest-income persons is an objective? What utilization patterns might be developed? Could changes in patterns of utilization be documented? Could changes in health status be demonstrated?

The original intent was to test social-action techniques for improving health and for fighting poverty in certain communities. Those showing success were to be taken to other parts of the nation. The potential for a significant leap in the scientific knowledge of development theory and its influence on the quality of care was tremendous. OEO efforts in community participation and action represented perhaps the greatest effort that a Western nation ever made to involve the formerly denied and excluded citizens in social change. However, the experiment was not allowed to run its full course, and a rigorous evaluation of the degree of impact that maximum feasible participation had on the health care system could never be completed. OEO and its critics were shortsighted in not having conducted more scientific analyses of programs which were remarkably successful (as well as those that failed).

Neighborhood health centers and rural comprehensive health centers, which gave health consumerism its biggest initial push, were not immune to the effects of OEO shortsightedness. The assumption that representation of the poor on neighborhood boards would ensure access to and influence upon decision-making structures was not enough to remove the critical barriers for improving the quality of care. Simply to place poor people on boards-of-health programs and expect them to compete with the traditional health care industry was foolhardy. They frequently lacked certain technical knowledge and resources, as well as the accepted language with which to gain even more.

Although reform-oriented professionals agreed that community people had a role to play in reshaping health care, they held varied notions of what it should be. Few had the insight and skill to involve community people in planning strategies for improving such health problems as high rates of hypertension, infant mortality, uncontrollable diabetes, drug abuse, and depression—all usually found in low-income communities. Too often the professional staff perceived the community board of a health center as the public-relations division promoting the center's services to the people. Board members, on the other hand, often wanted to focus agency resources on issues like unemployment, poor housing, drug abuse, and crime in the streets. These boards soon discovered that such problems were not within the scope of the agency's mandate or within the realm of professional competencies held by health center staff. These differing perceptions of the priorities frequently resulted in conflicts between professional staff and community members.

Consumer involvement in health care was not a new reform idea of the 1960s. Volunteer organizations such as the Red Cross, Alcoholics Anonymous, the Heart Fund, the National Foundation for Birth Defects, and the national efforts focusing on cancer and mental retardation are well known to most Americans. Their struggles and triumphs are well documented.[11]

Religious and ethnic organizations had also been responsible for the development of health care services. Health care operated by ethnic groups emerged from many of the same concerns that led to the emergence of services sponsored by religious groups. These problems included the feeling that existing services would not provide the type of care or the amenities essential to the welfare of its members and the refusal of established services to provide care to their people solely on the basis of their identifications with a minority group.

Black hospitals were organized because at that time most existing hospitals absolutely refused to accept black patients and because the few that accepted black people refused to grant staff privileges to black physicians. The presence of black hospitals in rural Mississippi, Alabama, Tennessee, and other poverty areas provided concrete evidence for the role that a denied population could take in providing itself with needed services. A hospital in the Mississippi Delta was opened in 1940, at a time when the mean family income of the sponsoring body's membership was less than $400 annually.

In 1929, Michael A. Shadid, a physician in Oklahoma, began a cooperative health care program known as the Farmer's Union Cooperative Hospital Association. That effort was subject to prolonged harassment by county and state medical societies. The principal issues in dispute were the following:

1. the right of people to organize for their own medical care;
2. the right of doctors to make agreements with patients on other than a fee-for-service basis;
3. the right of medical societies to be judge and jury in the matter of ethics.

The Pacific Supply Co-operative, a farmer's group, sponsored a tour by Shadid to speak to farmers' cooperatives about cooperative medicine. A dozen or so communities responded with interest, setting up committees, and soon the idea became primarily urban in character. It was carried to Washington and led to the establishment of the Group Health Cooperative of Puget Sound. Its success was due to the following favorable circumstances:

1. *Legal Counsel:* The committee secured a firm of attorneys which was familiar with cooperatives.
2. *Group Practice:* The Group Health Cooperative merged with a clinic staffed by fifteen generalists and specialists which had operated under contracts to various local industries.
3. *Consumer Constituency:* The original subscribers receiving prepaid health care from the group practice supported the Group Health Cooperative approach.

Other examples of consumer-based health care approaches can be found among the numerous efforts of organized labor to secure health care for its members. Two, in particular, had great influence on the national patterns of health care. The first health program was developed and sponsored by the United Mine Workers (UMW). Miners' health care prior to World War II was poor. A common practice was to provide just enough care for injured individuals to reduce their dependency on whatever workmen's compensation was available in the mining community. Following the mining strikes of World War II, the miners won an agreement that included a royalty payment from the companies into a health and welfare fund. In 1946, the unions formed an advisory committee of miners to develop a health program for the care of the workers and their families.

The resulting UMW health program soon indicated that working with the existing health delivery system was not a sound approach. The quantity and quality of care were extremely low. When discrepancies between miners' care and health care for other groups were brought to the attention of the local and state authorities, the UMW program was informed that no one other than a practicing physician was capable of judging medical performance. Eventually, the UMW decided to drop from its list of approved physicians those doctors and hospitals that had been the most lax. The quality of care then began to improve.[12]

The UMW also stimulated the formation of group practice plans for miners and their families. These plans had three basic structural similarities:

1. a sponsoring nonprofit board of directors composed largely of miners themselves, with a trained administrator as their representative;
2. medical practice in the hands of a group of generalists and specialists under the leadership of a medical director;
3. extensive prepayment mechanisms jointly supported through the UMW fund and personal contributions.

The second example of consumer-based health programs comes from the Teamsters Union. In 1945, a committee of union members was formed to identify a good comprehensive medical care plan for their families and to determine the best means for including this plan within their available incomes. They found that existing medical insurance plans provided only incomplete coverage. As a result, a patient-oriented pattern of insurance coverage was developed. Funding was procured through a collectively bargained agreement that provided for contributions by the employer. Physicians would work on a part-time basis, being paid at an hourly rate based on the median incomes of physicians in the community.[13]

Unlike these union and cooperative efforts that have involved consumers in health care, OEO-sponsored health programs did not draw on a constituency with sharply defined issues. Nor were they held together by membership in a formally structured group with prior experience in negotiating. The constituencies of neighborhood health centers were and remain predominantly poor, and not prepared to "pay their way" within the terms of financial responsibility as generally defined in the United States.[14]

Rather than placing the primary organizing effort at the community level and expecting local representatives of the poor to have a direct impact on health care in their communities, an alternative strategy would have been to organize regional coalitions of several communities. By pooling their resources, they might have been able to hire professionals who were responsive to poor people and who also possessed skills in such key areas as health, ressource planning, economics, clinical epidemiology, and law that would have been useful in shifting toward those priorities the coalitions perceived as primary.

Neither the professional nor the community people were given the type of training that would have enabled them to maximize their potential. Perfect understanding between the intentions of providers and the priorities of communities is perhaps an unachievable dream. But liberal reforms such as the Economic Opportunity Act could have brought them closer to a common understanding, if the experiences of consumer-oriented efforts like the documented successes of cooperatives and labor unions had been used.

In retrospect, it is ironic that in neither the planning for nor the implementation of maximum feasible participation was there input from the poor and underserved communities. At the very best, the OEO movement attracted well-meaning professionals to act as advocates for the poor rather than involving the poor themselves in strategy design. No one among the staff at OEO headquarters had ever been a community organizer.

Much of the confusion at the community level can be traced to the unrealistic, and at times wild, criteria used to identify local leaders. In some cases respected and influential members of the community, such as schoolteachers, preachers, and funeral directors, were categorically excluded from participation. Past performance and ability to involve other community members were frequently not taken into consideration. While some OEO administrators were fully aware of the critical brokerage role played by such "gatekeeper" persons, they saw such roles as barriers to broader participation of the poor in the management of their own affairs.

Although it was true that some gatekeepers were wedded to the status quo, many were genuinely interested in the welfare of their community and could have added valuable skills and leadership to the task of redefining what was meant by the control and quality of care. Instead, those individuals who generated the most steam and who were most militant were too often perceived by OEO Washington administrators as being community leaders. In many cases, they tended to hold policy positions on boards far beyond their actual base of grass-roots support. A decision was made in Boston, for example, to recruit pimps as staff for community improvement programs because they were bright, had a strong self-image, and tended toward action. When placed in positions of sanctioned authority, they, of course, proceeded to replicate in the community the type of relationship they had previously established with their women. Strategies such as these frequently resulted in disabling communities rather than in strengthening them, as advocates of these actions had surely intended. As struggles for influence and control within service delivery organizations intensified, staff professionals often became the scapegoats.

What OEO failed to recognize is that the struggles for change of those poor who have nothing differ from the struggles of those who have jobs and a stake in the existing order. The difference is in the means for effecting change—from burning buildings to negotiating through nonviolent means. For a true involvement of the poor in the program of a health center or of community action, the task is very different from that of organizing a one-shot militant protest or mass meeting.[15] The community leaders have usually been drawn from the pool of the men and women who are a little more stable financially and of a higher status, who serve as role models, and who therefore have a constituency in the community. Young militants wearing dashikis in the 1960s were not those leaders. They were more specifically representatives of a movement and an ideal of the time. They did not fit in with the mainstream of poor communities.

OEO programs were often planned as if poor communities had no viable social organization or structure. They, therefore, sought to create or sanction new structures rather than to conduct a hard analysis of what existed. In addition to ignoring the existing leadership and local decision-making patterns, long-established social-support networks were overlooked. For example, the Community Action Program guidelines stipulated that community participation be brought about by forums, discussions, nominations, block elections, referendums, petitions, newsletters to neighborhood leaders, and the ability to protest or propose changes. These traditional democratic means frequently appeared absurd because they were so alien to the traditional community mechanisms for eliciting involvement. In some communities, when elections were held, nobody voted. Charges and countercharges of scandal plagued many programs as a result of the competition that these democratic means instilled. Maximum feasible participation as interpreted by OEO staff sometimes did more to divide poor communities than to bring them together.[16]

However, changes did occur in the health service delivery system and among the communities directly influenced by OEO programs. Community health and action programs were successful in stimulating awareness among those who were better off and among professional health workers of the smoldering discontent found among the poor and near poor. Community participation provided an opportunity for expression as well as a catharsis of sorts for the poor to ventilate their feelings within a structure rather than through the burning of cities. It encouraged people to see their right to health care and to demand that it be accessible and delivered with human dignity. The experiences of comprehensive health centers such as the Tufts-Delta project and of the people of Bolivar County, Mississippi, have certainly influenced the redefinition of health care to encompass nutrition, housing, water, and sanitation. It happened because of the voice and insights of the people living daily with these problems.[17]

John Hatch, one of the authors of this chapter, spent three months picking cotton in the Delta area to listen and learn about the people's perceptions, experiences, and needs before the project began. The information proved invaluable to the project staff for bridging the gap between the medically oriented intentions of providers and the community development needs of the consumers. Communitywide meetings were held in each of the ten towns to be served, in order to introduce the project and to elicit people's opinions, suggestions, and involvement. Several community members who were eventually hired as staff aides or placed on community boards had first been noticed at these meetings. The participation of poor people in shaping an alternative model for health service delivery presented a hope for liberal reforms in medical care.[18]

Community participation and control helped to reorient health care institutions to include staff persons who had not gotten their credentials in the usual way. Life experience, ability to communicate in the local language and language styles, intimate knowledge of the local community, and willingness to live in the local community became important factors in selecting staff when community health center boards were involved in the selection process. It was also persuasively argued that workers from the community could perform such tasks as conducting needs assessments and providing outreach to enhance the difficult process of health behavior change

—and do them more effectively than workers with professional credentials, because they did not face class barriers that often separated professional from client. On-the-job training and paid leave for education were encouraged. Personal development was built into many new career tracks. A number of persons who began as community aides, outreach workers, and the like went on to earn degrees from recognized institutions and to join the ranks of certified professional workers.

To the vast majority of participants, opportunities opened up by OEO represented the best chance they had ever had for personal development, and many of these individuals used the experiences as a bridge to mainstream participation. Experiences gained as board members were taken to other community organizations and activities. In many communities, OEO program participation provided a mechanism for establishing links among people with shared interests. Although poor people had been involved in ward politics in a few urban communities, most places lacked a forum for the discussion of problems of particular concern to them. Health center boards provided such a forum. Political awareness and involvement grew out of these experiences. Today throughout the nation it is possible to identify skilled and respected civic and political leaders of the poor who were stimulated to engage in these activities through early involvement with community board experiences during the 1960s and early 1970s. Those aides who moved on to midlevel and professional positions brought a new dimension to the training institutions that had prepared them and to the field of practice itself as they continued their work for poor communities.

Documentation regarding the numbers of persons who completed technical and professional training as a direct result of all OEO activities is not available. However, Ms. L. C. Dorsey, who was on the staff of the Tufts-Delta Comprehensive Health Center, has shared data from a study in progress on those persons who received technical or professional training as a direct result of assistance gained through the Tufts-Delta project in Mound Bayou, Mississippi. Bolivar County, Mississippi, is located in the Delta region of the state. In 1960, it was the third-poorest county in the nation. Sixty-five percent of the county's population of 39,000 was black, and over half of it was living in poverty. Between the years 1968 and 1978, 62 persons from Bolivar County gained technical and professional credentials in health care and related career fields. Six became physicians, thirteen became registered sanitarians, eleven became registered nurses, fifteen earned L.P.N. certifications, seven gained master's degrees in social work, one earned a Ph.D. in that field, three got degrees in administration, five got master's degrees in public health, and one person earned a Ph.D. in clinical psychology. Nineteen young people from the community completed training in a field not directly related to health care. The Mound Bayou experience provided the stimulus and direction to many talented people who might otherwise have been trapped into roles considerably less significant to regional development and human betterment. Dorsey herself is representative of this group.[19]

Before joining the health center's community organization staff in 1967, Dorsey had been involved as an organizer in the civil rights movement but had relied on field work on cotton plantations to support herself and her six children. After joining the center staff, she was able to complete requirements for high school certification and then enrolled in extension courses offered at the health center through Mary Holmes Junior College. In 1969, Dorsey was selected to be director of a poor people's food-producing cooperative by that organization's board of directors. Several years later she accepted a fellowship to work toward a master's degree in social work at the State University of New York at Stony Brook. Since completing the degree requirements in 1975, Dorsey has served as state director of the Prisoners Defense Organization in Mississippi and been active in a number of civil rights and human-service organizations. She is also a staff writer for a local black newspaper and has written a book of poetry. Two of her six children have completed college, three are currently enrolled, and one is a senior in high school.

With results such as these one could, as some did, feel that citizen participation on boards and the development of individual careers came into existence as one means for controlling the passions of minorities in poverty: that is, that the spending of money to bring them into the structure would be less expensive than the presence of police required for repressing potential destruction that rebellion would bring. However, several of these individuals did in fact move into the political arena to bring about change.

During the same year when Dorsey joined the Tufts-Delta Center staff, Johnny Todd was also hired as a community organization worker. Todd was involved in the development of the health council and the farm cooperative, and was the promoter-manager of the first bookstore in the region offering materials on black history and liberation. Several years later Todd was accepted as a graduate student in community organization at the Atlanta University School of Social Work. After completing his studies, Todd returned to Mississippi and joined the faculty of a local college as an instructor for the undergraduate social work program. He continued his interest in community development and became involved with self-help and development organizations of his home community. In 1978, Todd was elected mayor of Rosedale, Mississippi. Despite continuing agitation and harassment by conservative and reactionary interests in the town, Todd is making progress in improving the quality of municipal services. He has been successful in attracting outside resources and is well along in the development of a sewage plant. Before Todd's election, the black section of Rosedale did not have paved streets or sewers.

In Rosedale, political control by a mayor and a city council responsive to the needs of low- and modest-income black people has resulted in a dramatic improvement in their quality of life. When Todd's reelection in 1980 was reaffirmed by a special referendum called by the opposition, the *Delta Democrat Times* reported that people were dancing in the streets. For the first time poor and near-poor blacks are being treated like first class citizens. Fear of the police and of injustice before the local court is giving way to feelings of trust and hope. Todd now controls the resources he had a decade ago hoped only to influence positively.

It is unrealistic to expect most people to have the energy and talent of an L. C. Dorsey or a Johnny Todd. They are exceptional individuals, and programs based on community participation and control recognized them as such. However, without maximum feasible participation, persons with unrealized potential would not have had the opportunity or the experience to overcome barriers to personal development and to pursue their interest in community service. Through pathways created by the Tufts-Delta project, an uncommonly high percentage of the children of community workers and of nursing, social worker, nutrition, and other aide-level workers have attended college and entered health care technical and professional schools. There are now trained people from among the community persons who were directly associated with the center, and from among their children, to fill technical and professional positions to serve the people in the five-county area of the Delta Health Center and Hospital.

Clearly the particular economic, social, and political history of all the people involved—the community people, political leaders, civic leaders, business persons—made each project unique. Places that appeared to be demographically similar reacted quite differently to the notions of citizen participation. Some community decision makers used community participation to broaden the base of personal influence, while others saw broader participation as an effort by the federal government to bring underserving and irresponsible people into positions of trust and responsibility. Ironically enough, no matter how community participation and control were defined or executed in the past, evidence that this was considered a good idea can be found in the health legislation following the Economic Opportunity Act of 1964.

COMMUNITY PARTICIPATION
BY WHOM?

Another policy area in which the participatory concept was developed was in the 1966 Comprehensive Health Planning (CHP) and Public Health amendments. They cited the need for "an effective partnership, involving close inter-governmental collaboration, official and voluntary efforts, and the participation of individuals and organizations." State Health Planning Councils were to be established, on which the majority were representatives of the local consumers of health services. For the first time in America, consumers were explicitly recognized as necessary participants in the planning process of health service delivery.[20]

In 1974, the National Health Planning and Resources Development Act, passed as an improved version of the CHP legislation, sought to enhance consumer participation in the planning and development of health care at the community and state levels. Over 200 regional Health Systems Agencies (HSAs) and over 50 state-wide Health Coordination Councils were established throughout the country. Representatives of local residents were to constitute between 51 and 60 percent of these planning boards. Subarea advisory councils were also provided for in order to enable HSAs, if they so desired, to expand the participation of consumers by forming a recognized constituency for those consumer representatives on HSA boards of directors.

HSA legislation, unlike the earlier CHP, specified who qualified as a health provider and a health consumer on the various governing boards; it also described the roles, functions, and responsibilities of these bodies. More significant, however, is that the HSA mandate solidified the federal government's commitment to community participation. But there is no doubt today who remains in control. Like OEO and CHP, HSA has yet to deal effectively with the questions surrounding the degree of community board members' representativeness of intended constituencies and their ability to influence decision-making.

Who represents whom has not been an easy question to answer, and has definite implications for the selection process of community board members. Health policy-makers and practitioners have resorted to statistical analysis and quantifiable measures for deciding who represents whom. Community leaders and their constituents are assumed to match up on demographic, geographic, and socioeconomic status characteristics across the board. The fallacy is that these indicators can be used as valid criteria for ensuring representativeness of specific constituencies by describing "service areas" or "target populations" through tables and graphs, and then selecting board members whose characteristics match the data. The truth of the matter is that community is synonymous neither with target population nor with service areas. Leadership does not usually occur on a matching basis with its constituents. And, criteria that most communities use for determining who can most accurately represent their priorities, values, and perspectives are not usually drawn from census-type data.

If one of the purposes of community participation is to establish a dialogue between consumers and providers, as partners, then it is crucial to assess existing patterns of communication between representatives and their particular communities. Surprisingly, very little attention has been given to the role of communication between representatives and their constituents. In some cases community representatives may not even have constituencies, because individuals were designated by noncommunity professionals or selected by non-community-based methods. It would, therefore, seem more appropriate to focus on identifying communities rather than on individuals and then to allow the separate communities to choose their own representative, using their own accepted process. If HSAs and similar health planning efforts in the future are truly committed to the concept of community participation, then encouraging continuing relationships rather than creating temporary ones is the more appropriate route. After more than fifteen years of experimentation, one key lesson should have been learned: one can never assume that a community has no institutions, decision-making patterns, leadership structure, or social support mechanisms of its own. Through necessity they have been functioning to varying degrees for purposes of survival. When given the opportunity to exercise control over decisions that directly affect their lives, members of a community can certainly determine who is best able to represent them. People were making decisions, setting priorities, and surviving long before a health policy was set in order to consider involving communities in the planning process.

Another important lesson concerns the potential impact of community participation and control on established institutions and power structures. Health care can become a force for social change that is not always universally desired. The medical care system has as much vested interest in maintaining the status quo as do the political and economic systems. Health status is intricately tied to social and economic status, to access and control over resources. If one seeks change in health status through community participation and control, then one will certainly alter the existing economic and political systems. Those programs that sought to improve the health of the poor while developing their awareness that the quality and the control of care are closely related met varying degrees of resist-ance from the political, economic, and medical care systems. The history of liberal reforms in health care provides insight into how this relationship operates when one compares the different impact that community participation and control had on the rural South and the urban North in the United States.

In the North, city politicians were not opposed to federal legisla-tion allocating funds to poor people; they were concerned with who was to control them. They resented the use of tax dollars to weaken their influence over the allocation of jobs and other resources tradi-tionally used to support political organizations.

These conflicts were not sharply divided along racial lines. In such urban centers as Chicago, Boston, New York, and Detroit, many powerful blacks questioned the value of direct federal influence at the local level. They were more threatened by community participa-tion they did not directly control. As a result, federally sponsored community participation initiatives met a higher degree of in-tracommunity and intraethnic conflict in the North than in the South. Undesirable conditions of poverty and ill health, so the rhetoric went, had been due to the lack of militancy toward the existing political system or to the degree of blackness. Unfortu-nately, some city officials and health professionals agreed. Some of those following the super black militant movement were sincere; others were urban hustlers taking care of business. The distinction was not always made.

Finely tuned combinations of arrogance and ignorance led to excesses in some urban communities. In a health center in Califor-nia, the local director of illicit trade in drugs and prostitution be-came the chairman of the health center board and used threats of violence to influence the pattern of decision making among the board members.

On balance, however, there is no reason to believe that health programs sponsored by federal reforms were any more or less cor-rupt than other federally funded activities such as highway con-struction, defense, and agricultural subsidies. In the urban North, there was an established mechanism for allocating resources in terms of services, jobs, and money to the poor and predominantly black communities. Those who controlled them were not at all immune to the idea of receiving federal money to improve the quality of health care for the poor. Most northern black leaders possessed the basic skills and savvy for making community deci-sions within the existing social order. Federal reforms might have improved the health care by ensuring their participation in deci-sion-making bodies. However, those in power in the existing social order wanted to be sure that *they* would still control who could participate. Thus, the intracommunity conflicts and underestimation of the power of the political machinery in the urban North contributed to the weaker community participation in the North than was the case in the South.

In the South, the majority of the black population, especially those having the greatest need, lived in rural places and in towns under 50,000. In many of these areas, blacks and whites had had no prior experience in participating as equals. The act of sitting in the same room was perceived by many, both black and white, as radical change. Clearly, many such neighborhoods preferred to bypass federal money if accepting it would in any way increase the influence of black people. Although resistance was based on the philosophical ground that legislated reforms such as OEO, CHP, and HSA exceed the constitutional powers of the federal government, the real objection rested on the realistic concern that blacks would be less amenable to exploitation if they had links with the federal government and control over substantial amounts of money.

Southern rural and small-town politicians rightly saw community participation legislation as a continuation of the civil rights movement. While there were struggles within southern black rural communities on the issues of representativeness and control, the strong resistance from white elected officials tended to stimulate cohesiveness in situations in which it would otherwise not have developed. Class, education, and philosophical differences among southern blacks were set aside in the face of the threat posed by the opponents of development for black people. Strong black leaders in the South, who emerged in the fight for civil rights, and faith in Washington among southern blacks because of the protection that the federal government offered during desegregation heightened expectations for change.

In the South, the community health center was frequently the first health care facility opened to people unable to pay. Participating on boards and working as aides often provided blacks with their first opportunity outside of the church to acquire the basic skills for initiating and fostering community development. It was, therefore, more possible in the rural South to provide poor people with a sense of personal advancement and community progress with much less than would have been required for similar bonding in the North.

The implications for the health care system in the future for the United States as a whole, however, do look hopeful. The momentum begun by the liberal reforms continues to influence the health care establishment. The notion of citizen participation and self-help is accepted by liberal and conservative policymakers alike. Concern is growing among all consumers about skyrocketing costs of medical care and a service delivery system that is not yet sufficiently flexible to accommodate need in a rapidly changing society. Such alternatives to the more traditional models of health programming as HMOs, physician extenders, self-care, health activation, and birthing rooms demonstrate a movement toward greater responsiveness to the needs of the consumer.

Several health centers have successfully taken steps to develop and provide excellent examples of new and creative approaches to solving the problems of poor health, rural poverty, and neglect. The Sea Island Comprehensive Health Care Center and the Beaufort-Jasper Comprehensive Health Center in South Carolina, the Lee County Health Center in Marianna, Arkansas, the Delta Center in Mound Bayou, Mississippi, and the Jackson-Hines Comprehensive Health Center in Jackson, Mississippi, are outstanding examples of rural development stimulated and inspired by concern for health improvement.

It is imperative to continue this creativity and momentum in community-oriented health programming for poorer and less well served citizens of this country. It is important for health planners and providers working with these communities to broaden the definition of health so that it goes beyond the reduction in morbidity and mortality and includes such social characteristics as underemployment, poor schools, oppression, poor housing, and self-reliance. The movement of the 1960s and early 1970s has provided stimulus and identified pathways that, if followed, will lead the American people to a more realistic notion of the determinants of health. The right to health care is much too critical to be left solely to the mercurial powers of legislation or visions of need from a professional perspective. Rather, it is through community participation and control that this right can be secured.

11.

holism and self-care:

CAN THE INDIVIDUAL SUCCEED WHERE SOCIETY FAILS?

Larry Sirott
Howard Waitzkin

In the 1980s, it has become clear that capitalist society cannot provide for some of its citizens' most basic needs. Economic stagnation fosters unemployment and financial insecurity. Overexpanded credit and high interest rates make it harder to find adequate housing and to obtain needed goods and services. Profound inflation reduces the standard of living to which people are accustomed. Many countries in the Third World that previously provided raw materials and cheap labor resist continued exploitation of their resources, a stance that leads to shortages of petroleum and other essential products. Partly because of fiscal instability, state-supported public services are cut back. With such problems, people lose confidence in their leaders and institutions, and the legitimacy of the whole system comes into question. Patterns of racism, sexism, ageism, and social-class deprivation persist. Environmental and occupational hazards threaten the very survival of humanity. Under these circumstances, society cannot assure our needs for material and spiritual sustenance.

Holism and self-care have emerged as major developments in medicine, while social conditions have deteriorated. Although there are many variations on the theme of holism and self-care, these trends have certain characteristics of social movements. At times, holism and self-care seem to offer great hope for transcending the more dismal features of our social and material environment. At other times, they seem to be full of contradictions and delusions about their potential accomplishments and distract us from looking at the conditions that foster poor health.

DEFINITIONS AND EXAMPLES

One problem in understanding holism and self-care derives from their diversity. The terms have been used loosely and applied to different activities in various settings. Written discussions of these trends diverge from actual practices. The definitions and examples that follow are selective but try to give the meanings that holism and self-care generally convey.

Holism comprises the health disciplines that view the person as an integration of body, mind, and spirit. In general, holism stands opposed to Western medicine, which claims a scientific, technological base. Holistic therapies view the individual as a totality, rather than as a collection of interrelated organ systems. In particular, the social and psychological dimensions of the person receive attention, along with physical problems. In some forms of holistic therapy, the political and economic nexus of a person's life can be a focus of change, although, as discussed below, these dimensions of health problems often escape attention in holistic medicine. Examples of the holistic approach include massage therapies, postural and structural integration, acupuncture, transcendental meditation, yoga, psychic healing, iridology, orthomolecular nutrition, and colonic irrigation. Obviously, these therapies vary widely in their theoretical basis and in their technical methods. Yet each sees a person as a whole being, illness as a disruption of personal integration, and therapy as aiming at a healthier reintegration of the total being.

Self-care involves the attitudes and techniques by which individuals assume responsibility for maintaining health and treating illness. One purpose of self-care is to remove healing from professional control and to foster the capabilities of clients and support groups, who usually are lay people. Although the self-care approach emphasizes the individual's capacity for healing, self-care often takes place in a group setting. For instance, many women's organizations and community clinics have developed programs that train individuals in self-care or that offer treatment by supportive lay people. Self-care almost always encourages prevention: that is, by maintaining a life-style that contributes to health rather than to illness, individuals can presumably prevent medical problems before they need treatment.

There are numerous examples of self-care that involve many different approaches. One of the best known is the preparation of self-care manuals. These books and articles contain descriptions of specific medical syndromes and plans that people can use in caring for themselves. When a person begins to feel symptoms, he or she can consult the manual, perform a simple routine that leads to a diagnosis or a decision to seek help from a more fully trained professional, and obtain treatment as appropriate. Similarly, these publications emphasize the concrete actions that individuals can take to prevent disease. Such actions include the reduction of smoking and alcohol intake, better nutrition, increased exercise, and the correction of psychological difficulties. In addition, prevention usually includes the reduction of stress. The individual's ability to institute these life-style changes usually depends on available socioeconomic resources.

Beyond the level of the individual, self-care groups have formed to help deprofessionalize prevention and treatment. In particular, the women's movement has encouraged self-care for a variety of gynecological and obstetrical problems that previously fell within the province of professionals. Many other groups deal with specific medical problems that have psychological dimensions. Examples are Alcoholics Anonymous, groups dealing with other addictions, stroke clubs, ostomy clubs, and organizations for the overweight.

The self-care approach has received the blessing and support of numerous corporate, governmental, and philanthropic agencies during the past decade. Agencies of the U.S. government have published manuals promoting self-care and prevention and have funded the formation of self-care programs. Philanthropies have granted financial support to publications and new organizations devoted to self-care. A number of position papers and government pronouncements have appeared that place the primary responsibility for health on the individual's life-style. Such pronouncements have often questioned the advantages of further public spending on health care services, attributing the major responsibility for health to the individual and calling for wider attempts at self-care. From this perspective, self-care is usually assumed to be cheaper and less burdensome than professional attention.

Self-care and holism are not always interrelated in theory and practice. Certain holistic disciplines encourage prevention and treatment by lay persons, while others maintain a prominent role for practitioners who possess specialized knowledge and skills. For example, some massage and yoga therapies encourage the popularization of knowledge so that lay people can care for themselves. On the other hand, psychic healing, chiropractic techniques, and acupuncture tend to involve the maintenance of esoteric and often arcane concepts that a limited number of practitioners try to maintain as a private sphere of competence. Similarly, self-care is not always holistic: that is, specific manuals and instructions are published so that clients can learn to recognize and treat specific disorders. Some of these publications encourage individuals to assess the totality of their lives and to make larger changes. But self-care approaches often focus on particular areas of prevention and treatment, without adopting a more holistic approach. In short, although holism and self-care are at times interrelated, they are not always complementary.

PROBLEMS THAT HOLISM AND SELF-CARE AIM TO RECTIFY

Since the midtwentieth century, a series of problems have arisen, both within medicine and within the broader society, that holism and self-care aim to rectify. Some of these pertain to the organization and practice of medicine itself. Others are apparent in the society of which medicine is a part. Still other problems concern the interrelationships between medicine and society.

Perhaps the primary difficulty that holism and self-care seek to correct has to do with the alienating features of Western technological medicine. Until approximately the first two decades of the twentieth century, the practice of medicine in the United States and in other countries was technically backward but often emotionally supportive. Many healing traditions existed. Folk healers, homeopaths, midwives and other women healers, and a variety of traditional practitioners attended to people's needs when they were sick. The physical success of these therapies was difficult to assess, but practitioners of traditional medicine did attract adherents throughout most sectors of society.

With the emergence of modern laboratory medicine, based particularly in bacteriology, the emphasis gradually shifted to scientific medicine. Beginning first in western Europe, the practice of medicine oriented to laboratory sciences gained prominence. In 1910, the Flexner report was published.[1] This report, discussed in the chapter on medical education in this volume, was financed by large philanthropies closely linked to capitalist industries, and called for the promotion of laboratory-based scientific medicine and criticized traditional practices. More than ninety medical schools closed within the next decade and traditions of medicine that were not rooted in scientific practice became discredited and disenfranchised.

Ironically, the comparative effectiveness of traditional as opposed to scientific techniques in improving morbidity and mortality has never been studied in detail. The findings of modern epidemiology make it quite clear that scientific medicine itself had little impact on broad morbidity and mortality patterns. Instead, the major improvements in disease patterns and early death derived from better nutrition, sanitation, and economic development. Whether scientific medicine is more effective than the traditional therapies that it displaced is still impossible to know with any certainty. This is not to say that scientific medicine is inappropriate for specific problems in certain patients, particularly for such infectious diseases as pneumonia and meningitis. However, its impact on the health and survival of large populations is difficult to demonstrate.[2]

The technological emphasis in medicine, on the other hand, has led to a more alienating experience of medical care for many patients. When they fall ill, people become subject to a variety of complicated and painful tests. When diagnoses are reached, treatments also tend to be technically based. The humanistic relationship between a practitioner and patient has tended to deteriorate, as many observers have noted. Hospitals and other health care institutions have grown large and relatively impersonal. Technological innovations have taken precedence over the more human qualities of caring relationships. The frustrations that technology has engendered account for much of the hopefulness attached to holism and self-care. Practitioners and clients have believed that holistic practices, as well as heightened emphasis on one's care for oneself, would reduce these alienating features of modern medicine.

Fragmentation by specialty is another problem that holism and self-care aim to modify. Closely linked to the proliferation of technology, medicine has become more highly specialized since approximately the end of World War II. A variety of specialists and subspecialists have received advanced training in the normal and pathological functioning of particular organ systems. Specialists tend to practice close to medical centers, often affiliated with schools of medicine, which are usually located in large cities. While priding themselves on the expert diagnosis and management of problems within their specialties, they often do not feel capable of caring for even the simplest problem outside their narrow spheres of competence. The availability of generalists, who could take care of the spectrum of problems that might arise for patients and their families, has declined. Although this trend was reversed somewhat during the 1970s, with the renewed growth of family practice, its general impact on North American medicine has been quite profound. Holism and self-care try to reduce the impact of fragmentation by specialty. By attending to the patient's total experience and by encouraging self-care, these orientations seek to avoid the narrow attention to specific organ systems that specialization has encouraged.

In addition to specialization, professional dominance and its abuse have stimulated the growth of holism and self-care. The expertise that medical practitioners have derives from their technical training, and it has historically justified their dominance in the doctor-patient relationship. Professionals possess knowledge that is often esoteric and difficult for patients to understand. Even when patients can comprehend simple explanations, doctors have tended not to provide them. The insufficient communication of information about diagnosis and treatment has been patients' most frequently expressed dissatisfaction with North American medical care. The technical basis of the professional's dominance has led to many perceived abuses. In particular, doctors have been in a position to recommend unnecessary surgery. This problem has been a major focus of contention for women, who often have undergone unnecessary hysterectomies and other gynecological surgery. In addition, doctors have recommended expensive laboratory tests and treatments that may or may not have been needed. The dominant position and attitude of professionals that derives from the possession of technical knowledge has created widespread discomfort and reaction. Holism and self-care have tried to demystify technical knowledge and to encourage patients' assuming skeptical and more equal roles in their relations with professionals.

A subtle problem that holism and self-care address is the psychic and physical dependency that patients feel vis-à-vis their doctors. This dependency is closely tied to professional dominance. Because professionals have controlled medical knowledge, patients have tended to be dependent on their doctors for both preventive and curative care. The dependency for physical problems has engendered an emotional dependency as well. Many persons have become so attached to their physicians that they frequently have been unable to manage their physical and emotional difficulties with any degree of independence. Personal autonomy has declined in the process. Dependency on the medical profession has become a common focus of frustration. Holism and self-care seek to reduce this dependency and foster personal autonomy.

The high costs of medical care have also motivated a search for less expensive therapies. The problem of costs is complex. It derives in part from specialization and professional dominance. The technological orientation of scientific medicine encourages the use of diagnostic and therapeutic procedures that demand high technology and require extensive financial resources. The escalation of medical costs is related historically to the expansion of technological approaches in medicine. Because doctors dominate the process of decision making about diagnosis and therapy, they have been in a position to use expensive procedures rather than less costly ones. Patients have in general not been able to criticize costly practices. Private and public insurance programs have subsidized expensive medical techniques, so that their critical appraisal has been limited. The sources of costly practices within medicine are a focus of holism and self-care. Both of these orientations encourage the use of relatively inexpensive methods of diagnosis and treatment. It is assumed that individuals' ability to care for themselves and to use appropriate techniques of prevention ultimately will have the impact of reducing costs.

Another impetus to the development of holism and self-care is the recognition of illness-generating life-styles. During the past two decades it has become clear that a variety of individual behaviors lead to illness and early death. These include (but are not limited to) smoking, alcohol abuse, inappropriate drug use, lack of exercise, and poor diet. Stress in the workplace and family are also elements of life-style that are said to contribute to disease. Some of these behaviors, such as smoking and drinking, are actually amenable to individual change. Other life-style changes are often more difficult for individuals to achieve; these include the reduction of familial and occupational stress. Holism and self-care aim to modify illness-generating components of personal life-style. Practitioners encourage clients to undertake changes in their behavior that will foster health and reduce the risk of disease and early death. In short, holism and self-care tend to shift responsibility for a healthy life back to the individual by emphasizing changes in life-style. This shift is easier for some people to make than for others. Life-style changes may be simpler for wealthier people than for the poor. Moreover, the emphasis on life-style may inappropriately transfer the burden for maintaining health from society to the individual. These considerations will be discussed later. For now, it is enough to say that illness-generating life-styles have become a widely recognized problem and have been a impetus for the growth of holism and self-care.

More fundamental social problems that transcend medicine have also been important factors in the holistic and self-care movements. The social problems of advanced capitalist societies are extremely difficult ones for many people. Economic insecurity has become an ever more troubling condition of day-to-day life. Sources of oppression in racism, class structure, sexism, and aging frustrate personal aspirations. Family life has become less stable, and communities provide less interpersonal support than they did in the past. Under these circumstances, individuals frequently face isolation and loneliness. Organizing in the community and workplace has historically provided roots of mutual aid and support to deal with social problems. Clearly, social and political organizing still can and should be a technique to deal with social problems that are the causes of personal unhappiness. Meanwhile, the social supports that organizations provide are not always available. The holistic and self-care movements have provided directions by which individuals can try to transcend their personal problems, either alone or in association with small groups that are therapeutically oriented. Without doubt, the availability of holistic and self-care techniques has allowed many individuals to adjust to social conditions that generate dissatisfaction and unhappiness. Whether these techniques can address and change the underlying social causes, however, is a question that needs more attention later.

To summarize, a series of problems have emerged both in Western medicine and in the wider society. These problems have helped stimulate the growth of holistic medicine and self-care. The problems are certainly real. The extent to which holism and self-care can provide solutions is more questionable.

HISTORICAL AND PHILOSOPHICAL ROOTS

One of the most striking features of holism and self-care is the diversity of their origins. These approaches emerged during the 1960s and 1970s from a variety of directions, rather than from a single source. The diversity of their backgrounds accounts for many of the divergences that practitioners in these fields currently manifest.

An important philosophical root of holism and self-care lay in Eastern philosophies. Although many Eastern traditions influenced holism and self-care, these sources are especially clear in acupuncture, transcendental meditation, yoga, and some forms of psychic healing. Specific theories and techniques have derived from principles in Zen Buddhism, Confucianism, Hinduism, and other religious traditions of the Far East and India. The Eastern philosophies generally encourage a more holistic approach to the totality of a patient's existence. Because of this orientation, the Eastern philosophical roots of holism and self-care have provided a balance to the more technological focus of Western practices. In addition, the Eastern philosophies generally emphasize the integrity and autonomy of the individual. In some instances a dominant gurulike figure has maintained professional control over the healing process. In general, however, the Eastern approaches try to develop clients' mastery over techniques that reduce the dependency on professional healers.

Another important source of holism and self-care was the counterculture movement of the 1960s. The counterculture movement expressed rebellion against many forms of tradition and authority in North American society. The movement was closely tied to the opposition against the military stance of the U.S. government, particularly in Indochina. The movement went further, to advocate a different culture from that of the mainstream society. In particular, the counterculture movement took on an antitechnological orientation. It opposed the impact of technology, in medicine as well as in other areas. Doctors and other professionals who controlled technology became sources of opposition. The counterculture movement sought to develop alternative forms of living and healing. The emphasis on self-care and holistic practice was but one manifestation of a more general attack on cultural traditions that were seen as alienating and dehumanizing. A third major influence on the emergence of holism and self-care was the women's health movement which is discussed elsewhere in this volume.

The community clinic movement was another impetus that encouraged holistic practice and self-care. This movement was in part a reaction against the dominant traditions of Western medicine that failed to provide humanistic and responsive care for large segments of the population. In particular, low-income and minority people suffered from a lack of access to reliable services. Complaints often arose that professionals working in private practice or medical centers lacked concern for the special problems that low-income and minority groups faced. Neighborhood health centers had appeared in various cities earlier in the twentieth century, but they expanded quickly in the 1960s and 1970s. The governing structure and professional staffing of these clinics differed markedly. (For more discussion of these differences, see the first chapter.) One common assumption, however, was that the totality of clients' situations and concerns should be addressed. Another emphasis was the encouragement of clients' autonomy in caring for their own needs.

Some of the roots of the holistic and self-care approaches reach farther back in time. The emphasis on mutual aid that characterizes many of the clinics oriented to holism and self-care derives in part from the tradition of anarchism. Anarchist principles of mutual aid were widespread during the nineteenth century both in Europe and in North America and have recurred sporadically during the twentieth century. Anarchist philosophy questioned the capability of government and large institutions to respond to people's everyday needs. Mutual aid, as envisioned by Kropotkin and others in the anarchist tradition, encouraged popular education and a deprofessionalization of services.[3] The emergence of cooperative economic institutions in various parts of the United States was only one reflection of the anarchist emphasis on mutual aid. An anarchist approach to popular education and deprofessionalization was an important part of the counterculture movement of the 1960s. Although the roots of holism and self-care in historical anarchism are not straightforward by any means, efforts in these areas have shown anarchist leanings.

One other sociohistorical root of holism and self-care needs brief mention. Narcissism has emerged as an important cultural and psychological predisposition during the last two decades. With the weakening of the family, the economic system, the educational system, and traditional religion, the social supports that have historically provided grounding for individuals have become less effective. In these circumstances, individuals have suffered a growing sense of isolation. From a psychocultural viewpoint, an emphasis on the concerns of the solitary individual's growth and development has become a major feature of life in North America. The orientation toward the self has been trivialized as the "me first" generation. As Christopher Lasch and other social critics have pointed out, however, the narcissistic emphasis on the individual reflects a growing deterioration of social relationships under advanced capitalism.[4] Although seldom acknowledged, similar factors probably have stimulated the emphasis on self-care in medicine. Designs to enhance the capability of caring for oneself often express themes that resemble the more general narcissistic orientation of the past two decades. The positive effects of self-care should be noted, but this negative aspect is one that is rarely discussed. The narcissistic element leads to a question about other possible negative effects of holism and self-care in modern society. These orientations have exerted a damaging impact on certain social policies, which now need to be considered.

IDEOLOGISTS OF HOLISM AND SELF-CARE

To begin, it is necessary to consider a major trend in health policy analysis emerging since the mid-1970s, which might be called the new reductionism. The approach emphasizes holism and self-care. Two analyses, by Ivan Illich and Victor Fuchs, are representative of this approach and have exerted a wide influence on major policy decisions.[5] Since both involve criticisms of modern medicine, they superficially seem to convey progressive messages. For this reason, these works and their policy implications deserve appraisal.

In general, Illich believes that the institution of modern medicine exerts a pernicious effect on society and should be dismantled. Fuchs is less extreme, although he expresses many similar themes. Both place responsibility for health squarely on the individual; they find the sources of illness in personal life-style. Explicitly or implicitly, they urge a reversion to a more primitive society, where people's life-styles support health and where the pressures, habits, and tensions of modern life are absent.

Much of the critique of modern medicine is persuasive. The difficulty is that both Illich and Fuchs reduce social problems to individual ones. Few would argue that an individual's life-style is an important determinant of health. But individuals very often lead unhealthy lives because of the social structural conditions—at work, in the family, and so forth—with which they must contend. Structural injustices will not evaporate if society is demedicalized.

The emphasis on personal life-style has a seductively progressive ring. But dismantling medicine without fundamentally changing many other institutions of modern society will do nothing to correct the structural bases of ill health. Moreover, isolated from broader structural changes, the policy thrust emerging from these analyses promises to be quite conservative.

Illich. The arguments of *Medical Nemesis* resemble those of Illich's earlier books on education and energy. In this perspective, the basic problem is the emergence of strong and coercive institutions in industrial society; medicine is but one example. Because these institutions limit the individual's capacity for personal growth and self-care, they should be dismantled.

Illich has mounted a devastating polemic against modern medicine. At the outset, he summarizes the growing and convincing epidemiological evidence of modern medicine's technical ineffectiveness in improving the health of large populations. This literature has not been widely available to the general public. Illich's review is comprehensive. His propagandization serves a useful purpose in demystifying many of modern medicine's technical claims.

Having questioned the assumption that medicine is effective, Illich then focuses on the ways in which it is pernicious. Medicine's bad effects he lumps together in the term *iatrogenesis*. He sees iatrogenesis occurring at three levels—the clinical, social, and structural. *Clinical iatrogenesis* refers to iatrogenic disease, the clinical problems that result from doctors' unintended mistakes or from complications of treatment. According to Illich, it includes "all clinical entities for which remedies, physicians or hospitals are the pathogens or 'sickening' agents." *Social iatrogenesis* comprises the unintended consequences of the sick role or of illness behavior in society. Illich's comments on the "medicalization of life" resemble the analyses of several social scientists who find that the sick role is an important social-control mechanism, which contains deviance and protest. By creating a far-reaching dependency on the institution of medicine, according to Illich, the profession helps excuse people from the task of reconstructing society. *Structural iatrogenesis* refers to the loss of autonomy for the individual, and particularly the loss of the capability for self-care. Responsibility for health passes from the individual to the medical profession—a process that Illich views as the most evil effect of modern medicine. According to him, people are punished for their dependency on medicine and medicalization. The punishment is medical nemesis, with its three tiers of iatrogenesis.

Illich does not have a political program. In a draft of *Medical Nemesis* issued during 1974, Illich mentions that in the future someone might "propose a political program in which this criticism could become operational."[6] This statement does not appear in later editions published in Britain and in the United States. Rather than explicit policy suggestions, Illich offers a nihilistic critique of current policy options that he believes will not work. The danger here is that Illich's analysis of medicalization, coupled with his nihilism regarding policy, can easily be used by policymakers to justify cutbacks in needed health and welfare programs. He claims that current proposals—usually thought of as progressive—for consumer control, redistribution of services, nationalization, alternative healers, and preventive and environmental health programs are all misguided: "The political remedies for these shortcomings have one thing in common: they tend to reinforce further medicalization. Only a substantial reduction in total medical outputs could foster autonomy in health and in sick care, and thereby make it effective."[7]

At the level of social policy, Illich makes no recommendations. Instead, with classic reductionism, he shifts the burden to the individual. He advocates the development of the individual's capacity for coping with pain and suffering. Claiming that primitive cultures provided a "health-granting wholeness" and that "culture makes pain tolerable by integrating it into a meaning system," he argues that industrialized society, with medical help, has lost the meaning of pain and suffering. The individual's stolid coping with pain, suffering, and death is Illich's ideal.

The policy implicit in this idealization of the past and rancor about the present is quite reactionary: let people suffer in peace. This is why Illich has tickled the medical profession rather than threatened it. His critique legitimates a decrease in social responsibility for health care. Consequently, he frees the profession, and others who control the health sector, from blame.

For example, to cite some clinical problems, farmworkers tend to suffer from crippling back disease. This disease does not occur because of industrialization in the abstract or because of farmworkers' individual life-styles. Instead, it develops because farmworkers have been forced to work for long hours in a stooped posture with the short hoe, a tool that capitalist agribusiness claims is more efficient and less costly than the long-handled hoe. Farmworkers' children frequently develop kidney and cardiac complications of streptococcal infections, anemia from parasitic infections and poor nutrition, and many other health problems. These children grow more slowly and have a shorter life expectancy than children who enjoy greater access to what Illich calls medical "torts." Farmworkers understand these elementary facts; this is why they want more stringent occupational health regulations and more rather than fewer medical services. Should farmworkers accept Illich's counsel that they learn self-care, in order to cope more effectively with the pain that the capitalist system inflicts?

All this is not to deny general validity of much of Illich's critique of the medical profession. Because he has stated his message so baldly, however, his work provides a legitimation for a social policy of cutbacks in health programs. Signs of this trend have appeared at both the national and the local levels in the United States, where officials have considered reductions in public health programs as part of economic austerity measures. The rationale, following Illich, is that more health care does not necessarily mean better health indices in modern society.

His arguments consistently overlook or downplay the importance of social class. In a class society, low-income people often depend on health services from the public sector; higher-income people can buy needed care from the private sector. As usual, cutbacks justified by Illich's line of analysis will disproportionately affect low-income people who cannot afford regular access to the private medical system. Because Illich makes a nihilistic attack on current policy options while providing no alternatives, his work (perhaps unintentionally) supports regressive health policy decisions.

Fuchs. Although to a slightly lesser extent than Illich, Fuchs also puts the responsibility for health on the individual or on factors that are more in the individual's sphere of control than subject to societal intervention. He says, "Current variations in health among individuals and groups are determined largely by genetic factors, environment, and life-style (including diet, smoking, stability of family life, and similar variables)."[8] Life-style and variation in personal behavior, he argues, are the major determinants of "who shall live."

How does Fuchs, an economist, reach his conclusion that individual differences in life-styles are among the most important determinants of health? His argument is tortuous and loaded with a reductionism that converts social issues to problems of individual psychology and behavior. Fuchs's principal data come from a comparison of death rates in Nevada and Utah, in a passage subtitled "A Tale of Two States." These data show generally higher mortality and morbidity rates in Nevada, especially from cirrhosis and lung cancer. Fuchs attributes these differences to the quiet, stable, devout lives of Mormons in Utah, who do not use tobacco or alcohol and do not participate in the frenetic life-style prevalent in Nevada. He also compares mortality rates in Sweden and the United States; in general, U.S. rates are higher.

Methodologically, this analysis suffers from the well-known "ecological fallacy"—drawing erroneous or misleading inferences about individuals from aggregate rates for large populations.[9] Fuchs cannot statistically infer anything about the life-style of individuals, simply because those individuals live in states or countries with different presumed, stereotypical cultural patterns. Nevertheless, he states a conclusion about causality that bears a tenuous relation to the data he reviews: "At present . . . the greatest potential for reducing coronary disease, cancer and the major killers still lies in altering personal behavior."[10]

Fuchs does not consider the institutionalized expectations that pattern individual behavior. Individual men and women cannot simply start relaxing, as he implies the Mormons do, when the many institutional structures that affect them—the occupational system, schools, family, and so forth—pattern the ways they act. It is just not possible for the vast majority of individuals who face the contradictions of social life in capitalist society to heed Fuchs's suggestion that they slow down, drop out, and change their life-style. Again, Fuchs ignores the social issues that are often at the root of personal troubles like illness and premature death.

The principal problems of the health system, as Fuchs sees them, are three: high costs, inaccessibility for some groups, and poor health levels as compared with other countries. He outlines some incremental proposals for dealing with costs and inaccessibility. But he claims that we cannot expect these proposals to improve the overall health of the population, since "the greatest potential for improving health lies in what we do and don't do to ourselves"[11] —that is, in self-care.

Implications. These analyses are important and potentially dangerous. The implications of Illich's recommendations, such as reduced resources for health care, are negative and reactionary. In extolling individual pain and suffering, he shifts the burden from collective to individual responsibility. Fuchs's conclusions are reductionistic; he assumes that life-style is determined by the characteristics of individuals, rather than by the nature of the social institutions in which individuals live and work. Fuchs, too, encourages a reactionary-policy inference: Why spend more money on or develop programs for health care if there is little chance of improving health?

The new reductionism justifies a collective abdication of responsibility during a period of fiscal crisis. In a class society, this analysis will not affect the ability of the wealthy to buy the medical care they need. On the other hand, Illich, Fuchs, and their supporters may provide a justification for policy changes that will lead to further deprivation for the poor. In a time of economic instability, these arguments help rationalize cutbacks in health and welfare services.

Furthermore, the new reductionism resonates with other dominant ideologies that legitimate current patterns of class structure and oppression. This perspective assigns the burden of care to the individual, while deemphasizing the social origins of illness and illness-producing behavior. Consistent with the wider ethos of individualism, medical reductionism encourages victim blaming.[12] From this viewpoint, the individual's sickness or early death is ultimately the individual's own fault. As many have pointed out, the medicalization of *social* problems has had many damaging effects. But the demedicalization of *medical* problems promises even worse repercussions. Self-care is fine, but it does not substitute for health services when they are needed. Nor can self-care offset the necessity of struggle against illness-generating conditions in the workplace, environment, and organization of society. Despite its progressive ring, the new reductionism fosters change that is reformist at best and—to the extent that it supports a suffering acquiescence in the social status quo—reactionary at worst.

STRENGTHS OF HOLISM AND SELF-CARE

In short, holism and self-care are ambiguous. On the one hand, they can justify negative policy positions and obscure the social origins of many health problems. On the other hand, they also support more positive trends, and these need to be emphasized as well.

First of all, holism and self-care foster the individual's autonomy and personal control over health and medical services. The holistic and self-care movements have provided education regarding medical diagnosis and treatment. Through this knowledge, individuals can assume control over major parts of their own care. In particular, they can learn to recognize health problems early and to prevent them when possible. They can develop a greater ability to choose their sources of care in order to maximize their own satisfaction. Because of greater personal knowledge, they can appraise professionals' recommendations more critically. Through such challenges, clients can assume a more equal position in their relations with practitioners. These emphases on personal control are worthwhile and should be encouraged.

In addition, these approaches have drawn greater attention to the importance of the person as a whole human being. In health or sickness, individuals are totalities, rather than the sum of their separate organ systems. The holistic and self-care movements have emphasized the totality of experience and the need to care for clients as whole beings, rather than the sum of their parts.

Holism and self-care also provide an important alternative to technological approaches in modern medicine. Technology has played an important role in dehumanizing and alienating many medical practices. In addition, technological innovations have contributed to the high costs of medical care. Holism and self-care generally advocate interventions that use little or no technology. When technological methods are needed, they urge that they be used sparingly. The effectiveness of nontechnological approaches is very important to assess. Because they have encouraged the use of nontechnological methods in diagnosis and treatment, holism and self-care have provided a useful balance to the frequent overemphasis on advanced technology in modern medicine.

Perhaps more important, although holism and self-care focus on the individual's capacity for autonomy, they also encourage group processes and organizing. Holistic practices and self-care experiments often take place in alternative clinics or in other health care programs. Frequently, these group efforts have emerged from the women's movement and community organizing. The call for greater individual autonomy has often been linked to groups' trying to obtain greater power for people who previously were underserved. The emergence of groups and other organized efforts that emphasize holism and self-care has decreased individuals' isolation, both in the medical system and in society more generally. Although self-care can at times place inappropriate responsibility on the individual, it can also encourage greater social responsibility for health and illness when it is linked to wider organizing.

CRITIQUES

Despite these real or potential advantages, holism and self-care have also manifested a number of serious problems. Sometimes these problems have arisen despite the best conscious intents of the advocates of holism and self-care. At other times, the ideology of holism and self-care has functioned to legitimate oppressive social conditions. In addition to recognizing the strengths of holism and self-care, then, one must give careful attention to their drawbacks.

First of all, holism and self-care allow reductionism and victim blaming. Although the ideologists of these approaches, such as Illich and Fuchs, have often remained quite separate from actual organized programs, their analyses have led to some potentially dangerous conclusions. In particular, by focusing mainly on the individual, holism and self-care downplay social problems and social solutions. Generally, advocates of these approaches see illness as arising from inappropriate behavior or life-styles at the individual level. They encourage individual changes and adjustments that are sometimes very difficult to attain. Programs emphasizing holism and self-care rarely devote attention to the social conditions that impede the individual's efforts to change. In particular, they tend to overlook important structural sources of oppression in the workplace, environment, family, and other major social institutions. In short, the reforms that holism and self-care encourage are not really holistic—or they are holistic only at the individual level of analysis. That is, these reforms generally do not advocate wider social changes that could foster individuals' capabilities to care for themselves in a meaningful way.

In emphasizing the individual, holism and self-care tend to deemphasize a variety of social structural problems that both cause illness and impede self-care. These problems of society need special attention. Only a few of them can be enumerated here.

For example, social class is related to the incidence and prevalence of a variety of diseases and mortality patterns. In general, working-class people are subject to a higher probability of contracting many diseases and suffering an earlier death than are non-working-class people. Much of this excess morbidity and mortality is attributed to the greater stress of working-class life, with its associated economic insecurity.[13]

Racism is also a major determinant of ill health and early death. Blacks, Latinos, native Americans, and other minority groups in the United States show a relatively high incidence of hypertension, a variety of infectious diseases, infant mortality, and many other medical problems.

Ageism likewise is a determinant of ill health and inadequate medical care. Although Medicare legislation provided limited financing of services for elderly people, the accessibility of these services still remains problematic. Nursing facilities are expensive and, when private resources are limited, often provide care of dubious quality. The special medical needs of the aged transcend individuals' abilities to care for themselves all or even most of the time.

Environmental and occupational problems have become a major source of illness and early death in advanced capitalist societies. Toxic chemicals have accumulated at a devastating rate. Even more important, nuclear wastes, emissions from nuclear power plants, and the dangers of thermonuclear war pose threats to humanity's very survival. In comparison with the enormity of these risks, the advocacy of holism and self-care as simple solutions is profoundly limited.

Finally, medical care remains maldistributed. In rural areas and low-income districts within cities, people who are at risk for disease and early death have difficulty in getting access to needed services. Maldistribution is another social structural problem that the emphasis on self-care and holistic therapies does little if anything to correct. Ironically, the maldistribution of holistic services, especially with respect to income and class, parallels and often exceeds the maldistribution of nonholistic medicine.

Advocacy of holism and self-care does not necessarily imply a deemphasis of social structural problems. However, social structure has received relatively little attention in the holistic and self-care movements until this time. There is no intrinsic reason that social structure cannot be analyzed within a movement that encourages holism and self-care. The balance of these orientations needs greater scrutiny.

Finally, perhaps the greatest danger of holism and self-care lies in their potential regressive social policy implications. As was noted above, major analyses adopting an orientation that encourages holism and self-care have placed responsibility for health almost exclusively on the individual. These analyses have questioned the overall effectiveness of medicine, based on the morbidity and mortality patterns of large populations. They voice skepticism about whether existing health and welfare programs exert a significant impact on morbidity and mortality; the impact of social class, racism, and other systematic patterns of deprivation tends to be overlooked. If health is the individual's responsibility, the argument goes, health and welfare programs may be detrimental and unneeded.

In this view, cutbacks in publicly financed facilities and services can easily be justified. These cutbacks can have a devastating impact on individuals' ability to obtain even the most basic services. Since the late 1970s and early 1980s, many public hospitals and clinics have closed in major cities throughout the United States. Other preventive and curative programs have been reduced or eliminated. Predominantely, these cutbacks have affected low-income and minority groups. The new reductionism in health policy, placing responsibility for health mainly on the individual, has provided an ideological legitimation of these cutbacks. Again, such cutbacks are not necessarily entailed by the encouragement of holism and self-care, but these orientations can be manipulated to justify regressive policy decisions. These trends deserve criticism and opposition.

IMPLICATIONS FOR ACTION

Holism and self-care are exciting orientations that have attracted wide attention in the past two decades. Their contradictions are troubling. Understanding these contradictions implies taking certain necessary actions.

First, holism and self-care should be encouraged, but with a clear view of their limitations. The individual's capacity for autonomy and sound health practices is a desirable goal. In addition, an emphasis that fosters attention to the totality of human experience can and should be an important part of medical practice. On the other hand, holism and self-care should be viewed within the context of society; that is, they should be truly holistic, in seeing how individual life is embedded within the realities of social structure. It is not enough to put responsibility for health strictly on the individual. Since the nature of society both creates and reproduces many problems of illness and early death, there must be continuing social responsibility for health care as well. This responsibility extends both to the prevention of socially caused illness and early death and to the provision of needed health services.

Second, ideologies that place the chief responsibility for prevention and cure on the individual should be resisted. It is foolhardy to argue that individuals have no responsibility for their own health. Clearly, individuals do have the capability to make major decisions that can be beneficial. On the other hand, the difficulties that society imposes on an individual should be clearly recognized. Even in such areas as exercise and diet, the stresses of work and family life make it difficult for individuals to change their behavior. Certainly, sources of stress that derive from work and economic insecurity are often beyond the individual's control. In short, responsibility for health involves a combination of individual and social responsibility. Holism and self-care should emphasize the social component of responsibility as much as the individual component.

Regarding political action, holism and self-care should be part of a broader struggle that aims to change the social structural conditions that cause illness and suffering and that impede self-care.[14] Only a few examples can be mentioned; these efforts attack social structural problems that have been discussed previously. The detrimental impact of class structure and economic insecurity needs to be a major focus of political action. Organizing efforts in communities, workplaces, unions, and service institutions should continue the struggle for economic security for the individual and family. Obviously, the struggle for a transformed class structure will be a protracted one. But because of the impact of social class on health, holism and self-care must occur within a larger struggle to change the negative effects of class. Similarly, organizing needs to combat racism. The conditions that create ill health and inadequate care for the aged also need much greater attention, as do patterns of continuing sexism in society. Organizational efforts to combat environmental and occupational health problems are an extremely important focus of political action. Given the magnitude of these problems, efforts that encourage holism and self-care at the individual level but exclude attention to the environment and workplace will remain incomplete and misguided.

Holism and self-care, then, must be one phase of a broader political strategy that encompasses both medicine and society. Holistic medicine must be holistic in its most meaningful sense. It should encompass both the totality of individual existence and the totality of society. Likewise, self-care needs to occur within the context of mutual aid and broader political organizing. Unless holism and self-care take place as part of a wider political struggle, they will continue to shift the burden inappropriately to the individual. In doing so, they will allow the most troubling problems that create ill health and early death to persist. Holism and self-care must aim at the social reconstruction that is a precondition of individuals' caring for themselves.

part V

SUMMARY AND CONCLUSIONS

12.

toward the twenty-first century

Ruth and Victor Sidel

What do these in-depth accounts of attempts to reform a major social institution tell us about the nature of that institution and about the problems of producing lasting change in American society? Our first conclusion is that some reforms efforts can, at least for limited periods of time, lead to dramatic improvements in health care and medical care for selected groups of people. There is no doubt that those served by community health centers received vastly improved primary care, that the elderly and many poor people had greater access to medical care because of Medicare and Medicaid, and that the protection of the health and safety of many workers was markedly strengthened and the care of many workers improved because of the workers' health and safety movement. Nor is there any doubt that women have achieved greater control over their health care and have brought about definite changes, such as improved consent procedures for sterilization and the legal right to abortion, that the self-help movement has become a significant element within the health care system, that an important cadre of physician's assistants and nurse practitioners was trained, that many dedicated people who could not have attended medical schools were enabled to do so, and that many students received a more humane medical education, more focused on preventive medicine and primary care, because of the reform efforts of the 1960s and 1970s.

Another conclusion that seems equally indisputable is that even though significant changes were made in health care for many Americans, the health care system is formidably resistant to change. As neighborhood health centers were being organized, they met powerful opposition from black as well as white physicians working within the private sector in the targeted communities. Once the health centers were established, many of the innovations for which they were to become justly famous were staunchly resisted by health officials in federal and local government. The AMA has vigorously and often viciously resisted a national health insurance plan, and opposed Medicare and Medicaid until it was clear that Congress would inevitably pass some federal financing plan during the 1960s. Doctors, medical care institutions, and drug companies have resisted women's insistence on greater knowledge about their bodies and their health care as well as their greater participation in caring for themselves. Medical schools resisted rethinking admissions policies, an effort that was essential in order to admit increased numbers of minority students and women. And what is, perhaps, the most pervasive example of institutional resistance to change, health professionals, administrators, and financing agencies overtly and covertly opposed strong community participation in health care planning.

The more difficult question is whether these reforms have had a significant impact, in either the short or the long term, on the health care system as a whole. We believe the reform efforts can, in an analysis of their overall impact, be grouped into three major categories: those that were resisted so successfully—if not overtly, then covertly—that they never really took hold in any significant way; those that were indeed implemented but were co-opted or absorbed by the system in ways that left the structure of the system fundamentally unchanged; and those that after a brief period of success were essentially destroyed through underfunding and a fundamental lack of commitment on the part of health care professionals and of government at all levels. We recognize that these categories may be somewhat arbitrary and that some of the contributors to this volume may disagree with our analysis; nevertheless, we are attempting a critical overview in the hope that it will stimulate further discussion of the forces that permit and limit reform not only in the health care system but in other elements of American society as well.

Reforms that were resisted so successfully that they never really took hold include minority admission to medical schools and community participation and control. As Strelnick and Younge point out, blacks and other minority students have been systematically excluded from American medical schools—with the exception of the "black" medical schools—throughout our history. Until the late 1960s, blacks, who then made up 12 percent of the U.S. population, constituted no more than 2.5 percent of the medical students, and most of these were concentrated in the "black" schools. Through a variety of affirmative action techniques, black enrollment increased from 2.0 percent in 1965–66 to a peak of 6.3 percent in 1974–75. The total enrollment of black, Hispanic, and native American students reached its peak in 1975–76, at 8.2 percent, compared with their percentage in the overall population of 18 percent. These figures are all the more revealing when we consider the astonishing rise in the number of female medical students—from approximately 10 percent in 1970 to 30 percent in 1980. The federally funded scholarship and loan programs that had increased the numbers of minority students were significantly decreased by 1976. Medical schools, which had been under pressure to alter their admissions procedures, did so to a limited extent, but they have nonetheless continued to emphasize grades, MCAT scores, and performance in basic science in determining admission and to neglect commitment to providing primary care to underserved populations or identification with the needs of a specific minority group. In other words, the medical profession was willing, for a brief period of time, to permit small numbers of minority students to enter the educational process if, and only if, the admissions process itself was not fundamentally changed. By the middle and late 1970s, chilled by the *Bakke* decision, the major push for real equality of opportunity for minority students—and for minority people to be able to choose a minority physician—was over.

Community participation and control in health care is another reform that encountered so much resistance that it never truly took hold except in a few isolated model programs. Community participation was an essential component of the neighborhood health center movement and the community mental health movement. As Hatch and Eng point out, "Through 'maximum feasible participation,' issues of policy and control were to be examined and reshaped by those outside any mainstream establishment. Poor communities were provided with a direct financial link to the federal government through community participation and control." While significant community involvement was achieved in a small number of health centers—in the Tufts-Delta project in Mound Bayou, Mississippi, the NENA Health Center on the Lower East Side of New York, and the Martin Luther King, Jr. Health Center in the South Bronx, to a name a few—community participation and control spread little beyond these sites and has essentially no place in current health care organization. Neither health professionals nor government officials nor local politicians were willing to relinquish real power to community residents, who were often poor or working-class minority people with little formal education or previous opportunity to deal with complex medical issues beyond their immediate experience. The same was true of the Community Health Planning Agencies and the subsequent Health Systems Agencies, which were grossly underfunded for their tasks, were given insufficient power, and were largely controlled by health care providers and government officials.

Let us turn now to the second group of reform efforts—those that were implemented but were largely co-opted or absorbed into the medical establishment and that supported its current structure or even intensified its problems rather than contributing to significant lasting change in the system. Quentin Young describes the attempts to improve urban public hospitals, with emphasis on the efforts at Cook County Hospital in which he himself played a major role. There is no doubt that much was accomplished to improve the medical care and the quality of hospital life of patients and the working conditions for the staff at Cook County and in a number of other public hospitals in the United States. The efforts at Lincoln Hospital, a public hospital in the South Bronx, have been movingly described by Fitzhugh Mullan, one of the contributors to this volume, in *White Coat, Clenched Fist.* Without these efforts, care for the poor and for racial minorities would surely be worse than it is. But it is also clear that these efforts in some ways helped to support and strengthen a two-class medical care system and that there was a systematic retreat from many of the advances that had been made when federal or other special funding was no longer available or when those who pressed for the reforms left or were forced from the scene. A number of public hospitals have been closed, and others have through various methods passed into private hands or other forms of management less responsive to public pressures. In short, the reforms in public hospitals, with few exceptions, were transient in their impact and did little to improve the long-term quality of care for those most in need or to change the basic structure of the medical care system.

E. Richard Brown, describing another example in this group in the chapter "Medicare and Medicaid: Band-Aids for the Old and Poor," notes that the enactment of Medicare and Medicaid was the result of years of political compromise. Medicare, available to the elderly of all economic levels, has carried significantly less of a stigma than Medicaid, but it nonetheless removes only part of the financial burden from recipients. With the explosion of medical care costs (in part generated by Medicare itself) and with the deductibles and copayments built into the Medicare structure, the aged today pay more out-of-pocket in current dollars than they did in 1965, when President Lyndon Johnson signed the bill into law. They pay less in inflation-adjusted dollars, but this is of small comfort to the many who have to live on savings or on fixed incomes.

Although Medicaid has greatly increased the use of health services by the poor, it has engendered many major problems, even more than has Medicare. Brown has detailed the differences between the two systems. It is clearly not accidental that the program that provides care for the poor—a scorned and stigmatized group in the United States—has had to endure state-controlled restrictions and severe financial cutbacks, scams such as unneeded return visits and the "Ping-Ponging" of patients from one doctor to another, and limited eligibility and coverage. The incorporation of reimbursement mechanisms like Medicare and Medicaid into a largely uncontrolled fee-for-service system has meant, in short, that the reforms have magnified many of the flaws in the system and that they have failed to be levers for needed change. These reforms ended up encouraging hospitalization rather than ambulatory or home care, high technology and specialization rather than primary care, and in some cases the basest instincts of doctors and institutions.

Rocio Huet-Cox, in her chapter on changes in medical education, points out that during the 1960s and early 1970s existing medical schools were expanded, new schools were created, and medical education was shortened in a number of medical schools in order to increase the number of physicians trained. While the increase of medical students has continued, leading, some feel, to a "glut" of doctors, most of the experiments in shortening the curriculum have ended. In addition, in an effort to be relevant to the needs of the 1970s, medical schools added courses such as those in community medicine, ethics, drug abuse, geriatrics, and occupational health. Independent-study programs have also been developed in many U.S. medical schools in order to enable students to follow their own particular interests rather than going lockstep through medical school. Yet Huet-Cox reports that only 1.5 percent of the actual curriculum time is devoted to preventive medicine and public health. She goes on to state, "The greater number of physicians being produced in 1980 are being trained in curricula that have been rearranged but that are essentially unchanged since 1960. Despite the increased flexibility, interdepartmental teaching, and limited exposure to disciplines outside the basic biomedical sciences in today's curriculum, medical students graduating in 1980 are still being taught to focus on a disease in the individual patient as the graduates of 1920 and 1960 had been." Again, the reforms, rather than fundamentally changing the medical curriculum, were absorbed by the medical schools.

The training of physician's assistants (PAs) and nurse practitioners (NPs) during the 1960s would, it was hoped, provide midlevel health workers who would both ease the problem of the physician shortage and curtail rising health costs. Since these health workers presumably would not erect the same authority and class barriers as physicians did, they would be able to relate more personally to patients, provide services to the underserved, and allow mobility within an otherwise rigidly hierarchical profession. Although it has indeed been found, as Molly Backup and John Molinaro indicate, that the quality of care and the patient acceptance of physician's assistants and nurse practitioners are high, that these health workers are more accessible to patients and are seen as less elite than physicians, that training costs are far lower, and that these new health professionals tend to order fewer expensive tests, many problems nevertheless remain. The program originated when a doctor shortage was perceived to be a major problem; what will happen to PAs and NPs when, as is currently predicted, we will have an "oversupply" of physicians? But perhaps the most critical issue is the use of PAs and NPs as assistants to physicians in private practice. This use of the new health professional to increase the physician's private practice and profits rather than to provide care to sectors of the population that are underserved is already a significant problem and may well worsen as the number of doctors increases. Once again we see a program that started as a reform being exploited by the private, fee-for-service segment of American medicine.

Larry Sirott and Howard Waitzkin have analyzed many of the central problems from which the concepts of holism and self-care have sprung. Like many of the other reform efforts, this movement has responded to the needs of many groups and individuals in American society: the desperate need for greater autonomy, for less reliance on professionals, for the support that small-group participation provides. However, we and many others in the health field feel that significant disadvantages have emerged as well.

While we see the self-help movement overall as an important and encouraging development, it is often, in our view, a response to symptoms rather than to underlying social problems and may in some instances lead to an exacerbation of deeper problems. Medical self-help groups may, for example, help to perpetuate the basic inequities that characterize our health care and medical care system. By relieving some of the pressure on the society to provide preventive services, self-help groups help to perpetuate the disparity between the resources our society devotes to medical care and those it devotes to prevention. Since these groups cannot serve entire segments of the population and since they frequently serve those who are most actively interested rather than those who are hardest to reach, the self-help movement may be helping to maintain the inequality of care in our society by providing care to and thereby neutralizing those who might, out of dissatisfaction with the system, vocally protest medical inequities. Thus, self-help in the absence of equity may serve to perpetuate inequity.

In a third group, several of the reform efforts discussed in this book, including neighborhood health centers, the National Health Service Corps, and occupational health and safety, had significant success for a limited time in limited areas and looked as though they might produce useful structural change but were then undermined by gross underfinancing and dismantling. Although myriad studies have demonstrated and documented the overwhelmingly positive achievements of neighborhood health centers—not only in improving the health status of the patient population but in reducing health care expenditures as well—the Reagan administration has continued the Nixon and Ford policies of undermining, in fact destroying, neighborhood health centers as they were originally envisaged.

The National Health Service Corps (NHSC) appeared to many to be an important opening wedge for fundamental change in the U.S. medical care system. Federally salaried physicians and other health workers, many of them supported by NHSC scholarships during their training, were sent, usually in teams, to staff health centers in underserved areas. Many communities received, and some continue to receive, needed care from these professionals. But the corps was not merely a means of meeting immediate needs. Many people also perceived it as an alternative model to a system that required students to make enormous outlays for their medical education, to be compensated for later by enormous incomes from fee-for-service practice. It was, however, not to be. Determined opposition by organized medicine led to the adoption of a "private practice option" that permitted professionals who had been supported by NHSC scholarships to fulfill their obligations simply by entering into private practice in underserved areas. An even greater blow was dealt by the Reagan administration, which beginning in 1981 cut off all new scholarship support (whereas an average of 1,300 new scholarships a year had been awarded in the period 1976–80) and reduced the active-duty complement of the corps to 2,000 professionals (compared with the goal of 8,000 to 9,000 set under the Carter administration).

Similarly, the reforms in occupational health and safety brought significant short-term improvements and a promise of further change that has not been fulfilled. After important changes in regulation (in standard setting, in inspection, and in enforcement) and in workers' rights (in organization around health and safety, in the "right to know," and in workers' participation in health and safety decisions), events starting in 1981 have reversed many of the gains. Not only has the Reagan administration directly decimated the work of NIOSH and OSHA, but rising unemployment and falling real income have reduced the power of workers and their unions to demand the maintenance and expansion of labor's health and safety gains in the workplace.

The reforms of the 1960s and 1970s were not the first ones attempted in U.S. medicine that failed, either partially or in toto, to alter substantially the health care system. One of the leading examples of what are usually considered reforms in American medicine were the efforts of Abraham Flexner, described in several of the chapters in this book. Flexner's 1910 report on the quality of facilities and instruction in the 155 medical colleges in the United States and Canada had an enormous impact. As a result of that study, many schools were closed; others, often with foundation support, made extensive changes in their admissions policies and their curricula. There is little doubt that much of the impact was positive: many patients in the United States in succeeding years were spared treatment by technically incompetent physicians. But there is also little doubt that a significant price was paid. Emphasis in many schools shifted from clinical medicine to the preclinical sciences. All the schools that had admitted large numbers of black students—with the exception of Howard and Meharry—were closed. The total numbers of schools and of graduates were sharply reduced, with a consequent decline in the physician-to-population ratio in the United States and the disappearance of physicians from many poor rural and urban areas. Indeed half a century passed before some of the direct negative consequences of the Flexner "reforms" began to be reversed.

Perhaps even more significant, this reform effort in medical education left intact the basic structure of medical care in the United States. Indeed, by keeping out of medicine a large group of physicians who, while poorly trained, might have stimulated other changes and by shifting the direction of medical education toward more academic and more specialized areas, the reform may have prevented, or at least delayed, more significant change.

Other medical reform efforts of the past fifty years—such as those in the regulation of food and drugs, the development of group practice, both fee for service and prepaid, the expansion of private health insurance, and the Hill-Burton hospital construction act—shared the same characteristics. Many people received improved care as a result of the reforms; some of the positive consequences were long-lived, lasting to the present day. But these efforts also led to severe distortions of the system and to delays of more fundamental reform. For example, the food-and-drug reforms protected many, the delay of the introduction of thalidomide being its most publicized triumph, but the structures that were produced by these reforms delayed the introduction of many useful materials and helped raise the price of many others. Group practice, particularly prepaid group practice, pioneered new methods of medical care delivery and—with the federal support for "health maintenance organizations" in the 1970s—reached many people but hardly affected the patterns or cost of medical care for most. Private health insurance spread some of the burden of the cost of care for the middle class and well off, but it did little to help the poor and contributed to the emphasis on hospital-based high-technology medicine and to the explosion of costs. The Hill-Burton program placed hospitals where none had existed, providing some patients with life-saving care, but contributed to the proliferation of small, inefficient hospitals and to duplication and fragmentation in the system.

What lessons can be drawn from the reform efforts in health in the past and particularly in the past quarter century? A central issue, it appears to us, is the need to transfer power from one group to another in order to implement the reform with any degree of success. In the establishment of neighborhood health centers and community mental health centers, administrators, health professionals, and funding agencies were expected—indeed required—to share power with the community. Hatch and Eng have suggested that a key problem in community participation and control is the identification of legitimate community representatives; though we think that this has often been a difficult dilemma, we do not consider it the fundamental reason that effective sharing of power with community representatives was relatively rare and, when it took place, short-lived. Rather, we would assert, very few of the groups involved were genuinely prepared to share power with nonprofessionals, and once the rather euphoric period of believing that real reform was possible had passed, that sharing of power was the first concept to be discarded.

A major thrust of the occupational health and safety movement and of the women's health movement has been the right to know —the workers' right to know the specific substances with which they are working and the potential hazards of these substances, and women's right to know about a broad range of issues affecting their health. In addition to the right to know, both groups have claimed their right to participate in decision making in matters affecting their health. The "right to know" is itself, of course, a form of power, an essential one in this highly technological and specialized age. Work in these two areas has resulted in a far more successful transfer of power than has the attempt to transfer power to community groups. Why has this been so? It seems clear that workers have been most successful when the effort has been spearheaded by major unions (such as the Oil, Chemical, and Atomic Workers), groups that already have legitimate power within the society. According to Max Weber, power is considered legitimate only if people generally recognize that those who apply it have the right to do so; it is perceived as illegitimate if people believe that those who attempt to assert it do not have that right. While labor unions may indeed be losing some of their support in American society, there is no question that they are widely seen as having the legal and moral right to represent their dues-paying workers, to bargain with employers on their behalf, and to try to protect the workers from harm on the job. Because of their legitimate power, some unions, those that have considered it a priority to do so even at times at the cost of deferred gains in wages and other "bread-and-butter issues," have been able to secure real benefits for their workers in the areas of occupational health and safety. The Reagan administration has already seriously eroded some of these gains, and severe unemployment promises to erode them still further, but they were nevertheless real.

Similarly, the women's health movement has made significant advances—most notably in the areas of abortion, sterilization abuse, and women entering the field of medicine but also, to a lesser extent, in childbirth practices and participation in medical decision making. Much of the success of the women's health movement, we believe, is due to the fact that it has involved women of all classes, specifically including upper-middle-class women and health professionals, groups that are also considered by the society and by other health professionals to have legitimate power. The legitimate power or authority of these women, we contend, is class based and newly won. It has been through the adamant insistence of the women's movement that women, particularly upper-middle-class women, be taken seriously that they have gained some measure of authority. It is through a broad-based coalition of women utilizing the authority of a few and the active support of many to advance issues that would benefit all women that the women's health movement was able to bring about significant change.

This coalition of women is reminiscent in some ways of the civil rights movement, which was a broad-based coalition of groups within the black community (far more broad-based than the women's movement has been in this country) that borrowed heavily on the legitimate power or authority of the black clergy. Black ministers had enormous standing in their own communities, and by virtue of their being ministers, they had at least some standing in segments of the white society. In short, the civil rights and women's movements—movements that produced significant reforms that benefit all classes—have been movements in which middle- and upper-middle-class people, often professionals themselves, played a significant role.

These examples of the use of "legitimate power" to bring about reforms for a wide spectrum of groups—including the traditionally powerless—stand in stark contrast to the attempt to share power with impoverished, frequently minority community residents. Reformers may see the urban and rural poor as being legitimately entitled to some measure of power over their lives (in this case over basic services like health and education), but the majority of Americans, particularly those currently holding power, apparently do not share this view. The attempted participation in decision making by the poor and the underserved is therefore seen as a grab for illegitimate power, and the professionals who support these efforts, and who often initiated them, come to be viewed as utopians at best and incompetent troublemakers at worst.

An essential principle of successful reform within a society in which power is systematically denied to the poor, to members of minority groups, to most women, and to other disadvantaged, stigmatized groups must therefore be to develop programs that benefit not only them but also more privileged groups, so that the "legitimate power" of the privileged can be used to gain advantages for all.

Medicare and Social Security are programs that illustrate the importance of developing a constituency across class lines. The Reagan administration has been able to decrease budget allocations for essentially all the health and social welfare programs that serve only the poor—food stamps, Medicaid, categorical programs, work training programs—but its efforts to cut Medicare and Social Security have been met with far greater resistance than have its cuts in services to the poor and have therefore been prevented or at least minimized.

The events of the last decade clearly indicate the need for building coalitions in support of reform efforts—for reaching out to unions, the middle class, professionals, people with clout, people with power—and, even more important, for developing reforms such as broad entitlements that benefit people across class, race, and ethnic lines. It is clear by now that programs for the poor and for minority people are the first to go when economic, political, or social circumstances change; programs that also benefit the middle and upper-middle class have at least a fighting chance.

Of course, the only effective and lasting way to achieve an equitable distribution of income and of services in a society is the fundamental redistribution of power within that society for the benefit of those who have the least. Short of that, any reforms are likely to be incomplete, short-lived, or, even worse, supportive of the inequitable distribution of wealth and power. But in a society that seems unlikely in the short run to achieve any fundamental redistribution of power—except possibly to the benefit of the wealthiest—it appears to us important to develop methods for reform that have the greatest chance of success within the inequitable system.

Defenders of reforms in the medical care system—and those who advocate more fundamental changes in its structure—must respond to a basic criticism of such efforts. The reforms described and analyzed in this book, and structural changes such as comprehensive national health insurance or a national health service, aim to make medical care more accessible, acceptable, effective, efficient, and humane, both for underserved populations and for the population at large. The premise underlying such efforts is that improvement in medical care services will, ipso facto, lead to improved health or at least to greater longevity and possibly to a better quality of life. This premise is based on a model—the "medical" model—that emphasizes the prevention, detection, and alleviation of disease rather than on the "social" model, which emphasizes the complex effects of the economy and of social organization.

There is, however, significant evidence that health status is more closely related to class status than to the medical care services—or even to the formal health care services—that a given population receives. The Report of the Working Group on Inequalities in Health, also known as the Black report, published in August 1980 by the United Kingdom Department of Health and Social Security, deals with the issue of inequality in health in Great Britain over the past thirty years. Despite the three-decade effort of the National Health Service to provide comprehensive health care "to everyone regardless of financial means, age, sex, employment or vocation, area of residence or insurance qualification," the working group found significant inequality in health status among the five social classes (defined by occupation) in Great Britain—significant differentials in infant mortality, in death rates, in causes of death, in "longstanding illness," and in brief illness causing restricted activity, with rates generally rising markedly as class levels decline. The group's report also describes similar findings in several other European countries, the only exceptions appearing to be in Norway and Sweden.

If, as the Black report and numerous other studies seem to indicate, health status is far more closely related to class status, to occupation, housing, nutrition, and control over one's environment than to medical services, why did health professionals focus so much effort on reform of the medical care system, which treats existing disease rather than attempting to alter social conditions that produce disease? First, medical reformers felt they might have some impact on the medical care system and on a few of its associated health care tasks, whereas many of them despaired of being able to effect fundamental societal change. It was, after all, within the medical care system that they had some leverage, some expertise, some power. If blacks were struggling with civil rights issues and women with feminist issues, what better place for doctors, nurses, health economists, and other health professionals to start than medicine? Second, many health workers hoped that by reforming the medical and health care system, they might alter the larger society as well. If poor people were trained to become health workers, might they not, with their greater expertise and power, help to make changes in the larger society? If communities were empowered to participate in running health centers, would those communities not attempt to be heard in regard to other basic needs as well? If workers and women asserted control over what was being done to their bodies, would they not assert greater control in other areas as well? There was clearly the hope that significant change in the medical care system would, both directly and indirectly, lead to change in the nonmedical sectors of society. And finally, these reforms were attempted because of the manifest inequities within the medical and health care system. If adequate medical and health care is a fundamental right of all people—as most of the reformers believed—then surely all segments of American society are entitled to accessible, humane, high-quality services.

There can be, we feel, little quarrel with the last premise. Even if medical care services (as contrasted with health care services) contribute little to the improvement in life expectancy and to other conventionally defined measures of health, they can when properly provided have a great impact on the quality of life. One important function of medical care, often overlooked, is the reassurance of the "worried well" that no evidence of physical illness can be found through appropriate technical evaluation. Another is the relieving of symptoms through the appropriate use of medications, replacement therapy (such as thyroid hormones for hypothyroidism), and surgery. Methods of "definitive" treatment of illness—"cure" rather than "care"—such as antibiotics and, rarely, surgery can if rigidly controlled be extremely helpful to the sufferers and even lifesaving. Furthermore, medical care facilities and personnel can—again, if appropriately structured—be important sources of health care: prenatal care, well-baby care, blood pressure screening, and health education, for example. In short, *appropriate* medical care—using techniques of demonstrated effectiveness for those patients who can benefit from them and interweaving elements of health care—can be extraordinarily important and ought not be denied because of barriers of poverty, race, or ignorance.

A society at the level of economic development of the United States must, we believe, ensure and if necessary provide adequate and equitable services for all segments of the population. The word *equitable* (rather than *equal* or *equivalent*) is crucial, because it implies that those groups that have greater need—such as the elderly and the poor—should have greater access to appropriate services. Thus, while efforts to promote greater equality among classes in American society through income redistribution, full employment, improved housing, nutrition, day care, and education may be crucial to minimizing inequalities in health status, reforms of the medical care system itself are essential as well.

It is in this context that the Reagan administration's attacks on the fruits of the reform efforts of the 1960s and 1970s can best be seen for what they are. As this chapter is written, the United States has the highest level of unemployment in forty years and the number of people living below the official poverty line increased by 2.2 million between 1981 and 1982, to the point where 31.8 million people, one person in seven, now live in poverty. But because of administration policies the number of recipients of Medicaid benefits is expected to fall sharply, and many states have reduced not only eligibility but also available benefits to those enrolled. Funding for community health centers was further cut through a variety of methods. Support for the NHSC, as we have seen, has been drastically curtailed. These cuts in services that primarily benefit the poor and the underserved are not based on "cost containment" and budget cutting; those goals would be accomplished far more effectively by change within the medical care system, such as the introduction of a national health service, or by change outside medicine, such as the reduction in a bloated military budget. No, these efforts to withdraw needed services from the underserved are specifically redistributive, designed to make the wealthy richer at the expense of the poor.

What, in this period of Reaganomics and of Reaganism, remains of the previous years of reform? What remains of the optimism, the sense of mission, the attempts to modify and to humanize the health care system from within and to make it accessible to all in need? First, many accomplishments of that era remain—increased accessibility of health care to the poor, increased admission of women and of some minority students to the profession, a powerful self-help movement, and genuine changes in women's health care, to cite just a few examples. Second, even for those reforms that have essentially been dismantled, the bold, truly creative ideas of the 1960s and early 1970s remain, available for future implementation —albeit with modifications to suit them to another time—or as springboards to new reforms. The concepts of the neighborhood health center, of community participation and control, and of the National Health Service Corps are now part of the consciousness of those concerned with ways of improving health services for all Americans. When the political climate is more favorable—as one day it must be—these strategies, which are fundamental to the development of an equitable, accessible, humane health system, will be available. They have been thought through and tried out; many of their deficiencies as well as their strengths are known. We will not need to start from scratch.

A third, and perhaps the most important, legacy from this most recent American reform era is the fundamental belief on the part of many in our society that ordinary people have a right to take part in decision making on issues that will have a significant impact on their lives. For the 1960s were above all a time of questioning the power of experts and, occasionally, even their expertise. Those who fought for a nuclear test ban treaty questioned both the expertise and the power to make decisions of the scientists who told us repeatedly that atmospheric nuclear testing was not harmful. Mothers and other lay people insisted that they—even though they did not have scientific training—had a right to participate in a decision that might affect the health and well-being of their children and their children's children. The anti–Vietnam War movement was the most dramatic assertion in the 1960s and 1970s of the right of ordinary citizens to have a voice in decisions that had formerly been thought to rest appropriately with experts. And, of course, in health this questioning of professionalism, of the almost absolute right of professionals to make decisions for the rest of society, was felt in every sphere. The women's health movement is perhaps the clearest example of an attempt to demystify medicine, to challenge the power of the physician and with him the entire medical establishment—the questioning of the pill, of sterilization abuse, of the medicalization of childbirth, of the overprescribing of tranquilizers, and particularly of the attitude of the medical care system toward women. But the questioning of professional dominance reached into other areas. The entire notion of community participation is based on the belief that community residents have unique expertise and understanding that professionals cannot have, and that members of the community therefore must have input into the system. The self-help movement rests on the premise that nonprofessionals who have experienced similar problems can frequently be more effective in helping those in need than professionals can, in part because of the absence of class and other barriers. Many patients now routinely question the need for X rays, seek second opinions, and actively participate in decision making in regard to treatment plans. We do not mean to suggest that physicians are not still dominant or that patients are not still intimidated by powerful, technological medical care institutions, but significant change has occurred over the past twenty years.

And that change—that questioning of the infallibility of professionals, that recognition that people without technical training have the right to participate in decisions that will have an enormous impact on their lives and on the lives of their children—is clearly evident in several other areas today. The environmental movement, particularly the protests against the dumping of toxic chemicals, has been spurred on by the angry efforts of residents of affected areas. No one can doubt that the dramatic lobbying of Lois Gibbs and the other members of the Love Canal Homeowners Association, working together with a few scientists and reporters, was instrumental first in publicizing the Love Canal tragedy and then in pressuring lawmakers finally to take actions against the Hooker Chemical Company and on behalf of the residents. Similarly, the opposition to nuclear reactors has been mounted, in large part, by outraged and frightened people living in areas in which reactors have been built. Again, these citizens have utilized the expertise of scientists to present their case; some would say that experts have led the movement, but, in any event, the "antinuke" effort requires mass support in order to be effective. Another example of popular participation in decision making in highly technical matters is the anti-nuclear war movement. Reactivated in recent years both in this country and in Europe by a combination of mass protest, lobbying and political action, and efforts by scientists, physicians, and other professionals who are using their expertise and their status to educate and activate others, this movement is having a significant impact on the thinking about nuclear war. Again, the assumption that nonprofessionals have the right—indeed the responsibility—to take part in the nuclear debate is taken for granted. The thousands of town meeting members across the United States who recently debated the nuclear freeze constituted the clearest expression of the view propounded in the 1960s that experts must not be given unlimited authority in technological matters and that nonprofessionals can and must play a significant role in making what are essentially political decisions.

As we approach the twenty-first century, a series of escalating problems will find the U.S. health care and medical care system—with or without the reforms of the past quarter-century—shamefully inadequate. Medical technology will grow explosively, due to internal imperatives and the desire for profit and prestige on the part of its developers and promoters. This will happen with little examination of the consequences, and ineffective methods for constraint. The number of older people will increase rapidly, both in absolute numbers and as a proportion of the population, without appropriate planning for new medical and social needs. Chronic illness will become an increasingly important part of medical practice, with much of medical education and most medical institutions still geared to the treatment of acute short-lived illness. Medical care costs will continue to rise faster than the general rate of inflation, extracting resources from other needed public health and social services. And environmental despoilment—or its ultimate, the omnicide of nuclear war—will threaten the biological life of the planet. Our current health care system, and efforts at piecemeal reform, cannot survive such fundamental challenges.

Assuming that the goals for a nation's health care system include assuring equitable access, emphasizing the promotion of health and the prevention of illness, making health care community based, and developing ways for nonprofessionals to play a major role in the decision making that affects our health and the quality of our lives, where do we go from here? We have elsewhere discussed our specific proposals for approaching these goals, including fundamental changes in the work of health care personnel by changing their selection, training, and supervision and in medical care organization by moving toward a national health service that would essentially eliminate fee-for-service medicine in the United States. We continue to believe that in medicine it will be difficult if not impossible to get over the chasm in our care with anything less than a single radical leap. But the chapters in this book suggest to us that while we wait for—and strive to build—the political climate that will permit such change, specific types of reforms, pursued in specific ways, may move us closer to the goal. What we need and must work for are reforms that move the system in new directions rather than solidifying current dysfunctional structures, that actively involve not mainly professionals but communities and their people, and that cut across class and racial lines and build coalitions rather than contributing to the divide-and-conquer techniques that encumber us. When our nation moves back—as it must—toward a climate that permits progress in our health care and medical care system, we must select objectives to work for that will bring effective reform in the short run, will withstand adverse political winds, and will contribute to broader change.

Basic questions remain. Can there be significant, lasting change in one social institution, such as the formation of a national health service with universal entitlement, abolition of fee-for-service reimbursement, and strong community control, without significant changes in a basically inequitable, exploitative society in which wealth and power are concentrated in the hands of a few? More broadly, can health be adequately protected and promoted in our nation unless it moves toward an end to the arms race, guarantees full employment and appropriate family supports, places industry under the control of its workers and its community, and takes greater steps to end the racism, sexism, ageism, and other attitudes that foster injustice and divide and demean us? The answer is almost certainly no. As we strive for short-term reforms and more fundamental long-term change in medicine, we must also strive for basic change in our society, for the movement of our nation and of others toward a world in which we can be just, secure, peaceful, communal, and healthy.

notes

Chapter 1.
COMMUNITY HEALTH CENTERS

1. Michael Harrington, *The Other America* (New York: Macmillan, 1962).
2. Raymond Wheeler, "Health and Human Resources," *New South* 26 (1971): 3–4.
3. H. Jack Geiger, *Tufts Comprehensive Community Health Program* (Proposal to the Office of Economic Opportunity, February 1965). The full outline of the proposal cited here is available in H. J. Geiger, "A Health Center in Mississippi—A Case Study in Social Medicine," in *Medicine in a Changing Society,* ed. L. Corey, S. E. Saltman, and M. F. Epstein (St. Louis: C. V. Mosby, 1972).
4. Ibid.
5. Robert M. Hollister, Bernard M. Kramer, and Seymour S. Bellin, "Neighborhood Health Centers as a Social Movement," in *Neighborhood Health Centers,* ed. R. M. Hollister, B. M. Kramer, and S. S. Bellin (Lexington, Mass.: Lexington Books, D. C. Heath, 1974), 13.
6. H. Jack Geiger, "Health and Social Change: The Urban Crisis," in *Metropolis in Crisis: Social and Political Perspectives,* ed. J. K. Hadden, 2d ed. (Itasca, Ill.: F. E. Peacock, 1971), 241–51.
7. Rashi Fein, "An Economic and Social Profile of the Negro American," *Daedalus* 94 (Fall 1965): 815–46.
8. Oscar Ornati, "Health and Poverty," in *Poverty amid Affluence* (New York: Twentieth Century Fund, 1966).
9. Robert L. Eichorn and Edward G. Ludwig, "Poverty and Health," in *Poverty*

in the Affluent Society, ed. H. H. Messner (New York: Harper & Row, 1966), 172–80.

10. Karen Davis and S. Schoen, *Health and the War on Poverty* (Washington: Brookings Institute, 1978), tables 2–6, p. 42.

11. Ibid., 43.

12. House Committee on Education and Labor, Subcommittee on the War on Poverty Program, *Examination of the War on Poverty Program: Hearings,* 89th Cong., 1st sess., April 12–15, 1965.

13. William P. Walton, "Effect on Families and Individuals in a Rural Community Where Poor Relief Was Exhausted: A Study of 162 Cases in Clermont County, Ohio," *Cincinnati Journal of Medicine* 45 (1964): 226–27.

14. John W. Hatch, "Contributions of Minorities, Particularly Black Americans, in Medicine as Providers and as Health Care Recipients: An Historical Perspective," National Health Service Corps Monograph (in press); Fein, "The Negro American."

15. A. Yerby, "The Disadvantaged and Medical Care," *American Journal of Public Health* 56 (1966): 5.

16. George Rosen, "The First Neighborhood Health Center Movement—Its Rise and Fall," *American Journal of Public Health* 61 (1971): 1620–37.

17. John D. Stoeckle and Lucy M. Candib, "The Neighborhood Health Center —Reform Ideas of Yesterday and Today," *New England Journal of Medicine* 280 (1969): 1385–91.

18. *The Health Units of Boston, 1924–1933* and *1934–1944* (Boston: Boston Printing Department, 1933 and 1945).

19. Committee on the Costs of Medical Care, *Medical Care for the American People* (Chicago: University of Chicago Press, 1932).

20. J. Adair and K. Deuschle, *The People's Health: Medicine and Anthropology in a Navajo Community* (New York: Appleton-Century-Crofts, 1970).

21. I. H. Pearse and L. H. Crocker, *The Peckham Experiment: A Study in the Living Structure of Society* (London: Allen and Unwin, 1943).

22. Conrad Seipp, *Health Care for the Community: Selected Papers of John Grant* (Baltimore: Johns Hopkins University Press, 1963).

23. S. L. Kark and G. W. Stewart, eds., *A Practice of Social Medicine* (London: Livingstone, 1962).

24. H. Jack Geiger, "Family Health in Three Cultures: Implications for Medical Education" (M.D. thesis, Case Western Reserve University, 1958).

25. H. Jack Geiger, *Tufts Comprehensive Community Action Program* (Proposal to the Office of Economic Opportunity, February 1965). The full outline of this proposal is available in Geiger, "Health Center in Mississippi."

26. Ibid.

27. Economic Opportunity Act, as amended; 42 U.S.C. 2809.

28. Department of Health, Education, and Welfare, *Delivery of Health Services for the Poor,* Program analysis (Washington, D.C.: GPO, 1967).

29. Daniel I. Zwick, "Some Accomplishments and Findings of Neighborhood Health Centers," *Milbank Memorial Fund Quarterly* 50 (1972): 387–420.

30. Ibid.

31. H. Jack Geiger, "Community Control—or Community Conflict?" in *Neighborhood Health Centers,* 133–42; Milton S. Davis and Robert E. Tranquada, "A Sociological Evaluation of the Watts Neighborhood Health Center," *Medical*

Care (1969): 105–17; Peter K. New, Richard M. Hessler, and Phyllis B. Cater, "Consumer Control and Public Accountability," *Anthropological Quarterly* 46 (1973): 196–213.

32. H. Jack Geiger, "Of the Poor, By the Poor or For the Poor: The Mental Health Implications of Social Control of Poverty Programs," in *The Health Gap: Medical Services and the Poor,* ed. R. L. Kane (New York: Springer, 1976), 86–98.

33. Zwick, "Neighborhood Health Centers."

34. H. H. Tilson, "Characteristics of Physicians in OEO Neighborhood Health Centers," *Inquiry* 10, no. 2 (1973): 27–38.

35. H. H. Tilson, "Stability of Physician Employment in Neighborhood Health Centers," *Medical Care* 11 (1973): 384–400.

36. Zwick, "Neighborhood Health Centers."

37. Ibid.

38. Ibid.

39. See, for example: Seymour S. Bellin, H. Jack Geiger, and Count D. Gibson, "Impact of Ambulatory Health Care Services on the Demand for Hospital Beds," *New England Journal of Medicine* 280 (1969): 808–12; Michael Klein et al., "The Impact of the Rochester Neighborhood Health Center on Hospitalization of Children, 1968 to 1970," *Pediatrics* 51 (1973): 833–39.

40. "Neighborhood Health Centers," *Health-PAC Bulletin,* no. 42 (1972): 1–2.

41. Office of Health Affairs, Office of Economic Opportunity, "OEO Activities to Improve Health Care and Health Delivery Systems in Low-Income Areas" (Unpublished memorandum, 1967), 5.

42. Zwick, "Neighborhood Health Centers."

43. C. L. Orso, "Delivering Ambulatory Health Care: The Successful Experience of a Neighborhood Health Center," *Medical Care* 17 (1979): 111–26.

44. *A Decade of Epidemiologic Research in East Boston: A Bibliography* (East Boston: East Boston Neighborhood Health Center, 1980).

45. Geiger, "Health Center in Mississippi."

46. A. James, "Tufts-Delta Administers Environmental Treatment," *Journal of Environmental Health* 31 (1969): 437–46.

47. Geiger, "Health Center in Mississippi."

48. Karen Davis, M. Gold, and D. Makuc, "Access to Health Care for the Poor: Does the Gap Remain?" *Annual Review of Public Health* 2 (1981): 159–82.

49. Bellin, Geiger, and Gibson, "Ambulatory Health Care Services."

50. Joyce C. Lashof, "Medical Care in the Urban Center," *Annals of Internal Medicine* 68 (1968): 242–45.

51. T. J. Colombo, E. W. Saward, Merwyn Greenlick, "The Integration of an OEO Health Program into a Prepaid Comprehensive Group Practice Plan," *American Journal of Public Health* 59 (1969): 641–50.

52. Karen Davis, "Primary Care for the Medically Underserved: Public and Private Financing" (Paper presented at the American Health Planning Association and National Association of Community Health Centers Symposium on Changing Roles in Serving the Underserved, Leesburg, Va., October 11–13, 1981).

53. H. K Freeman, *Community Health Centers: An Initiative of Enduring Utility* (Los Angeles: University of California Institute for Social Science Research, 1981), 1–132.

54. B. C. Duggar, B. Balicki, and A. Zuvekas, "Costs and Utilization Patterns for

Comprehensive Health Center Users" (Paper presented at the Medical Care Section, American Public Health Association Annual Meeting, Los Angeles, November 2, 1981).

55.   Mildred A. Morehead, "Evaluating Quality of Medical Care in the Neighborhood Health Center Program of the Office of Economic Opportunity," *Medical Care* 8 (1970): 118–31.

56.   F. Goldman and R. Grossman, "The Responsiveness and Impacts of Public Health Policy: The Case of Community Health Centers" (Paper presented at the Medical Care Section, American Public Health Association Annual Meeting, November 2, 1981).

57.   Ibid.

58.   R. E. Anderson and S. Morgan, *Comprehensive Health Care: A Southern View* (Atlanta: Southern Regional Council, 1973).

59.   Andre Chabot, "Improved Infant Mortality Rates in a Population Served by a Comprehensive Neighborhood Health Program," *Pediatrics* 47 (1971): 989–94.

60.   B. J. Vaughan, "Maternal and Infant Care Projects: Results in Dade County, Florida," *Southern Medical Journal* 61 (1968): 641–645.

61.   M. R. Gold and R. G. Rosenberg, "The Use of Emergency Room Services by the Population of a Neighborhood Health Center," *Health Services Reports* 89 (1974): 65–70.

62.   L. Gordis, "Effectiveness of Comprehensive Care Programs in Preventing Rheumatic Fever," *New England Journal of Medicine* 289 (1973): 331–335.

63.   Davis, Gold, and Makuc, "Access to Health Care."

64.   Robert M. Hollister, "Neighborhood Health Centers as Demonstrations," in *Neighborhood Health Centers,* 11.

Chapter 2.
THE URBAN HOSPITAL

1974 Statistical Profile of Public General Hospitals (Chicago: American Hospital Association, 1976).

The Future of the Public General Hospital: An Agenda for Transition. Report of the Commission on Public-General Hospitals (Chicago: Hospital Research and Educational Trust, 1976).

Readings on Public General Hospitals (Chicago: Hospital Research and Educational Trust, 1978).

Geraldine Dallek, *The Struggle to Save Public Hospitals: An Advocacy Guide* (Los Angeles: National Health Law Project, 1981).

Committee to Save Cook County Hospital, *Newsletter* vol. 1 (available from 1032 W. Altgeld, Chicago).

Jeffrey Schwartz and Marilyn Rose, "Opening the Door of the Non-Profit Hospital to the Poor," *The Clearinghouse Review* 7 (1974): 655–661.

Fitzhugh Mullan, *White Coat, Clenched Fist: The Political Education of an American Physician* (New York: Macmillan, 1976).

Quentin D. Young, "Structural Reforms in Health-Care Delivery," *Archives of Internal Medicine* 135 (1975): 904–909.

Ivan Illich, *Medical Nemesis: The Expropriation of Health* (New York: Pantheon, 1976).

Chapter 3.
MEDICARE AND MEDICAID

1. The Committee on the Costs of Medical Care was a foundation-funded project created to conduct policy-oriented research on problems in the organization and financing of medical care and to recommend solutions to those problems. Between 1927 and 1933 it produced twenty-six research studies, summarized in I. S. Falk, C. Rufus Rorem, and Martha D. Ring, *The Costs of Medical Care* (Chicago: University of Chicago Press, 1933); and a landmark final report, *Medical Care for the American People* (Chicago: University of Chicago Press, 1932).

2. Computed from data in Falk, Rorem, and Ring, *Costs of Medical Care,* 599.

3. Theodore R. Marmor, *The Politics of Medicare* (Chicago: Aldine, 1973), 7–9; and James G. Burrow, *AMA: Voice of American Medicine* (Baltimore: Johns Hopkins University Press, 1963), 185–204.

4. Marmor, *Politics,* 9–14; and Burrow, *AMA,* 205–27, 293–301, 340–77.

5. Elton Rayack, *Professional Power and American Medicine: The Economics of the American Medical Association* (Cleveland: World, 1967), chap. 5; and Burrow, *AMA,* 228–51.

6. Cambridge Research Institute, *Trends Affecting the U.S. Health Care System* (Washington, D.C.: Health Resources Administration, 1976), 184–85.

7. Marjorie Smith Mueller, "Private Health Insurance in 1973: A Review of Coverage, Enrollment, and Financial Experience," *Social Security Bulletin* 38, no. 2 (1975): 21–40.

8. Ibid.

9. Robert H. Bremner, *American Philanthropy* (Chicago: University of Chicago Press, 1960), 12–15, 98.

10. Robert Stevens and Rosemary Stevens, *Welfare Medicine in America: A Case Study of Medicaid* (New York: Free Press, 1974), 11; and Eugene Feingold, *Medicare: Policy and Politics* (San Francisco: Chandler, 1966), 193–200, 219–27.

11. Marmor, *Politics,* 13–23.

12. Mueller, "Private Health Insurance."

13. Stevens and Stevens, *Welfare Medicine,* 23.

14. Marmor, *Politics,* 29–54.

15. Stevens and Stevens, *Welfare Medicine,* 26–30.

16. Ibid., 31–36.

17. Marmor, *Politics,* 39–54; and Stevens and Stevens, *Welfare Medicine,* 46.

18. Stevens and Stevens, *Welfare Medicine,* 46; and Marmor, *Politics,* 54–57.

19. Marmor, *Politics,* 61–62; Stevens and Stevens, *Welfare Medicine,* 46–47; and Feingold, *Medicare,* esp. 157–294.

20. Richard Harris, *A Sacred Trust* (New York: New American Library, 1966), 187.

21. Marmor, *Politics,* 69.

22. Harris, *Sacred Trust,* 4; Marmor, *Politics,* 63–74; and Stevens and Stevens, *Welfare Medicine,* 47–48.

23. "Medicare: Persons Enrolled, 1979," *Health Care Financing Notes* (Baltimore: Health Care Financing Administration, January 1981), 3.

24. Stevens and Stevens, *Welfare Medicine,* 48–51.
25. Ibid., 58–61.
26. *The Medicare and Medicaid Data Book, 1981* (Baltimore: Health Care Financing Administration, 1982), 13.
27. Medicaid/Medicare Management Institute, *Data on the Medicaid Program: Eligibility, Services, Expenditures,* rev. ed. (Baltimore: Health Care Financing Administration, 1979), 41.
28. Beverlee A. Myers and Rigby Leighton, "Medicaid and the Mainstream: Reassessment in the Context of the Taxpayer Revolt," *Western Journal of Medicine* 132 (1980): 550–61.
29. Medicaid/Medicare, *Data on Medicaid,* 57.
30. Ibid., 6.
31. Ibid., 62–63; and Karen Davis, Marsha Gold, and Diane Makuc, "Access to Health Care for the Poor: Does the Gap Remain?" *Annual Review of Public Health* 2 (1981): 159–82.
32. Medicaid/Medicare, *Data on Medicaid,* 62–63.
33. Stevens and Stevens, *Welfare Medicine,* 2.
34. Davis, Gold, and Makuc, "Access"; and *Health, United States, 1979* (Hyattsville, Md.: DHEW, 1980), 132.
35. *Health of the Disadvantaged* (Hyattsville, Md.: DHHS, 1980), 61.
36. Ibid., 59, 61; and Davis, Gold, and Makuc, "Access."
37. Ibid.; and Lu Ann Aday and Ronald M. Andersen, "Equity of Access to Medical Care: A Conceptual and Empirical Overview," *Medical Care* 19, no. 12, suppl. (1981): 4–27.
38. Davis, Gold, and Makuc, "Access"; and *Health of Disadvantaged,* 43–51.
39. Davis, Gold, and Makuc, "Access."
40. Ibid.; and Martin Ruther and Allen Dobson, "Equal Treatment and Unequal Benefits: A Re-Examination of the Use of Medicare Services by Race, 1967–1976," *Health Care Financing Review* 2, no. 3 (1981): 55–83.
41. Davis, Gold, and Makuc, "Access"; *Health of Disadvantaged,* 68, 70; Aday and Andersen, "Equity of Access"; and Margaret C. Olendzki, Richard P. Grann, and Charles H. Goodrich, "The Impact of Medicaid on Private Care for the Urban Poor," *Medical Care* 10 (1972): 201–6.
42. Davis, Gold, and Makuc, "Access."
43. Janet Mitchell and Jerry Cromwell, "Medicaid Mills: Fact or Fiction?" *Health Care Financing Review* 2, no. 1 (1980): 37–49. See also John E. Kushman, "Participation of Private Practice Dentists in Medicaid," *Inquiry* 15 (1978): 225–33.
44. Ira L. Burney et al., "Medicare and Medicaid Physician Payment Incentives," *Health Care Financing Review* 1, no. 1 (1979): 62–78.
45. Dewey D. Garner, Winston C. Liao, and Thomas R. Sharpe, "Factors Affecting Physician Participation in a State Medicaid Program," *Medical Care* 17 (1979): 43–58.
46. Charles R. Fisher, "Differences by Age Groups in Health Care Spending," *Health Care Financing Review* 1, no. 4 (1980): 65–90.
47. *Changing the Structure of Medicare Benefits: Issues and Options*. Washington Congressional Budget Office, March 1983, p. 23. With insurance premiums included, the figure is actually higher.

48. Jack Hadley, "Physician Participation in Medicaid: Evidence from California," *Health Services Research* 14 (1979): 266–80.

49. Robert M. Gibson and Daniel R. Waldo, "National Health Expenditures, 1980," *Health Care Financing Review* 3, no. 1 (1981): 1–54.

50. Robert M. Gibson and Marjorie Smith Mueller, "National Health Expenditures, Fiscal Year 1976," *Social Security Bulletin* 40, no. 4 (1977): 3–22.

51. Stephen M. Weiner, " 'Reasonable Cost' Reimbursement for Inpatient Hospital Services under Medicare and Medicaid: The Emergence of Public Control," *American Journal of Law and Medicine* 3 (1977): 1–47.

52. Ronald Andersen, Richard Foster, and Peter Weil, "Rates and Correlates of Expenditure Increases for Personal Health Services: Pre- and Post-Medicare and Medicaid," *Inquiry* 13 (1976): 136–44.

53. *Capital Formation in Health Care Facilities* (Washington, D.C.: Health Resources Administration, 1979), 8–10.

54. Calculated from data in *Hospital Statistics* (Chicago: American Hospital Association, 1977), 4. Public Hospitals, having far less insurance revenues and more constraints on debt financing, fell further behind the private sector in assets related to physical plant, advanced technology, and accommodations. In 1955, public hospitals had 85 percent of the assets per bed that private hospitals had ($11,366 compared with $13,427), but by 1975 they had only 74 percent of the assets per bed available in private hospitals ($41,349 compared with $54,366).

55. Gibson and Waldo, "National Health Expenditures."

56. Ibid.

57. Robert A. Derzon and Connie L. Celum, "The Medi-Cal Program: Strategies for Constraining Costs in the Largest Single Expenditure in the State Budget" (Health Policy Program, University of California, San Francisco, December 1979).

58. *Health Care Costs and Services in California Counties* (Sacramento: California Department of Health, 1978), 19–20; and *California's Medical Assistance Program Annual Statistical Report, Medi-Cal Program 1978* (Sacramento: Center for Health Statistics, Department of Health Services, 1979), 7.

59. *Health Care Costs,* 14–15.

60. Ed Sparer, "Gordian Knots: The Situation of Health Care Advocacy for the Poor Today," *Clearinghouse Review* 15 (1981): 1–23.

61. E. Richard Brown, *Public Medicine in Crisis: Public Hospitals in California,* California Policy Seminar Monograph no. 11, (Berkeley: Institute of Governmental Studies, University of California, 1981).

62. Stevens and Stevens, *Welfare Medicine,* 293.

63. Quoted ibid.

64. Personal communication from William V. Opper, Illinois Department of Public Aid, to Ronni Scheier, *Chicago Reporter,* May 8, 1981.

65. Stephen F. Loebs, "Medicaid—A Survey of Indicators and Issues," in *The Medicaid Experience,* ed. A. D. Spiegel (Germantown, Md.: Aspen Systems Corporation, 1979), 10–16; and Myers and Leighton, "Medicaid."

66. Theodore R. Marmor, Donald A. Wittman, and Thomas C. Heagy, "The Politics of Medical Inflation," *Journal of Health Politics, Policy and Law* 1 (1976): 69–84.

67.   Joseph H. Hafkenschiel et al., *Mandatory Prospective Reimbursement Systems for Hospitals* (Sacramento: California Health Facilities Commission, 1982), 56.

68.   Milton I. Roemer et al., "Copayments for Ambulatory Care: Penny-Wise and Pound-Foolish," *Medical Care* 13 (1975): 457–66.

69.   Allen Dobson et al., "PSROs: Their Current Status and Their Impact to Date," *Inquiry* 15 (1978): 113–28; Robert H. Brook, Kathleen N. Williams, and John E. Rolph, "Controlling the Use and Cost of Medical Services: The New Mexico Experimental Medical Care Review Organization—A Four-Year Case Study," *Medical Care* 16, no. 9, suppl. (1978): 1–76; Anita Fulchiero et al., "Can the PSROs Be Cost Effective?" *New England Journal of Medicine* 299 (1978): 574–80; and Milton Westphal, Emma Frazier, and M. Clinton Miller, "Changes in Average Length of Stay and Average Charges Generated Following Institution of PSRO Review," *Health Services Research* 14 (1979): 253–65.

70.   Weiner, " 'Reasonable Cost.' "

71.   Hafkenschiel et al., *Mandatory Prospective Reimbursement Systems,* 10–41.

72.   Julianne R. Howell, *Regulating Hospital Capital Investment: The Experience in Massachusetts* (Hyattsville, Md.: National Center for Health Services Research, March 1981).

Chapter 4.
OCCUPATIONAL HEALTH AND SAFETY

1.   Susan Mazzocchi, ed., *Hazards in the Industrial Environment: District 2 Council* (Denver: Oil, Chemical, and Atomic Workers International Union, 1970), preface.

2.   The reader is referred to Alice Hamilton's *Exploring the Dangerous Trades* (Boston: Little, Brown, 1943), and Lorin Kerr and Frank Goldsmith's *Occupational Safety and Health* (New York: Human Sciences Press, 1982) for further reading on the history of occupational safety and health in the United States.

3.   Louanne Kennedy, "This Work of Living," *Health-PAC Bulletin* 12, no. 4 (1981): 5.

4.   Nicholas Askounes Ashford, *Crisis in the Workplace: Occupational Disease and Injury* (Cambridge, Mass.: MIT Press, 1976), 89–91.

5.   Ibid., 543; Tony Bale, "The Benefit and the Doubt," *Health-PAC Bulletin* 12, no. 4 (1981): 18.

6.   John T. O'Connor, "The '70 OSHA Act Offers Little Safety," *In These Times,* July 30–August 12, 1980, p. 8.

7.   Jane Halpern, M.D., occupational health consultant, Department of Labor, Office of the Assistant Secretary for Policy Evaluation and Research, personal communication; data source, OSHA Management Data System.

8.   Joseph A. Page and Mary-Win O'Brien, *Bitter Wages: Ralph Nader's Study Group Report on Disease and Injury on the Job* (Washington, D.C.: Center for Study of Responsive Law, 1972), 131.

9.   Bale, "The Benefit and the Doubt," *Health-PAC Bulletin* 12, no. 4 (1981): 20.

10. Ibid., 20.

11. U.S. Department of Labor, Assistant Secretary for Policy Evaluation and Research, *An Interim Report to Congress on Occupational Diseases* (Washington, D.C.: GPO, 1980), 1–4.

12. Ibid.

13. Susan Mazzocchi, "Training Occupational Physicians," *Health-PAC Bulletin,* no. 75 (1977): 10.

14. Ibid, p. 10; Ashford, *Crisis in the Workplace,* 427, 441.

15. William E. Morton, "The Responsibility to Report Occupational Health Risks," *Journal of Occupational Medicine* 19 (1977): 258–60.

16. "Code of Ethical Conduct for Physicians Providing Occupational Medical Services," (Adopted by the Board of Directors of the American Occupational Medical Association, July 23, 1976).

17. David P. Discher, *Pilot Study for the Development of an Occupational Disease Surveillance Method,* NIOSH Publication no. 75-162.

18. David Kotelchuck, "OSHA: The Movement Speeds Up," *Health-PAC Bulletin* 12, no. 4 (1981): 14.

19. Michael Silverstein, "Mortality Among Workers in a Die Casting and Electroplating Plant," paper presented at the NIOSH–UAW Scientific Symposium, Detroit, Mich., November 1980.

20. Hank Cox, "Carter Activists Create 'Baby OSHA,'" *Regulatory Action Network: Washington Watch.* U.S. Chamber of Commerce, March, 1981. S-1-S-4.

21. "Special Report: OSHA Saves Lives," *Viewpoint* (Industrial Union Department AFL-CIO), (Winter 1980): 10.

22. Ruth Ruttenberg, "Regulation Is the Mother of Invention," *Working Papers For a New Society* 8, no. 3 (1981): 42–47.

23. Samuel Epstein, "It Costs Us All More Not to Regulate," *In These Times,* August 12–25, 1981, p. 16.

24. Ruttenberg, "Regulation," 43.

25. Epstein, "It Costs Us All More," 16.

Chapter 5.
THE WOMEN'S HEALTH MOVEMENT

1. Sheryl Burt Ruzek, *The Women's Health Movement: Feminist Alternatives to Medical Control* (New York: Praeger, 1979).

2. The Boston Women's Health Book Collective, *Our Bodies, Ourselves* (Boston: New England Free Press, 1969).

3. Barbara Ehrenreich and Deirdre English, *Witches, Midwives, and Nurses: A History of Women Healers,* Glass Mountain Pamphlet, no. 1 (Old Westbury, N.Y.: Feminist Press, 1972); idem, *Complaints and Disorders: The Sexual Politics of Sickness* (Old Westbury, N.Y.: Feminist Press, 1973).

4. Seaman, *The Doctors' Case against the Pill* (New York: Avon, 1969).

5. Barbara Seaman and Gideon Seaman, *Women and the Crisis in Sex Hormones* (New York: Rawson Associates, 1977), 60–149.

6. Barbara Seaman, *Free and Female* (New York: Fawcett, 1972), 180–81.

7. Belita Cowan, "Going to Washington: The Women's Health Lobby," *Health Right* 2, no. 3 (1976): 4, 8.

8. Ruzek, *Women's Health Movement*, 44.

9. Barbara Ehrenreich, Mark Dowie, and Stephen Minkin, "The Charge: Gynocide; The Accused: The U.S. Government," *Mother Jones,* November 1979.

10. Stephen Minkin, "Depo-Provera: A Critical Analysis" *Women and Health* 5 (Summer 1980).

11. Ruzek, *Women's Health Movement*, 58.

12. Helen Marieskind, *An Evaluation of Caesarean Section in the United States* (Washington, D.C.: DHEW, 1979).

13. Ruzek, *Women's Health Movement*, 48.

14. Gena Corea, "The Caesarean Epidemic," *Mother Jones,* July 1980.

15. Ibid.

16. Laurie Olsen, Letter to Editor, in *Mother Jones,* August 1980.

17. Seaman, *Doctors' Case against the Pill,* 14.

18. Ibid., 20.

19. Ibid., 6.

20. Ibid., 16.

21. Hal Strelnick and Richard Younge, *Double Indemnity: The Poverty and Mythology of Affirmative Action in the Health Professional Schools* (New York: Health-PAC, 1980).

22. Helen Rodriguez-Trias, "Tragedies We Hope Never to Be Repeated," *Response* 14, no. 8 (1982): 22. (Cincinnati: General Board of Global Ministries, United Methodist Church).

23. Ruzek, *Women's Health Movement,* 22.

24. Ibid., 25.

25. Robert, E. McGarraugh, Jr., *Sterilization without Consent: Teaching Hospital Violations of HEW Regulations: A Report by Public Citizens' Health Research Group* (Washington, D.C.: Public Citizens' Health Research Group, 1975).

26. James E. Allen, "An Appearance of Genocide: A Review of Governmental Family-Planning Program Policies," *Perspectives in Biology and Medicine* 20 (1977): 300–306; Allen Chase, *The Legacy of Malthus: The Social Costs of the New Scientific Racism* (New York: Knopf, 1977).

27. *Morbidity and Mortality Weekly Report,* November 4, 1977.

28. Helen Rodriguez-Trias, "Sterilization Abuse" (Reid Memorial Lecture, Barnard Women's Center, 1978).

29. Relf v. Weinberger, 372 F. Supp. 1196. 1199 (D.D.C. 1974).

30. McGarraugh, *Sterilization without Consent;* Elissa Krauss, "Hospital Survey on Sterilization Policies: Reproductive Freedom Project," *American Civil Liberties Union Reports,* March, 1975.

31. New York City Health and Hospitals Corporation, *Why Sterilization Guidelines Are Needed* (New York: Office of Quality Assurance, 1975).

32. Claudia Dreifus, "Sterilizing the Poor," *The Progressive,* December 1975, p. 13; Joan Kelly, "Sterilization and Civil Rights," *Rights* 23 (September, 1977): 9–11 (New York: National Emergency Civil Liberties Committee).

33. "Why Sterilization Guidelines Are Needed."

34. New York City Health and Hospitals Corporation, *Guidelines on Sterilization Procedures* (New York: Office of Quality Assurance, 1975).

35. Gordon W. Douglas et al. and John L. S. Holloman et al., Civil Action File no. 76, CW6 U.S. District Court, January 5, 1976.
36. Department of Health, Education, and Welfare, Regional Hearings on Guidelines on Sterilization, unpublished testimony, 1978.
37. *Sterilization Abuse: What It Is and How It Can Be Controlled* (Washington, D.C.: National Women's Health Network, 1981).
38. José Vázquez-Calzada, "La esterilizacion femenina en Puerto Rico," *Revista de Ciencias Sociales* 17 (1973): 281–308.
39. Allen, "Appearance of Genocide."
40. General Accounting Office, Report to Hon. James G. Abourezk, Report no. B 16403(5), November 1976, p. 3.
41. "Uri Charges I.H.S. with Genocide Policy," *Hospital Tribune,* no. 13, August 1977.
42. Bonnie Mass, *Population Target* (Toronto: Latin American Working Group, 1976); Terry L. McCoy et al., *The Dynamics of Population Policy in Latin America* (Cambridge, Mass.: Ballinger, 1974).
43. *Our Bodies, Ourselves,* 1973 edition, p. 2.
44. *Sterilization Abuse.*

Chapter 6.
MEDICAL EDUCATION

1. Abraham Flexner, *Medical Education in the United States and Canada: A Report to the Carnegie Foundation for the Advancement of Teaching* (New York: Carnegie Foundation, 1910).
2. Carnegie Commission on Higher Education, *Higher Education and the Nation's Health: Policies for Medical and Dental Education* (New York: McGraw-Hill, 1970).
3. E. Richard Brown, *Rockefeller Medicine Men: Medicine and Capitalism in America* (Berkeley: University of California Press, 1979).
4. Ibid.
5. D. Wolfle, "The Implications of Specialism for University Education," *Journal of Medical Education* 36, no. 12, pt. 2 (1961): 35–41.
6. C. Jacobsen, "Introduction," *Journal of Medical Education* 51 (1976): xvii–xx.
7. G. Miller, "Setting the Stage," in *Medical Education and the Contemporary World,* ed. G. Miller, DHEW Publication no. (NIH) 77-1232, pp. vii–ix.
8. Flexner, *Medical Education,* p. 26.
9. Cecil G. Sheps, G. A. Wolf, and C. Jacobsen, eds., *Medical Education and Medical Care: Interactions and Prospects: Report of the Eighth Teaching Institute of the Association of American Medical Colleges* (Evanston: AAMC, 1961): 3.
10. Department of Health, Education, and Welfare, *Minorities and Women in the Health Fields,* DHEW Publication no. (HRA), 76-22.
11. Barbara Ehrenreich and John Ehrenreich, *The American Health Empire: Power, Profits, and Politics* (New York: Random House, 1971).
12. DHEW, *Minorities and Women.*
13. Ehrenreich and Ehrenreich, *American Health Empire.*
14. Cecil G. Sheps, "The Medical School—Community Expectations," in *Trends in New Medical Schools,* ed. H. Popper (New York: Grune & Stratton, 1967).

15.   "Health and Hospital Care," Message from the President of the United States, H. Doc. no. 85, *Congressional Record,* February 9, 1961: 2000-03.

16.   R. Graham and J. Royer, eds., *A Handbook for Change* (Chicago: SAMA Foundation, 1973).

17.   G. James, "Medical Education: Medical Technique or Disease Control," in *Trends in New Medical Schools,* 1–7.

18.   President's Commission on Heart Disease, Cancer and Stroke, *Report to the President: A National Program to Conquer Heart Disease, Cancer and Stroke* (Washington, D.C.: GPO, 1964).

19.   Ehrenreich and Ehrenreich, *American Health Empire.*

20.   Department of Health, Education, and Welfare, *Costs of Education in the Health Professions* (Washington, D.C.: National Academy of Sciences, 1979).

21.   Ibid.

22.   E. Ginzberg, "Medical Education in the Real World," *Journal of Medical Education* 51 (1976): 986–90; Graduate Medical Education National Advisory Committee, *Report of the Graduate Medical Education National Advisory Committee to the Secretary, Department of Health and Human Services* (Washington, D.C.: GPO, 1980); *Medical Education: Institutions, Characteristics and Programs* (Washington, D.C.: AAMC, 1981).

23.   Michael L. Millman, *Politics and the Expanding Physician Supply* (New York: Universe Books, 1980).

24.   Charles E. Odegaard, *Eleven Area Health Education Centers: The View from the Grass Roots* (Seattle: University of Washington Press, 1980).

25.   DHEW, *Costs of Education.*

26.   John S. Millis, *A Rational Public Policy for Medical Education and Its Financing: A Report to the Board of Directors of the National Fund for Medical Education* (New York: NFME, 1971).

27.   President's Commission, *Report to the President.*

28.   Lowell T. Coggeshall, *Planning for Medical Progress through Education: A Report Submitted to the Executive Council of the Association of American Colleges* (Evanston: AAMC, 1965).

29.   Carnegie Commission, *Higher Education.*

30.   P. Canfield, "Family Medicine: A Historical Perspective," *Journal of Medical Education* 51 (1976): 904–11.

31.   John S. Millis, *The Graduate Education of Physicians: Report of the Citizens' Commission on Graduate Medical Education* (Chicago: AMA, 1966).

32.   DHEW, *Costs of Education.*

33.   Carnegie Commission, *Higher Education.*

34.   James, "Medical Education."

35.   Jacobsen, "Introduction."

36.   Sheps, "Medical School."

37.   Paul Sanazaro, "Class Size in Medical School," *Journal of Medical Education* 41 (1966): 1017–29.

38.   *Medical Education.*

39.   Sanazaro, "Class Size."

40.   D. Matluck, "Changes in Trends in Medical Education," *Journal of Medical Education* 47 (1972): 612–19.

41.   DHEW, *Costs of Education.*

42.   GMENAC, *Report.*

43. R. Beran and R. Kriner, *A Study of Three-Year Curricula in U.S. Medical Schools* (Washington, D.C.: AAMC, 1978): 74.
44. Ibid., 73.
45. R. Beran, "The Rise and Fall of Three-Year Medical School Programs," *Journal of Medical Education* 54 (1979): 248–49.
46. *1979–80 AAMC Curriculum Directory* (Washington, D.C.: AAMC, 1980).
47. J. A. D. Cooper, "Major Factors Involved in Reconstructing the Medical Curriculum," *Journal of the American Medical Association* 170 (1959): 452–54; idem and A. Lein, "An Integrated Program for Premedical and Medical Education: Its Impact on the University," in *Trends in New Medical Schools,* 41–45.
48. Matluck, "Changes"; C. Campbell and G. DeMuth, "The University of Michigan Integrated Premedical-Medical Program," *Journal of Medical Education* 51 (1976): 290–95.
49. E. H. Blaustein and H. L. Kayne, "Boston University and Accelerated Medical Education: The First Five Cohorts," *Journal of Medical Education* 55 (1980): 202–4.
50. F. Hale, "Medical Education and Rural Health Care: The Impact of Federal Involvement," in *Workshops in Primary Care,* ed. S. Marlowe and M. McGowan (Waterville: National Rural Primary Care Association, 1980).
51. F. Hale et al., "The Impact of a Required Preceptorship on Senior Medical Students," *Journal of Medical Education* 54 (1979): 396–401.
52. Ibid.; Julius Richmond, *Healthy People: The Surgeon General's Report on Health Promotion and Disease Prevention,* DHEW Publication no. (PHS) 79-55071.
53. Hale, "Required Preceptorship"; D. H. Funkenstein, "Current Changes in Education Affecting Medical School Admissions and Curriculum Planning," *Journal of Medical Education* 41 (1966): 401–23.
54. Canfield, "Family Medicine."
55. GMENAC, *Report.*
56. R. V. Christie, *Medical Education and the State: The Changing Pattern in Ten Countries,* DHEW Publication no. (NIH) 76-943.
57. Ibid.; T. L. Leaman, "Predoctoral Education in Family Medicine: A Ten-Year Perspective," *Journal of Family Practice* 9 (1979): 845–54.
58. Hale, "Required Preceptorship"; Christie, *Medical Education.*
59. "Medical Education in the U.S.: 79th Annual Report," *Journal of the American Medical Association* 243 (1980): 849–66.
60. Statement of the Association for Teachers of Preventive Medicine to Congress, H.361–6.6, March 12, 1981: 329–44.
61. Ibid.; Canfield, "Family Medicine."
62. Mary E. Cunnane, "Recent Trends in Medical Education: Report of a Survey," in *Recent Trends in Medical Education,* ed. Elizabeth F. Purcell (New York: Macy Foundation, 1976), 1–7.
63. P. Lee, "Medical Schools and the Changing Times: Nine Case Reports on Experimentation in Medical Education, 1950–1960," *Journal of Medical Education* 36 (1961): 45–141.
64. Cunnane, "Recent Trends."
65. Gregory L. Trzebiatowski, "Independent Study Programs: The State of the Art," in *Recent Trends in Medical Education,* 111–26.
66. Ibid.

67. Funkenstein, "Current Changes."
68. DHEW, *Minorities and Women; Medical Education.*
69. Ibid.
70. Richmond, *Healthy People.*

Chapter 7.
AFFIRMATIVE ACTION
IN MEDICINE

1. Barbara Caress, "Medical School Sweepstakes: The Race Is Fixed," *Health-PAC Bulletin,* no. 76 (1977): 1–7.
2. E. Richard Brown, "He Who Pays the Piper: Foundations, the Medical Profession, and Medical Education," *Health Care in America: Essays in Social History,* ed. Susan Reverby and David Rosner (Philadelphia: Temple University Press, 1979).
3. Grace Ziem, "Medical Education since Flexner: A Seventy-Year Tracking Record," *Health-PAC Bulletin,* no. 76 (1977): 8–14.
4. James E. Blackwell, "In Support of Preferential Admissions and Affirmative Action in Higher Education: Pre- and Post-Bakke Considerations" (University of Massachusetts at Boston, 1977, Mimeographed).
5. Ruth M. Raup and Elizabeth Williams, "Negro Students in Medical Schools in the United States," *Journal of Medical Education* 39 (1964): 444–50.
6. Jerry L. Weaver and Sharon D. Garret, "Sexism and Racism in the American Health Industry: A Comparative Analysis," *International Journal of Health Services* (1978): 677–703.
7. Hal Strelnick, "Making the Dean's List," *Health-PAC Bulletin* 12 (1981): 7.
8. Institute of Medicine, *Health Care in a Context of Civil Rights* (Washington, D.C.: National Academy Press, 1981).
9. Lee Cogan, *Negroes for Medicine: Report of a Macy Conference* (Baltimore: Johns Hopkins University Press, 1968).
10. Ibid.; Charles E. Odegaard, *Minorities in Medicine: From Receptive Passivity to Positive Action, 1966–76* (New York: Macy Foundation, 1977).
11. Association of American Medical Colleges, *Report of the Association of American Medical Colleges Task Force to the Inter-Association Committee on Expanding Educational Opportunities in Medicine for Blacks and Other Minority Students* (Washington, D.C.: AAMC, 1970).
12. Sam Schildhaus and Franz M. Jaggar, *An exploratory evaluation . . . of U.S. medical schools' efforts to achieve equal representation of minority students,* DHEW Publication no. (HRA) 78-635.
13. Association of American Medical Colleges, *Report of the Association of American Medical Colleges Task Force on Minority Student Opportunities in Medicine* (Washington, D.C.: AAMC, 1978).
14. U.S. Commission on Civil Rights, *Toward an Understanding of Bakke* (Washington, D.C.: GPO, 1979), 58.
15. Joel S. Berke, Alan K. Campbell, and Robert J. Goettel, *Financing Equal Educational Opportunities Alternatives for State Finance* (Berkeley, Calif.: McCutcheon, 1972); Joel S. Berke and Michael W. Kurst, *Federal Aid to Education: Who Benefits?*

Who Governs? (Lexington, Mass.: Health, 1972); Alexander W. Astin, *The Myth of Equal Access in Public Higher Education* (Atlanta: Southern Education Foundation, 1975).

16. Hal Strelnick and Richard Younge, *Double Indemnity: The Poverty and Mythology of Affirmative Action in the Health Professional Schools* (New York: Health-PAC, 1980), 13–26.

17. Ibid., 48–49.

18. General Accounting Office, *Congressional Objectives of Federal Loans and Scholarships to Health Professions Not Being Met* (Washington, D.C.: GPO, 1974).

19. Department of Health, Education, and Welfare, *Health Professions Educational Assistance Program: A Report to the President and the Congress.* (Washington, D.C.: GPO, 1970).

20. Department of Health, Education, and Welfare, *A New Bureau, a Sharper Focus: Annual Report of Fiscal 1975 Activities, Bureau of Health Manpower,* DHEW Publication no. (HRA) 76-9.

21. Congressional Budget Office, *The Role of Aid to Medical, Osteopathic and Dental Students in a New Health Manpower Education Policy: Staff Working Paper* (Washington, D.C.: GPO, 1976).

22. Schildhaus and Jaggar, *Exploratory Evaluation, 71.*

23. American Medical Association, "Money Becoming Admissions Criterion," *American Medical News* (February 8, 1976).

24. Graduate Medical Education National Advisory Committee, *Summary Report of the Graduate Medical Education National Advisory Committee to the Secretary, Department of Health and Human Services,* DHHS Publication no. (HRA) 81-651.

25. Ibid., ii.

26. Ibid., 30.

27. Strelnick and Younge, *Double Indemnity,* 35–50.

28. Bernard W. Nelson, Richard Bird, and Gilbert Ruders, "Education Pathway Analysis for the Study of Minority Representation in Medical School," *Journal of Medical Education* 46 (1971): 745–49.

29. Boyd D. Sleeth and Robert I. Mischell, "Black Underrepresentation in United States Medical Schools," *New England Journal of Medicine* 297 (1977): 1146–48.

30. Bernard W. Nelson, "Expanding Educational Opportunities in Medicine for Blacks and Other Minority Students," *Journal of Medical Education* 45 (1970): 731–36.

31. Sleeth and Mischell, "Black Underrepresentation"; Vincent Tinto, "Dropout from Higher Education: A Theoretical Synthesis of Recent Research," *Review of Education Research* (1975): 89–120; Patrick T. Terenzini and Ernest T. Pascarella, "Voluntary Freshman Attrition and Patterns of Social and Academic Integration in a University: A Test of a Conceptual Model," *Research in Higher Education* (1977): 25–43; Larry G. Jones, *Black Students Enrolled in White Colleges and Universities: Their Attitudes and Perceptions* (Atlanta: Southern Regional Medical Board, 1979).

32. Strelnick and Younge, *Double Indemnity;* Student National Medical Association, *Minority Medical Students: Who They Are, Their Progress, Career Aspirations, Their Future in Medical School,* DHEW Publication no. (HRA) 78-625.

33. James L. Curtis, *Blacks, Medical Schools, and Society* (Ann Arbor: University of Michigan Press, 1971), 62.

34.   James R. Mingle, *Black Enrollment in Higher Education: Trends in the Nation and the South* (Atlanta: Southern Regional Education Board, 1978).

35.   Curtis, *Blacks, Medical Schools, and Society,* 64–72.

36.   J. N. Gayles, "Training at the Collegiate and Pre-Collegiate Interface: STRIKE as an Example," in *Minorities in Science: The Challenge for Change in Bio-Medicine,* ed. Vijaya L. Melnick and Franklin D. Hamilton, (New York: Plenum Press, 1977), 243–53.

37.   Willis R. Brewer, Merlin K. DuVal and Gloria M. Davis, "Increasing Minority Recruitment to the Health Professions by Enlarging the Applicant Pool," *New England Journal of Medicine* 301 (1979): 74–76.

38.   R. A. Warren, "Motivating Upper Elementary Level Mexican American Students toward Science Careers, in *Minorities in Science,* 255–58.

39.   Schildhaus and Jaggar, *Exploratory Evaluation,* 33.

40.   AAMC, *Report . . . on Expanding Educational Opportunities,* 5.

41.   R. E. Jackson, Addresses presented at the Macy Conference of leaders of programs to recruit minority group students for medicine, Ft. Lauderdale, Fla, April 21–23, 1971, pp. 111–13; W. D. Wallace, "The Harvard Health Careers Summer Program," in *Minorities in Science,* 231–35.

42.   Cogan, *Negroes for Medicine,* 17–18.

43.   Schildhaus and Jaggar, *Exploratory Evaluation,* 65.

44.   Harrison G. Gough, Wallace B. Hall, and Robert E. Harris, "Admissions Procedures as Forecasters of Performance in Medical Training," *Journal of Medical Education* 38 (1963): 983–98.

45.   Bart Waldman, "Economic and Racial Disadvantage as Reflected in Traditional Medical School Selection Factors," *Journal of Medical Education* 52 (1977): 961–67.

46.   Association of American Medical Colleges, *Final Report of the AAMC National Task Force with Recommendation for the Medical College Admissions Assessment Program Study* (Washington, D.C.: AAMC, 1973).

47.   Paul R. Elliott, "The Medical College Admission Test, in *Medical Education: Responses to a Challenge,* ed. William E. Cadbury and Charlotte Cadbury (Mt. Kisco: Futura Publishing Company, 1979), 157–73; James L. Angel, "The New MCAT: New Dimensions in Assessment," in *Minorities in Science,* 17–27.

48.   Association of American Medical Colleges, "Proceedings for 1969," *Journal of Medical Education* 45 (1970): 366–69.

49.   Robert Murden et al., "Academic and Personal Characteristics as Predictors of Clinical Success in Medical School," in *Proceedings of the 16th Annual Conference on Research in Medical Education* (Washington, D.C.: AAMC, 1977).

50.   William E. Sedlaeck and Glenwood C. Brooks, *Racism in American Education: A Model for Change* (Chicago: Prentice-Hall, 1976).

51.   D. H. Poorman, "Medical School Applicants: A Study of the Admissions Interview," *Journal of the Kansas Medical Society* 76 (1975): 298–301; Walter F. Char et al., "Interviewing, Motivation, and Clinical Judgement," *Journal of Medical Education* 50 (1975): 192–94.

52.   A. D'Costa et al., *Simulated Minority Admissions Exercise: Participants' Workbook* (Washington, D.C.: AAMC, 1974).

53. Helen H. Gee and John Cowles, eds., "Appraisal of Applicants to Medical School," *Journal of Medical Education* 32 (1957): 1–288; John S. Wellington and Pilar Montero, "Equal Education Opportunity Programs in American Medical Schools," *Journal of Medical Education* 53 (1978): 633–39.

54. William J. Oetgen and Max P. Pepper, "Medical School Admission Committees: A Descriptive Study," *Journal of Medical Education* 47 (1972): 966–68.

55. Wellington and Montero, "Equal Education Opportunity Programs."

56. Carnegie Commission, *Higher Education and the Nation's Health: Policies for Medical and Dental Education: A Special Report and Recommendations by the Carnegie Commission on Higher Education* (New York: McGraw-Hill, 1970).

57. Arthur Schatzkin and John Yergan, "The Case for Minority Admissions," *New England Journal of Medicine* 297 (1977): 554–56.

58. Schildhaus and Jaggar, *Exploratory Evaluation,* 41.

59. Wellington and Montero, "Equal Education Opportunity Programs."

60. Charles S. Ireland, Jr., "Orientation of Incoming Students," in *Medical Education,* 253–75.

61. Gregory Strayhorn, "Social Supports, Perceived Stress and Health: The Black Experience in Medical School, a Preliminary Study," *Journal of the National Medical Association* 72 (1980): 869–81.

62. *Office of Health Resources Opportunity Digest* (Washington, D.C.: DHHS, HRA, 1980).

63. Strelnick and Younge, *Double Indemnity,* 29–31.

64. Schildhaus and Jaggar, *Exploratory Evaluation,* 80.

65. Wellington and Montero, "Equal Education Opportunity Programs."

66. Henry P. Jolly and Thomas A. Larson, *Participation of Women and Minorities on United States Medical School Faculties* (Washington, D.C.: AAMC, 1976).

67. Elizabeth Higgins, "Participation of Women and Minorities on United States Medical School Faculties," *Journal of Medical Education* 54 (1979): 252.

68. Gail E. Wyatt, Barbara A. Bass, and Gloria Powell, "A Survey of Ethnic and Sociocultural Issues in Medical School Education," *Journal of Medical Education* 53 (1978): 627–32.

69. C. E. Odegaard, *Minorities in Medicine,* 85–89.

70. Marvin W. Peterson et al., *Black Students on White Campuses: The Impacts of Increased Black Enrollments* (Ann Arbor: Institute for Social Research, 1978); George M. Neely and Robert A. Green, "Predictors of the Impact of a Minority Program upon a Medical School," in *Proceedings of the 16th Annual Conference on Research in Medical Education* (Washington, D.C.: AAMC, 1977).

71. Robert H. Geertsuma, "A Special Tutorial for Minority Medical Students: An Account of a Year's Experience," *Journal of Medical Education* 52 (1977): 396–403.

72. Christina Grant, "The Role of the Foundations in Promoting Participation of Minorities in Medical Education," in *Medical Education,* 365–82.

73. Dietrich Reitzes and Heckmat Elkhanialy, "Black Physicians, Minority Group Health Care and the Impact of National Medical Fellowships," *Medical Care* 14 (1976): 1052–60.

74. Grant, "Role of Foundations."

75. "Fall Outlook Grim for Medical Student Aid," *New Physician* 30 (1981): 9.

76. *Office of Health Resources Opportunity Digest.*

77.   Richard E. Mantovani, Gordon L. Travis, and Davis G. Johnson, *Medical School Indebtedness and Career Plans,* DHEW Publication no. (HRA) 77-21.

78.   Richard E. Mantovani, *Medical Student Finances and Personal Characteristics, 1974– 1975,* DHEW Publication no. (HRA) 77-53.

79.   *Report of the GMENAC.*

80.   Schildhaus and Jagger, *Exploratory Evaluation,* 39–40.

Chapter 8.
THE NATIONAL HEALTH SERVICE CORPS AND HEALTH PERSONNEL INNOVATIONS

1.   Abraham Flexner, *Medical Education in the United States and Canada: A Report of the Carnegie Foundation for the Advancement of Teaching* (New York: Carnegie Foundation, 1910).

2.   John Duffy, *The Healers: A History of American Medicine* (Urbana: University of Illinois Press, 1976), 264–66.

3.   President's Commission on the Health Needs of the Nation, *Building America's Health* (Washington, D.C.: GPO, 1952), II, 115.

4.   Richard A. Harris, *A Sacred Trust* (New York: New American Library, 1966), 12.

5.   Department of Health, Education, and Welfare, *Health Manpower Perspective: 1967,* DHEW Publication no. 1667, Bureau of Health Manpower.

6.   Fitzhugh Mullan, *White Coat, Clenched Fist: The Political Education of an American Physician* (New York: Macmillan, 1976), 1–19.

7.   Ibid., 41–67.

8.   Carnegie Commission on Higher Education, *Higher Education and the Nation's Health: Policies for Medical and Dental Education* (New York: McGraw-Hill, 1970), 8–9.

9.   Department of Health, Education, and Welfare, Bureau of Health Manpower, *A Report to the President and the Congress on the Status of Health Professions Personnel in the United States,* DHEW Publication no. (HRA) 80-53, p. A-9.

10.   Department of Health and Human Services, Bureau of Health Professions, *Supply of Manpower in Selected Health Occupations: 1950–1990,* DHHS Publication no. (HRA) 80-35, pp. 10, 16.

11.   Eric Redman, *The Dance of Legislation* (New York: Simon & Schuster, 1973). Redman's book describes at length the political process that brought the NHSC into being.

12.   Public Law 91-623, Section 329(a).

13.   Ibid., Section 329(b).

14.   Julius B. Richmond, *The Blue Sheet,* 1977, no. 20, p. S 4.

15.   Graduate Medical Education National Advisory Committee, *Summary Report to the Secretary, Department of Health and Human Services,* DHHS Publication no. (HRA) 81-651.

16.   William B. Schwartz et al., "The Changing Distribution of Board-Certified Physicians," *New England Journal of Medicine* 303 (1980): 1032–37.

17.   Ibid., 1037.

Chapter 9.
NEW HEALTH PROFESSIONALS

1.   Harold Speert, *Obstetrics and Gynecology in America: A History* (Baltimore: Waverly Press, 1980).

2.   James Burrow, *Organized Medicine in the Progressive Era* (Baltimore: Johns Hopkins University Press, 1977).

3.   James Warren, "The Problem of Providing Health Services," *Annals of Internal Medicine* 69 (1968): 951–55.

4.   Ibid.

5.   E. Harvey Estes, "The Critical Shortage—Physicians and Supporting Personnel," *Annals of Internal Medicine* 69 (1968): 957–62.

6.   Editorial, *American Journal of Nursing* 70 (1970): 691.

7.   Paul Sanazaro, "Physician Support Personnel in the 1970's," *Journal of the American Medical Association* 214 (1970): 98–100.

8.   Russel Morgan, "Physician Assistants: Their Role in Medicine in the Years Ahead," *Journal of the Maine Medical Association* 59 (1963): 219–23.

9.   Andrew Nichols, "Physician Extenders: The Law and the Future," *Journal of Family Practice* 11 (1980): 101–8.

10.   Henry Silver, Loretta Ford, and Day Lewis, "The Pediatric Nurse-Practitioner Program," *Journal of the American Medical Association* 204 (1968): 298–302.

11.   Vernon W. Lippard, *A Half-Century of American Medical Education, 1920–1970* (New York: Macy Foundation, 1974).

12.   *Report of the National Advisory Commission on Health Manpower* (Washington, D.C.: GPO, 1967), II, 231–33.

13.   Association of Physician Assistant Programs, Statement on PA Education and Proposed Health Manpower Legislation, May 1980.

14.   H. Shultz, M. Zielezny, and J. Gentry, *Longitudinal Study of Nurse Practitioners,* DHEW Publication no. (HRA) 80-2.

15.   Graduate Medical Education National Advisory Committee, *Summary Report of the Graduate Medical Education National Advisory Committee to the Secretary, Department of Health and Human Services,* DHHS Publication no. (HRA) 81-651, 1981.

16.   Henry B. Perry and Donald W. Fisher, The Present Status of the Physician Assistant Profession: Results of the Association of Physician Assistant Programs' 1978 Longitudinal Survey of Graduates (Prepublication Draft, September 1980).

17.   Institute of Medicine, *A Manpower Policy for Primary Health Care* (Washington, DC: National Academy of Sciences, 1978).

18.   Harold Sox, "Quality of Patient Care by Nurse-Practitioners and Physician Assistants: A Ten Year Perspective," *Annals of Internal Medicine* 91 (1979): 459–68.

19.   Robert H. Brook et al., "Assessing the Quality of Medical Care Using Outcome Measures: An Overview of the Method," *Medical Care* 15 suppl. (1977): 1–84.

20.   Ibid.

21.   Eugene Nelson, Arthur Jacobs, and Kenneth Johnson, "Patients' Acceptance of Physician's Assistants," *Journal of the American Medical Association* 228 (1974): 63–67.

22. Susan Reverby, "The Sorcerer's Apprentice," in *Prognosis Negative,* ed. D. Kotelchuck (New York: Vintage Books, 1976), 215–229.

23. APAP, Statement.

24. Robert C. Mendenhall and Paul A. Repicky, Collection and Processing of Baseline Data for the Physician Extender Reimbursement Study: Executive Summary (Contract no. C5-100-75-0034, University of Southern California, 1978).

25. Robert Wood, Richard Tompkins, and Barry Wolcott, "An Efficient Strategy for Managing Acute Respiratory Illness in Adults," *Annals of Internal Medicine* 93 (1980): 757–63.

26. Health Manpower Committee Report, *New York State Journal of Medicine* 78 (1978): 1602.

27. Nichols, "Physician Extenders," 107.

28. Robert Taylor, *Family Medicine* (New York: Springer-Verlag, 1978).

29. Reverby, "Sorcerer's Apprentice," 228.

30. June Rothberg, "Nurse and Physician Assistant: Issues and Relations, *Nursing Outlook* 21 (1973): 154–58.

31. Editorial, "Physician Associate vs. Physician Assistant," *New York State Journal of Medicine* 75 (1975): 689.

32. Ibid.

33. Patrick B. Storey, *The Soviet Feldsher as a Physician Assistant,* DHEW Publication no. 72–58, 1972.

34. Nichols, "Physician Extenders," 105.

Chapter 10.
COMMUNITY PARTICIPATION
AND CONTROL

1. Department of Health and Human Services, Bureau of Health Resources Opportunity, *Health of the Disadvantaged* (Washington, D.C.: GPO, 1980).

2. Benjamin D. Paul, ed., *Health, Culture, and Community* (New York: Russell Sage Foundation, 1955).

3. John Hatch, "From Crisis to Disaster: An Account of the Struggles of Black Farm Laborers in the U.S." (Paper presented to the American Academy of Sciences, December 1971).

4. Kenneth B. Clark, *Dark Ghetto* (New York: Harper & Row, 1965).

5. John Hatch, "Self-Help and Consumer Participation in the Development of the Health Care System," *Annals of the New York Academy of Sciences* 310 (1978): 49–56.

6. Records of the Department of Preventive Medicine, Tufts University, 1965.

7. Clark, *Dark Ghetto;* Leslie Falk, "Community Participation in the Neighborhood Health Center," *Journal of the National Medical Association* 69 (1969): 493–97.

8. Daniel P. Moynihan, *Maximum Feasible Misunderstanding* (New York: Free Press, 1969); John Donovan, *The Politics of Poverty* (New York: Pegasus, 1967); Sanford Kravitz, "Community Action Programs: Past, Present and Future," in

On Fighting Poverty: Perspectives from Experience, ed. James L. Sundquist (New York: Basic Books, 1969).

9. Donovan, *Politics of Poverty.*

10. Richard Hall, "A Stir of Hope in Mound Bayou," *Life*, March 28, 1969; Seymour Bellin and H. Jack Geiger, "The Impact of a Neighborhood Health Center," in *The Health Gap*, ed. Robert Kane et al. (New York: Springer, 1976), 187–201; Office of Economic Opportunity, "For Those Who Need It Most," *Medical World News*, March 8, 1968.

11. Herbert Black, *People and Plows for Hunger* (Boston: Boston Globe Press, 1975); John Hatch, "Community Shares in Policy Decisions for Rural Health Centers," *Journal of the American Hospital Association* 43 (1969): 109–12; J. David Greenston and Paul Peterson, *Race and Authority in Urban Politics* (New York: Russell Sage Foundation, 1973); Lawrence Koseki and John Hayakawa, "Consumer Participation and Community Organization Practice: Implications of National Health Legislation," *Medical Care* 17 (1979): 244–54; John Hatch, "Discussion of Group Practice in Comprehensive Health Care Centers," *Bulletin of the New York Academy of Medicine* 44 (1968): 1375–77.

12. Milton I. Roemer, *Rural Health Care* (St. Louis: C. V. Mosby, 1976).

13. Ibid.

14. Falk, "Community Participation."

15. Hatch, "Community Shares."

16. Greenston and Peterson, *Race and Authority.*

17. Andrew James, "Tufts-Delta Administers Environmental Treatment," *Journal of Environmental Health* 31 (1969): 437–46; Cynthia Kelly, "Health Care in the Mississippi Delta," *American Journal of Nursing* 69 (1969): 758–63.

18. Black, *People and Plows;* Hatch, "Community Shares"; Hatch, "Discussion of Group Practice."

19. Hall, "Stir of Hope."

20. Greenston and Peterson, *Race and Authority.*

Chapter 11.
HOLISM AND SELF-CARE

1. Abraham Flexner, *Medical Education in the United States and Canada: A Report to the Carnegie Foundation for the Advancement of Teaching* (New York: Carnegie Foundation, 1910).

2. For a useful review of modern medicine's effectiveness, see Thomas McKeown, *The Role of Medicine: Dream, Mirage, or Nemesis?* (Princeton: Princeton University Press, 1979).

3. Peter Kropotkin, *Mutual Aid, a Factor of Evolution* (Boston: Porter Sargent, n.d.).

4. Christopher Lasch, *The Culture of Narcissism: American Life in an Age of Diminishing Expectations* (New York: Norton, 1979).

5. Ivan Illich, *Medical Nemesis: The Expropriation of Health* (London: Calder & Boyars, 1975); Victor R. Fuchs, *Who Shall Live? Health, Economics, and Social Choice* (New York: Basic Books, 1974). *Medical Nemesis* later appeared in a slightly revised edition for readership in the United States (New York: Pantheon, 1976).

6. Ivan Illich, *Medical Nemesis: The Expropriation of Health* (Cuernavaca: CIDOC, 1974), iv.

7. Illich, *Medical Nemesis* (1975), 66.

8. Fuchs, *Who Shall Live?* 144.

9. W. R. Robinson, "Ecological Correlations and the Behavior of Individuals," *American Sociological Review* 15 (1950): 351–57.

10. Fuchs, *Who Shall Live?* 46.

11. Ibid., 151.

12. William Ryan, *Blaming the Victim* (New York: Vintage Books, 1971), 3–29, 136–63; Robert Crawford, "You Are Dangerous to Your Health: The Ideology and Politics of Victim Blaming," *International Journal of Health Services* 7 (1977): 663–80.

13. See, e.g., Paul W. Newacheck et al., "Income and Illness," *Medical Care* 18 (1980): 1165–76; H. Brenner, "Mortality and the National Economy," *Lancet* 2 (1979): 568–73.

14. Howard S. Berliner and J. Warren Salmon, "The Holistic Alternative to Scientific Medicine: History and Analysis," *International Journal of Health Services* 10 (1980): 133–47; Victor W. Sidel and Ruth Sidel, "Beyond Coping," *Social Policy* 7, no. 2 (1976): 67–69.

contributors

Molly Backup, P.A., has been employed as a primary-care physician's assistant since her graduation from the Yale University Physician Associate Program in 1974, and has spent the last four years in a rural satellite health-maintenance organization under National Health Service Corps sponsorship. She received her B.A. in social anthropology from Radcliffe College. She has taught physician's-assistant, nurse-practitioner, nursing, and medical students as well as adult-education students studying occupational safety and health. She is involved in health promotion, patient education, health planning, and reform activities in a number of national organizations. She is also a delegate to the New York State Society of Physician's Assistants, and chairs the Professional and Continuing Educational Committee of the American Association of Physician's Assistants.

E. Richard Brown, Ph.D., is on the faculty of the School of Public Health at the University of California, Los Angeles. He is the author of *Rockefeller Medicine Men: Medicine and Capitalism in America* (University of California Press, 1980) and other publications on health policy, the history of health care, and the political economy of health. He has recently completed studies of problems facing public hospitals and their options, and community organizing efforts to assure access of low-income persons to health care. He is also developing cancer education programs for workers.

Molly Coye, M.D., M.P.H., is an assistant clinical professor, Department of Internal Medicine, University of California, San Francisco Medical Center. She received her medical and public health degrees from Johns Hopkins University and trained in family practice and occupational medicine at the University of California and at NIOSH. She has consulted on occupational health with the Pan-American Health Organization in Mexico and Nicaragua and with the Universidad Complutense in Madrid, Spain.

Eugenia Eng, Dr.P.H., is on the faculty of the School of Public Health at the University of North Carolina at Chapel Hill. Her work focuses on the cross-cultural aspects of integrating community development approaches with health care delivery in the rural communities of the United States and developing nations. Since 1970 she has been continually involved in international health projects in Togo, Benin, Upper Volta, Mali, Cameroon, and Tanzania. Her experience ranges from being a health education outreach worker and trainer of midwives and teachers to acting as consultant in environmental sanitation manpower development and as coordinator of a four-year USAID project in health education training.

H. Jack Geiger, M.D., is currently Arthur C. Logan Professor of Community Medicine at the School for Biomedical Education, City College, City University of New York. Most of his professional career has been focused on the problems of health and poverty and of civil rights in health care. He was instrumental in the development of the first two community health centers—in Boston and rural Mississippi—sponsored by the Office of Economic Opportunity in a network that grew to more than 800 centers serving some four million people in poverty. Since 1960 he has also been a leader in the opposition to nuclear arms and other military expenditures.

John Hatch, Dr.P.H., is professor of health education in the School of Public Health at the University of North Carolina at Chapel Hill. Prior to joining the faculty at Chapel Hill, he had been director of community health action at the Tufts-Delta Health Center in Mound Bayou, Mississippi, and worked as a community organizer in Boston. He is currently involved in issues related to health and development in the United States and in several African nations.

Rocio Huet-Cox, M.D., is completing her training in internal medicine at the University of Tennessee Memorial Research Center and Hospital. She received her M.D. degree from the University of Michigan Medical School. She was formerly coordinator of the Minority Affairs Committee of the American Medical Student Association and later served as AMSA national president. She is coordinator of the Knoxville area chapter of Physicians for Social Responsibility.

Anthony Mazzocchi is a member of the Oil, Chemical and Atomic Workers International Union, in which he served as director of the Occupational Safety and Health Program, director of the Legislative Office, member of the Executive Board, and vice-president. He is now on the executive committee of the Committee for Responsible Genetics and on the staff of the National Labor Education and Resource Center.

John Molinaro, P.A., is a primary-care practitioner in a health maintenance organization in upstate New York. He graduated from the now-closed Health Associate Program at Johns Hopkins. He experienced public-sector medicine while working at the Baltimore City Hospital and U.S. Public Health Service Hospital, before moving to New York State to work in a rural satellite clinic. Later, he was briefly involved in the National Health Service Corps Occupational Health Initiative Program, establishing an occupational medicine clinic within the Boriken Health Center in East Harlem.

Fitzhugh Mullan, M.D., is chief medical officer of the Office of Medical Applications of Research at the National Institutes of Health. From 1977 to 1981 he served as director of the National Health Service Corps. He is a board-certified pediatrician and the author of two books, *White Coat, Clenched Fist: The Political Education of an American Physician* (Macmillan, 1976) and *Vital Signs: A Young Doctor's Struggle with Cancer* (Farrar, Straus, & Giroux, 1983).

Helen Rodríguez-Trias, M.D., is a pediatrician who has been in New York since 1970. After medical school and residency training in Puerto Rico, she remained on the faculty of the School of Medicine of Puerto Rico in perinatal research and regional pediatrics. The challenge of social pediatrics led her to accept the directorship of pediatrics at Lincoln Hospital in the South Bronx in New York City in 1970, where she remained until 1978. She joined the staff of Roosevelt Hospital to direct the Children and Youth Program and, since the 1980 merger of St. Luke's and Roosevelt, she has been associate director of pediatrics for primary care at both hospitals.

Her work has centered on patients' rights, and she is a founding member of the Committee to End Sterilization Abuse and a charter member of the National Women's Health Network.

Ruth Sidel, Ph.D., is professor of sociology at Hunter College of the City University of New York. She is the author of numerous articles and books on health and human services in the United States and in other countries, including *Women and Child Care in China* (Penguin Books, revised edition, 1983) and, with Victor Sidel, *The Health of China: Current Conflicts in Medical and Human Services for One Billion People* (Beacon Press, 1982).

Victor W. Sidel, M.D., is professor and chairperson of the Department of Social Medicine at Montefiore Medical Center and the Albert Einstein College of Medicine in the Bronx. He is active in health service provision, education, and research in the United States and in other countries. His books include, with Ruth Sidel, *A Healthy State: An International Perspective on the Crisis in U.S. Medical Care* (Pantheon Books, revised edition, 1983). He is president of the Public Health Association of New York City and a member of the board of directors of Physicians for Social Responsibility.

Lawrence Sirott, M.D., is a family practitioner working in a health maintenance organization in Oakland, California. Prior to that he worked at La Clínica de la Raza in Oakland, California, for seven years. He has also worked in the Indian Health Service and the National Health Service Corps. He has been active in health-related political groups since helping to organize the Student Health Organization in 1966. He became interested in the politics of the Holistic Health Movement as a member of a health workers' study group studying this topic and also by virtue of living in California.

Mark D. Smith, M.D., is a member of the house staff in internal medicine at the University of California San Francisco Medical Center–San Francisco General Hospital. He received his bachelor's degree in Afro-American Studies from Harvard University and his medical degree from the University of North Carolina School of Medicine. He is a former coordinator of the American Medical Student Association's Task Force on Occupational and Environmental Health, and is currently a member of the Occupational Health Section Council of the American Public Health Association.

Hal Strelnick, M.D., is the coordinator of community health in the Residency Program in Social Medicine and the Department of Family Medicine at Montefiore Medical Center in the Bronx. He is a member of the faculties of the Albert Einstein College of Medicine and the Columbia University School of Public Health. Since 1979 he has been a member of the editorial board of the Health Policy Advisory Center (Health/PAC). He graduated from Princeton University and the Yale University School of Medicine and completed his training as a family physician at Montefiore before joining the National Health Service Corps and serving at the Dr. Martin Luther King Health Center.

Howard Waitzkin, M.D., Ph.D., is professor of medicine and social sciences at the University of California, Irvine, and practices internal medicine at the North Orange County Community Clinic in Anaheim. He has worked with community clinics in Boston and Oakland, as well as with the health programs of the United Farm Workers Union in California. He is co-author of *The Exploitation of Illness in Capitalist Society* (Bobbs-Merrill, 1974) and *The Second Sickness: Contradictions of Capitalist Health Care* (Free Press/Macmillan, 1983).

Quentin Young, M.D., is a general internist practicing in Chicago's Hyde Park area. He is clinical professor of preventive medicine and community health at the University of Illinois Medical School. He has been chairman of the Medical Committee for Human Rights and, for the decade ending in 1981, was chairman of the Department of Medicine at Cook County Hospital. He heads the Health and Medicine Policy Research Group and is editor of its journal, *Health and Medicine.* He chaired the Health Transition Team for Mayor Harold Washington.

Richard Younge, M.D., is a family physician at the Montefiore Family Health Center in the Bronx. He is a graduate of the University of California San Francisco School of Medicine, and completed his residency in the Department of Family Medicine at Montefiore Medical Center. He is a member of the faculty of the Albert Einstein College of Medicine and of the Sophie Davis Center for Biomedical Education of the City College of New York, a program to train physicians for inner-city primary care. He serves on the editorial board of the *Health/PAC Bulletin.*